DEVELOPMENT AND ASSESSMENT CENTRES

Two

Charles Woodruffe has worked as a management consultant for 15 years. His company – Human Assets Ltd – is based in London and specialises in creating and implementing strategies to ensure that clients have the staff they need now and in the future to fulfil their business strategies. Charles and his colleagues design systems for choosing and developing people as well as dealing with their motivation and retention. They work for a range of organisations in the private and public sectors. Present and past clients include British Airways, NatWest Bank, Nomura International, Esso, Unisys, HSBC, Canada Life, the Bank of England and the States of Jersey. Charles has been involved in assessment centres and development centres throughout his time as a consultant. Human Assets Ltd emphasises taking a tailor-made approach to ensure that each centre truly meets the client's particular needs. Charles has published widely on assessment and development centres, with articles in *Leadership and Organization Development Journal*, *People Management* and *Competency*. He is an active member of the IPD and a Chartered Occupational Psychologist.

Other titles in the series:

Appraisal (2nd edn)
Clive Fletcher

Benchmarking for People Managers
John Bramham

The Competencies Handbook
Steve Whiddett and Sarah
Hollyforde

Counselling in the Workplace
Jenny Summerfield and Lyn van
Oudtshoorn

*Employee Attitude and Opinion
Surveys*
Mike Walters

Empowering Team Learning
Michael Pearn

Flexible Working Practices
John Stredwick and Steve Ellis

From Absence to Attendance
Alastair Evans and Steve Palmer

I.T. Answers to H.R. Questions
Peter Kingsbury

The Job Evaluation Handbook
Michael Armstrong and Angela
Baron

Learning Alliances
David Clutterbuck

Performance Management
Michael Armstrong and Angela
Baron

Managing Redundancy
Alan Fowler

Project Management
Roland and Frances Bee

Recruitment and Selection
Gareth Roberts

360-Degree Feedback
Peter Ward

The Institute of Personnel and Development is the leading publisher of books and reports for personnel and training professionals, students, and for all those concerned with the effective management and development of people at work. For details of all our titles, please contact the Publishing Department:

tel. 020–8263 3387
fax 020–8263 3850
e-mail publish@ipd.co.uk

The catalogue of all IPD titles can be viewed on the IPD website:
http://www.ipd.co.uk/publications

DEVELOPMENT AND ASSESSMENT CENTRES

Charles Woodruffe

INSTITUTE OF PERSONNEL AND DEVELOPMENT

© Charles Woodruffe 1990, 1993, 2000

First edition 1990
Second edition 1993
   Reprinted 1995, 1998 (twice)
Third edition 2000

Design by Paperweight
Typeset by
Intype London Ltd
Printed in Great Britain by
The Short Run Press, Exeter

British Library Cataloguing in Publication Data
A catalogue record for this book is available from the British Library

ISBN 0–85292–852–1

The views expressed in this book are the author's own and may not necessarily reflect those of the IPD

**INSTITUTE OF PERSONNEL
AND DEVELOPMENT**

IPD House, Camp Road, London SW19 4UX
Tel: 020–8971 9000 Fax: 020–8263 3333
Registered office as above. Registered Charity No. 1038333
A company limited by guarantee. Registered in England No. 2931892

CONTENTS

Preface   viii

1   INTRODUCING DEVELOPMENT AND
    ASSESSMENT CENTRES   1

    What are development and assessment centres? –
    Some simplifying generalisations about centres –
    The overall shape of the centre – A brief history of
    development and assessment centres – Current usage

2   THE SEDUCTIVENESS OF ASSESSMENT
    CENTRES   11

    Behind the growth – The supply side – The
    indirect benefits

3   STRATEGIC FOUNDATIONS FOR THE CENTRE   22

    A centre based on HR strategy – The link to
    organisational strategy – The centres as part of an
    HR system – Choosing the purpose: selection or
    development

4   CENTRES FOR SELECTION   37

    Achieving the right atmosphere – External selection
    centres – Internal selection centres

5   DEVELOPMENT CENTRES   44

    Reasons for the growth of development centres –
    Development centre objectives – Development
    centre features – Line-manager involvement – A
    partnership approach

6   DECIDING TO HAVE A CENTRE   54

The validity of assessment centres – The validity
of development centres – Estimating the benefit
with utility analysis – Barriers to acceptance – Biding
time

7   PROJECT MANAGEMENT   76

Gaining commitment – Project stages – Project
personnel – Project timetable – Using consultants

8   THE COMPETENCY ANALYSIS   85

Defining a competency – Specifying the
competencies – Carrying out the analysis – Issues
around competencies

9   THE EXERCISES   115

The grid of exercises – Types of exercise –
Innovations in exercise design – Exercise production
– Harmonising the exercises – Trial of exercises –
Marking guides – Assessment centre exercise forms
– Off-the-shelf and customised exercises

10   NON-EXERCISE MATERIAL   149

Interviews – Ratings by self and others – Tests
and inventories – In-depth psychological assessment

11   GETTING READY FOR THE CENTRE; PRE-
     SELECTION, BRIEFING DOCUMENTS, AND
     TIMETABLES   157

Pre-selection – Briefing material – Timetables

12   THE PEOPLE AT THE CENTRE   169

A question of language – Assessors – The chairperson
– Role-players – Facilitators – The administrator –
Accommodation for the centre

13 HOLDING THE CENTRE   181

Observing and recording the exercises – Classifying
the behaviour – Rating the behaviour – The assessors'
meeting – Assessors' reports – Using information
technology (IT) with assessment centres

14 TRAINING FOR ASSESSORS/OBSERVERS   197

Training timetable – Training areas

15 AFTER THE EXERCISES   207

Feedback on exercise performance – Development
planning – Development actions – Feedback to the
resourcing function

16 VALIDATING THE CENTRE   220

Qualitative validation – Quantitative validation –
Developmental validation – Validating existing
centres – Inferential evidence: conformity to best
practice

17 VEXED ISSUES   233

The exercise effect – Reliability and validity – Equal
opportunities – International assessment centres –
Contrast effects – Conclusion

Appendix A: Guidelines and ethical considerations for
Assessment Center operations   251
Appendix B: Weblinks   266
References   267
Index   286

PREFACE TO THIRD EDITION

When I was asked by Richard Goff of IPD Books to prepare a third edition of this title I thought it would be a relatively simple matter. In the event, every chapter has been altered to a greater or lesser extent. One reason is to ensure that the book deals equally with development and assessment centres. The other is to remove the general tone in the 1993 second edition of certainty and predictability enjoyed by organisations. Reading it through made me appreciate how much organisational life had changed over the intervening seven years. Rather than layers of management, we have teams and team leaders. Rather than succession to jobs, we have potential for talent pools. Finally, of course, rather than memos, we have e-mails. These changes have benefited the cause of development and assessment centres. Choosing and developing people is seen as paramount to success in an age when organisations' ability to compete is directly related to the excellence of their staff.

Human Assets Limited has also changed since the second edition. I now have the good fortune to work with four other professionals, all of whom are living testimony to the validity of the assessment centre method. I am particularly grateful to Jo Rees, who read the draft of this edition and offered comments as well as ticks. To Jo as well as to Lindsay Dagg, Wendy Lyons and Julia Smith I am most grateful for their forbearance while I was 'working at home'. I am also indebted to these colleagues as well as to those who have passed through Human Assets for their ideas on assessment and development centres. Equally, I have benefited from excellent and thoughtful clients, and I would like to mention particularly Glynis Hibbeard of the States of Jersey and Robert Wylie of NatWest Group.

Finally, since the second edition the Internet has taken off and so Appendix B provides some weblinks. These will be kept up to date on our own website (humanassets.co.uk) and I would always welcome e-mail correspondence from you, the readers (cw@humanassets.co.uk).

1 INTRODUCING DEVELOPMENT AND ASSESSMENT CENTRES

What are development and assessment centres?

The terms 'development centre' and 'assessment centre' conjure up images of suites of rooms or whole buildings dedicated to development or assessment activities. As those of you who have experience of them will know, this is not quite correct. The terms, in fact, refer to a method or approach. Whilst some larger organisations do have physical space dedicated to their development or assessment work, this is certainly not the case for many organisations.

At their simplest, both development centres and assessment centres involve people taking part in a set of job-simulations. The simulations cover the essential components of the job upon which the centre is focused. People's performance in the simulations is recorded against the qualities needed for the job. For example, the centre for a headteacher would simulate the main components of the headteacher's job, such as a meeting with a parent, preparing the school budget and meeting with other headteachers in the neighbourhood. People participating in the centre would be observed taking part in the simulations and be measured against the qualities, such as problem-solving and empathy, that are required for the headteacher's job.

Development centres grew out of assessment centres. As the different names imply, they have contrasting purposes.

The purpose of a development centre is, not surprisingly, to help people develop. The purpose of an assessment centre is for the organisation to make decisions about people. Examples of the decisions might be to choose people to join the organisation, to promote them, or to put them onto a 'fast-track' development scheme. With assessment centres, there is always an element of selecting some people and excluding others from a desirable outcome.

What development centres and assessment centres have in common is that they seek to achieve their different purposes by assessing people accurately. Assessment centres must do this to enable valid decisions to be made about people. Development centres also need to assess people accurately. In this case, accuracy is necessary to give people feedback that is factual and that will steer them towards the right priorities for development.

All centres, therefore, aim to give accurate information about the participants' current or potential competence. This objective is true whether the centre is for selection or development. It might be competence to fulfil a particular job or it may be competence to succeed at a level of work (eg team leadership) within the organisation. In turn, the strategic objective of making this assessment of competence is to ensure that the organisation has the human resources it needs, through a combination of selection and development.

So, one defining and common characteristic of development and assessment centres is their objective: to obtain the best possible indication of people's current or potential competence to perform at the target job or job level. A second defining and common characteristic is how they aim to achieve their objective. The development centre and assessment centre approach combines a range of assessment techniques so that the fullest and clearest indication of competence is achieved. These techniques will include exercises that get participants to carry out simulations of the work involved in the target job or job level. Performance in the simulation is measured in terms of the competency dimensions that are important for the target job or level. The logic is straightforward. If the objective is to find out people's competence to perform a job, the surest route is to capture the

essence of the job in a set of simulations. People's performance at the simulations should be indicative of their
behaviour in the job itself.

Development and assessment centres therefore focus
squarely upon behaviour and include a set of exercises to
capture and simulate the major aspects of the job. To provide a
simplified example, let's take a team leader's job that involves
interacting with individuals (in meetings or by telephone),
meetings in groups and doing various kinds of written work,
such as responding to letters, faxes and e-mails and preparing
a report. A straightforward development or assessment centre
for that job might include:

❑ an 'in-tray' and an analytical exercise (to simulate the
written work)

❑ a meeting with a customer or team member (played by a
role-player and simulating the meetings with individuals)

❑ a group negotiation or a problem-solving meeting (to
reflect the meetings in groups).

Beyond the common objective and the inclusion of simulations, there are few hard and fast rules. Indeed, one of the
advantages of the method is that it is flexible: The centre
should be designed to meet the needs of the organisation, be
they development, selection, or some combination of the two.
This might mean that the centre includes one or more interviews, as well as psychological tests, self-assessment and
peer-assessment. On the other hand, it might consist only of
the simulations.

It is the fact that the centres make use of simulations that
contrasts them with work sample tests. Whereas centres ask
people to perform the sort of activities that they would carry
out in the job, the work sample gets people to perform 'hands-
on simulations of part or all of the job that must be performed
by applicants' (Schmidt and Hunter, 1998). For example,
asking an applicant welder to do a piece of welding is a work
sample. It is *precisely* the work the welder would be doing, if
selected. On the other hand, the assessment centre generally
contains exercises that are only, to a greater or lesser degree,
similar to the work the person would do. For example, they

will never at work have the very same group discussion as they have at the centre.

The distinction is, however, not perfect and an assessment centre's set of exercises might approach being work samples. For example, we designed an assessment centre for a new chief executive, and one of the exercises was *precisely* the strategic review that the successful candidate would need to carry out. Furthermore, some authors discuss assessment centre exercises as if they were work samples. For example, Anderson and Shackleton (1993) write that 'many ACs incorporate tests, work samples, and interviews within their design' (p35).

Some simplifying generalisations about centres

Although it is important to think freely and creatively in the design of a centre, from the above description there are four generalisations that can be drawn about the typical centre. The first is that participants in the centre are observed by a team of assessors. A ratio that works well is one assessor for each pair of participants. The effect is that each participant is assessed during the centre probably by three assessors. The rule can be stretched but not broken. A more developmental centre might rely largely on self-assessment and peer-assessment, but the people assessing must be trained in both the competency dimensions they are meant to be assessing and in the skills of observation and rating.

A second generalisation is that assessment is by a combination of methods, which must include simulations of the key elements of the job upon which the centre is focused. This means that it is likely that an assessment centre will last at least half a day. With centres for existing members of staff (which I shall call internal centres), the assessment can last two to three days, and the developmental component will then add further to this time.

Thirdly, all the information from the assessment techniques will be brought together, and usually this is done under the headings of the competencies that are crucial for high performance in the job. The alternative procedure is to gather the information under the headings of the simulation exercises that represent the various aspects of the job.

The competencies are behavioural dimensions. They frequently have as titles the traits or dispositions that could be used to 'explain' people's behaviour. The two broad classes of competency identified by Russell (1985) are problem-solving (eg analysis, breadth of awareness) and interpersonal (eg sensitivity, self-confidence). In effect, Russell's interpersonal competencies are those covered by the label 'emotional intelligence' (Davies *et al*, 1998; Goleman, 1998).

These first three generalisations make a development centre or assessment centre different from some other means of development or selection. The procedure would fall outside the parameters of development and assessment centres if it lacked the simulations, or the panel of trained observers or the pooling of information in a systematic manner. For example, a workshop on leadership is not a development centre. Equally, it is hard to justify the 'development centre' label for the process at Yorkshire Water, as reported in the *Employee Development Bulletin* (1993). As reported, it consisted of 'a battery of questionnaires', and there is no mention of simulations. This is not to be petty. The Yorkshire Water event might well have been extremely effective. It is, however, muddling to call it a development centre, in the same way that a set of psychometric tests and inventories should not be described as an assessment centre.

A final generalisation is that several people participate in the centre at the same time. Six is a very usual number in each batch of people, but there might be more than one batch running in parallel. The people in each batch take part together in the group exercises and complete the other exercises on their own. Having people participate in batches makes group exercises feasible, reduces the unit cost of the centre, and makes for a lighter approach than the individual assessment procedure of seeing people one at a time. However, unlike the other generalisations, it is not a defining requirement. If there were insufficient numbers of participants or very senior people were being assessed, they might be seen one at a time, perhaps using role-players for any group exercises.

The overall shape of the centre

As long as you work within the above basics of development centres and assessment centres, it is important to stress that the eventual centre that you design should be dictated by your precise requirements. Indeed, the whole centre should be designed to be congruent with its end purpose. You should not feel that an assessment centre must have a group exercise or that it must have an in-tray. You should not feel that participants in a development centre must be given a report at the end of the centre. Indeed, it will probably be much better if they write their own.

In essence, a centre should be designed to combine the objective of accurate observation with the equally important objective of acceptability and ownership. Technical accuracy, on the one hand, and acceptability, on the other, are the twin yardsticks by which practical assessment procedures are judged. For example, if the objective is people's development, it is crucial to design a centre that will marry the need for observations that are technically accurate with the requirement for participants to have an experience that is developmental. Practical and financial constraints must also be kept in mind. There is no point in designing a brilliantly accurate graduate assessment centre that lasts a week. Neither the graduates nor the assessors will be prepared to give up so much time in the interests of precision.

In conclusion, although there are definite rules about what makes a development centre or assessment centre, it is important to recognise that there is a great deal of flexibility within these rules.

A brief history of development and assessment centres

The history starts with assessment centres. They date back to the UK's War Office Selection Boards (WOSB), which were introduced in 1942 to select officers. Anstey (1989) recounts that the system the boards replaced had clearly broken down. A high percentage of people it passed had to be 'returned to unit' because of their lack of ability. The old system relied on interviewing people who had been judged as likely to be of officer quality. The judgement was formed on the basis of their background or their achievements in the ranks. These achievements could range from gallantry to exceptional smartness. With this method of pre-selection, the old system missed even the chance of interviewing many people who actually had officer potential. Furthermore, it incorrectly ascribed potential to large numbers of those it did get to assess.

The new system was devised by the Directorate for the Selection of Personnel and included leaderless group exercises, objective selection tests, and separate personal interviews by three assessors. Assessors were a senior and junior officer and a psychiatrist. Anstey describes how the new procedure resulted in a 'dramatic drop' in the percentage of people returned to unit. Its success led to its acceptance throughout the Army.

In the USA, the pioneering work was undertaken by the Office of Strategic Studies, which used the method to select spies during the Second World War (MacKinnon, 1977). This early US assessment centre was also derived from the WOSBs, but after the war the UK and US approaches diverged somewhat (Feltham, 1988a).

In the UK, assessment centres were developed by the Civil Service and by other parts of the public sector. They followed the model of the WOSB, and were sometimes labelled Extended Interviews. In the USA post-war development moved to the private sector. The pioneer was the American Telephone and Telegraph Company (AT&T), which used assessment centres in its Management Progress Study, which began in 1956 (Bray, 1964). The method was taken up by Standard Oil of Ohio in 1962 and then by IBM, Sears, General Electric and J C Penney (Finkle, 1976).

As Feltham (1988a) notes, the UK and US traditions have definite differences. In particular, the UK public-sector model relies more upon interviews than the US private-sector model. Indeed, the UK public-sector assessment centre is still sometimes called an Extended Interview. Other differences detailed by Feltham are the UK emphasis upon group exercises with an assigned leader, practical/physical group exercises, unstructured group discussions, and fairly long written exercises. On the other hand, US assessment centres place more emphasis on in-tray exercises, group exercises without a leader but with assigned roles, and on two-person role-plays.

Assessment centres in use today in the UK private sector probably owe more in direct terms to the developments in the USA and to the US assessment model than to the UK public-sector model. However, some of the centres in the UK private sector are modelled upon the old public-sector format, just as there are now some centres in the UK public sector that are in line with the private sector and the US tradition.

The 1980s saw the first development centres, and the 1990s saw these greatly increase in number. They came about in a rather circuitous way. Assessment centres were used both to select people into organisations and also to decide upon people's readiness for promotion and their potential to develop further. In essence, people passed or failed. The flow of information and benefit was very much a one-way street from candidates to the organisation. Broadly speaking, people were assessed in a rather cold and detached way by assessors who later told the assessees of the conclusions that had been reached. Not surprisingly, failure was demotivating. Organisations sought to overcome this problem by giving people a lot of feedback and emphasising the developmental benefits from attending the centre. Nevertheless, these were still assessment centres and people still felt demotivated if they failed. Organisations had to decide whether they wanted to make choices about people based on the assessment centre information or whether they wanted the centre to be developmental. In the 1990s, many organisations opted for the latter. This was thoroughly in keeping with the backdrop of asking people to take greater responsibility for their development and for their career progress. The development centre was a facility or opportunity provided by the organisation to its staff for them to gain an accurate picture of their strengths and development needs. It was up to staff to receive feedback in an adult and non-defensive manner and to make best use of it in a development plan.

Development centres place a much greater emphasis upon assessment being carried out collaboratively with participants, rather than it being something that is done to them. This new emphasis has led to some radical thinking about what should take place at the centre. In some cases, it might not be necessary to have assessors at all. People can assess themselves and each other to gain the insights that are required to plan out their development. The move to more collaborative centres is described by Iles and Forster (1994) in terms of a divide between Europe and the USA. They see the collaborative model as part of 'a European "social process" model of assessment and selection' (p59). They contrast this with the US psychometric model, which has much more psychological distance between the tester and the person being tested.

The three-stage move from traditional assessment centres to full development centres is well described in articles by Griffiths and Goodge (1994) and Goodge (1994a, 1994b, 1997), who talk about three generations of design. A case study of a particular organisation (NatWest) making the transition between the three generations is provided by Woodruffe and Wylie (1994).

Current usage

The use of assessment centres is widespread, particularly in North America and the UK. It has increased greatly since the 1980s. In the UK, in the mid-1980s, Robertson and Makin (1986) found that just over a quarter of organisations employing more than 500 people used assessment centres. They also found that the usage depended upon the volume of people the organisation recruited. Just over a third of large recruiters of managers used them compared with a tenth of the minor recruiters.

By the mid- to late-1990s, use had increased greatly. In the UK, a survey by the Industrial Society (1996), based upon 414 replies, found that 59 per cent were using assessment centres for a broad range of staff and 43 per cent were using development centres. A survey by Roffey Park Management Institute (1999) reported broadly similar results. Assessment centres were used by 62 per cent of respondents and development centres were used by 43 per cent. A majority of respondents

(57 per cent) also expected the use of both types of centre to increase. The Roffey Park respondents also foresaw a continued move from assessment to development centres. In the USA, Lowry (1996) conducted a survey of public-sector organisations and found that 62 per cent used assessment centres, while 19 per cent used development centres.

The Roffey Park results repeated those from earlier years by showing that both assessment centres and development centres were the province of larger organisations. Roffey Park found that assessment centres were used by 29 per cent of organisations employing up to 50 people, compared with the 72 per cent of organisations employing more than 5,000 staff.

2 THE SEDUCTIVENESS OF ASSESSMENT CENTRES

The growth in the use of development centres and assessment centres has occurred despite the cost of their installation and the on-going cost of operating them. The typical centre will take three managers away from their jobs to act as assessors for at least one day, and possibly quite a lot longer. If used with current employees it will also take them from *their* jobs. In addition, there is the need for administrative back-up, and in many cases the hire of suitable accommodation.

One reason that all this investment is seen as worthwhile is the belief in the quality of the assessment that is obtained. Accurate assessment is crucial in selecting people both for jobs and for career paths. It is also highly desirable for identifying people's development needs.

The assessment centre process has extreme credibility in terms of delivering accurate assessment. The belief in assessment centres is partly the result of a good deal of research evidence in their favour. This research evidence gets translated quite readily into the message that they have been proved to be virtually 100 per cent accurate. In fact, there are a number of questions raised about assessment centres in the more academic journals, and there are published instances of them not working. The doubts can be extended quite readily to development centres. These issues are dealt with in subsequent chapters. However, the fact is that these question marks have had little impact on the end user of either development or assessment centres. The doubts, anyway, do not take away from the overall belief that 'the assessment centre is the most effective selection method for predicting successful performance in the target job' (Association of Graduate Recruiters, 1993, p1).

Aside from the headline summary of the research evidence, people believe in assessment centres because of the persuasive logic of their design. The centres sample the participants' behaviour in a set of simulations of the target job. Participants are assessed against the dimensions of performance for that job, and these competency dimensions will be clearly visible in the simulations. Furthermore, there is the double-check that if the competency dimensions are not visible in people's performance of the simulations, then either the dimensions or the simulations are wrong. The rationality of the centres is extended by having assessors who are well trained in the observation, recording, classifying and rating of behaviour. The logical foundation to assessment centres was cited as a benefit by assessment centre users in a range of different countries when they were questioned by Imada *et al* (1985). These users saw the centre as a better tool for making decisions, and therefore it is also seen as a fairer approach.

The same plausibility is attached to development centres. People get the chance to take part in simulations of the job upon which their development is focused. They get high-quality feedback, and the opportunity to discuss this and to construct a development plan. In addition to the feedback on performance in the exercises, there can be other developmental aspects to the centre. For example, the centre might emphasise self-assessment and participants diagnosing their own and each other's strengths and limitations during the centre. It might also include consideration by participants of their career aspirations, and they can gain insights about themselves, such as becoming more aware of their learning style and career anchor(s). The process seems to speak for itself.

In the case of a development centre, aside from its logic and accuracy, its other obvious selling point is the impetus it gives to a management development programme. The centre will provide a clear and energised starting-point to the development process. A well-conducted centre is the best way of getting people to buy into and take responsibility for their own development plans. The planning will be based around behaviour that definitely took place during the exercises, and the priorities for development will be apparent. If the exercises are tailor-made, the areas of strength and weakness will have been identified within settings that belong to the organisation. This makes the feedback particularly persuasive. People can see that if they are to succeed within the organisation they must develop.

In summary, both development centres and assessment centres sell themselves. An uncritical summary of the more popular literature on centres, coupled with their intuitive appeal, means that they enjoy the support of assessors and participants. The assessors see how people behave in the centre and can place a lot of faith that this is a good preview of how the person would behave in the job. In addition, if used for selection, participants come through the centre feeling that the organisation has treated them fairly and that it has obtained sound evidence for its decision. They will also have enjoyed a taste of work with the organisation, which will give them a firm basis for deciding about any eventual offer of employment. If used for development, participants will gain valuable insights from their own experience of the centre and the feedback from observers, and maybe peers. As Strube et al (1986) have demonstrated, the need for accurate self-appraisal outweighs the need for self-enhancement, and centres undoubtedly appear to satisfy the former need, if not the latter.

In fact, all this faith is likely to be well founded only if the centre has been carefully and rigorously designed, and if checks are kept on its operation. Unfortunately, there are plenty of examples of centres with exercises that are poorly designed and that have little bearing on the target job; where information is gathered unsystematically and without its relevance being made explicit; where assessors are poorly trained; and where participants are alienated from the procedure. Yet the operators will often keep faith even with what outsiders see as the poorest centre. This is probably because of their personal investment in its design and because the credibility of centres is remarkably robust. It is easy to persuade oneself that the centre is working even when outsiders can see all its limitations.

Behind the growth

All the plausibility in the world would not explain the growth of centres if they were not also meeting a need. As I elaborate elsewhere (Woodruffe, 1999), both assessment and development centres can be core components in the attempt to choose, develop and retain talented people. Assessment centres appear to provide the best answer to the need for organisations to be more certain in choosing between applicants. Mistakes are ever more expensive. The mistake might be in terms of accepting people who do not work out, but nowadays the more important mistake for many organisations is rejecting people who could have made a valuable contribution. In the era of shortages of talent and experience, it is critical to recognise people who could contribute to the organisation's success. Furthermore, the way the organisation selects people must help it sell itself to potential recruits. Assessment centres do this very well.

A related and increasingly important aspect of the need for assessment is that it allows the organisation to place its new recruits wisely according to their strengths and interests. The organisation can make the best use of applicants' talent and, longer term, this will help to maintain people's commitment and motivation.

For people already in the organisation, development centres facilitate a joint approach in which the organisation and participants collaborate to make career plans and to arrive at development plans. The centres contribute to fostering and realising people's talent and to motivating people through their development.

The importance of recognising and developing talent should be seen against the need for organisations to have the highest quality of human resources. They need people who can enable them to respond to the challenges they face. The turbulent environment written about by Emery and Trist (1965) over 30 years ago has come of age. Organisations must be responsive in an uncertain world. Change and complexity have also resulted in the specification for the successful manager itself becoming more exacting. People are required who are adaptable and tolerant of the ambiguity of change.

They need both a high level of cognitive skills as well as strong interpersonal abilities. Couple these demands with talent shortages, and it is apparent that organisations simply cannot afford to waste the abilities of the people available to them. For example, Skapinker (1989b) reports how Triplex Lloyd set up a one-day assessment centre to help identify managerial talent amongst its shop-floor staff. The programme was a result of the chief executive's enlightened belief that many of these staff were more talented than their immediate superiors realised.

The supply side

The discussion so far has been of the demand side of the growth story. It should be added that the demand for development and assessment centres has been matched by supply. There is an increasing number of consultants in the area. Indeed, consultants have played an educational role and so they have to some extent fuelled the demand.

The indirect benefits

The growth of assessment centres can largely be attributed to their obvious uses in selecting people and helping to place and develop them. However, there is also a set of beneficial side-effects of having an assessment centre.

Development of assessors/observers

The process of being trained as an assessor carries the general benefit of imparting the skills of assessing people and of giving feedback. These skills will be useful in the assessor's normal job of managing people (Glaze, 1989). For example, Arkin (1991) reports how assessors at ICI said that it helped them manage people on a day-to-day basis. Similarly, observers at a development centre are given coaching in feedback skills. They also become more open to the culture of development. As Hardingham (1996) observes, the experience can result in their moving development higher up their personal agendas.

Assessors also benefit simply from being part of an assessor team. People from different parts of the organisation work together and build a network. Being chosen as an assessor can give the person a feeling of the confidence the organisation has in him or her. Assessors are being entrusted with a highly responsible task. Confidence is further built up by the process of having to present an opinion on participants regularly at assessors' conferences.

Analysis of competencies

The disciplined approach to assessment forces the organisation to analyse its jobs properly. It also results in the common language of the competency dimensions that differentiate the successful from the average performer. Through assessor training these dimensions can become part of the folklore of the organisation. As Glaze (1989) says, commenting upon the experience of Cadbury Schweppes, competencies become 'absorbed in the bloodstream of the organisation' (p44). One organisation that I worked with had a list of 12 competencies that became well known as the 12 Cs and were thoroughly internalised throughout the organisation. It even went to the point of a Yuletide humorist producing the 12 incompetencies, which he saw as a better representation of reality!

Of course, a thorough job analysis can be carried out quite independently of any decision about having a development or assessment centre. However, the design of a centre definitely requires that a thorough analysis is carried out, and so acts as a real impetus. Furthermore, as Jackson and Yeates (1993) point out, the use of the competencies in a large-scale assessment programme will result in their being disseminated throughout the organisation. In this way, the centre will have an impact on the organisation's culture.

Performance appraisal

The competencies can become part of an appraisal system. This will contribute to a rational and integrated overall system of human resource assessment and development, and will specifically improve the appraisal process because the competencies will be well understood. The appraisal system will further benefit from line managers who are also assessors being better able to carry out appraisal interviews and to give specific behavioural examples to substantiate their judgements on performance.

Recruitment and motivation

Assessment centres can be used to sell the organisation. Candidates see them as a sign that the organisation is thoroughly professional in its personnel practices. As evidence of this, Robertson *et al* (1991) report that candidates saw assessment centres as more adequate than a situational interview, and that these beliefs about adequacy predicted organisational commitment, which in turn predicts turnover and absenteeism. Successful applicants will also be subject to the psychological effect of feeling committed to an organisation that puts them through a rigorous selection before letting them in (Fletcher, 1989).

Smither *et al* (1993) found that people perceived simulations, interviews and cognitive tests with more concrete items (such as use of vocabulary) to have greater predictiveness than cognitive tests with more abstract items, personality inventories and biodata. In turn, perceived validity had a 'spill-over' effect on the applicant's willingness to recommend the organisation as an employer to other people. It also contributed to perceptions of the justice of both the procedure and of its outcomes (known as procedural and distributive justice, respectively). Smither *et al* suggest that procedures with less perceived validity are likely to be the subject of complaint and legal challenges.

Macan *et al* (1994) also found that candidates saw assessment centres as more valid than cognitive tests. In other words, the centres have a higher face validity than cognitive tests. In turn, applicants' perceptions of the tests and centres were related to their attitudes to the selection procedure, job and organisation. Furthermore, people's intention to accept or decline an offer of employment was related to their perception of the centre, although the stronger influences were their perceptions of the work and the organisation. These last two can, of course, be influenced by the centre. Applicants get a taste for the job. The centre should be realistic, but in so being it might well draw people's attention to the more positive aspects of the job. A realistic preview can boost people's overall opinion of the organisation. Meglino *et al* (1988) demonstrated the beneficial effects of a realistic job preview on trainees' turnover and on their perception of the organisation as caring, trustworthy and honest. Conversely, people who really are not suited to the work should have this made clear by the preview. The preview should thereby help to cut early turnover from unwise choices.

Of course, if a well-designed centre has a recruitment advantage, by the same token a badly designed and administered centre can lose potential recruits. Part of the design is to ensure that face validity of assessment centres is coupled with an attitude that the centre is not something inflicted upon candidates. Rather it is something that has a more collaborative feel to it. As noted in the last chapter, Iles and Forster (1994) see the focus on collaboration and attending to the social process of selection as within a European, as opposed to a US, tradition. This certainly seems borne out by the tone of an article by the US researchers Schmidt and Hunter (1998). They are strong advocates of cognitive testing, which they see as 'the most valid predictor of future performance and learning' (p262). They do not seem to pay much regard to the practical problem that people will not readily accept being selected mainly by cognitive testing.

Iles and Robertson (1997) link the collaborativeness of an assessment centre to the notion that it is less of an invasion of privacy than being tested. Centres also seem in accord with our norm of reciprocity. If the candidate tells a lot to the organisation, the organisation should give something back by revealing something about itself. Iles and Robertson maintain that candidates want to be given realistic information on which they can base their own decisions.

Assessment centres that are aimed at existing staff either to decide promotion or to identify people for fast-track schemes can also be more acceptable than other methods of selection. People see the system is fair and thorough. In general, the centres are able to satisfy people's need for a sense of procedural justice, assuming that they are properly designed.

The centre can also be sold to employees' representatives. Thornton (1992) provides an interesting case study of an assessment centre to select team members and team leaders at McDonnell Douglas. The company collaborated with the union, whose members were trained as assessors. Their involvement was seen to contribute to understanding and trust.

In the case of development centres, participants gain a sense of being valued by the organisation through being provided with the chance to attend. The centre is a clear sign of the organisation devoting resources to people's development. If the centre is well designed and developmental, participants should go away remotivated. They will see the organisation as concerned with their continued employability (Woodruffe, 2000). Again, the sting in the tail is that if it is badly designed they will depart demotivated. This is particularly likely if what was labelled a development centre turns out to be an assessment centre.

The acceptability of assessment centres to candidates and the potential of development centres to motivate people are a vital part of the story of their growth. Even if other methods (eg cognitive tests, biodata) might be shown academically to be as good a way of choosing people, they are not nearly as acceptable to candidates. Likewise, there are other ways of people becoming sensitive to their development needs (eg 360-degree feedback). However, a development centre can be particularly powerful as a way of motivating people. The existence of the development centre can be used to show that there is a strategy to provide the organisation with the talent it needs for the future and that those attending the centre are part of the strategy.

Assessment centres and equal opportunities enforcement

Assessment centres have been looked upon favourably by the courts. This helps explain the growth in their use, particularly in the USA. Thornton (1992) summarises the history of court cases involving assessment centres in the USA. He says that cases have generally been in the public sector and involved centres used for promotion. The cases have typically claimed the centres 'were not job-relevant, were administered in an inconsistent manner, and were biased against racial minorities' (p214). Thornton reported that there had yet to be a ruling against an assessment centre, and he links this to adherence to the US *Guidelines and Ethical Considerations for Assessment Center Operations* (Task Force, 1989 and reproduced in Appendix A). Assessment centres allow observation of job-related performance dimensions in job-related exercises. The decisions should be fair.

Furthermore, empirical studies have shown the results of centres generally to be even-handed. The 'pass' rates for different gender and ethnic groups are broadly similar (Huck and Bray, 1976, Ritchie and Moses, 1983). However, Walsh *et al* (1987) found that, in the assessment centre that they studied, females were rated more highly than males by male assessors. Various explanations might be advanced, but at least the study did not uncover an 'old boy' network. A further favourable impression is conveyed by Ballantyne (1999). He reports that 'Asian graduates seem to do slightly better proportionally in assessment centres than other ethnic groups' (p15).

Organisational development

There are various ways in which assessment and development centres can contribute to organisational change. The existence of a development centre shows a clear commitment to being a learning organisation. Getting senior people to act as assessors and observers is another sign of the importance of these activities. It can also seal these people's commitment both to the centre and to its objectives.

The competencies and exercises can be used to communicate a new definition of successful performance. The centre helps people match these new demands. The Industrial Society (1996) survey found that almost a quarter of respondents were using development centres to help manage a restructuring programme. Nearly one-third were using assessment centres for the same reason. Jackson and Yeates (1993) say that this typically requires running a large number of centres in a short period of time to allocate people to new positions. However, the use of assessment centres in connection with restructuring might also cover choosing people for redundancy. It is clearly important that the latter use does not cause centres generally to get a bad name in the organisation.

3 STRATEGIC FOUNDATIONS FOR THE CENTRE

The last chapter introduced the importance of explicitly locating the assessment or development centre within a human resource (HR) strategy. The centre also needs to be integrated with the rest of the HR system, and a clear choice needs to be made between a development centre that is purely for development and an assessment centre that makes decisions about people. If any of these issues are avoided, the foundations of the centre will be weakened.

A centre based on HR strategy

Centres are expensive in terms of time and money. If they are not seen to be a core component of delivering an agreed strategy, these costs will be resented and ultimately reined in by the executive of the organisation.

The centre should be part of an HR strategy, and the HR strategy needs to be linked to the business strategy. The aim of the HR strategy is to ensure that the organisation can meet its strategic objectives by having competent people. The organisation might seek to ensure that it has people with the competencies required for its jobs by selection, development, or – more probably – a combination of the two. Development and assessment centres can help to deliver both. First, assessment centres are used to choose people who already have the required competence or who have the potential to develop. If the assessment centre is used purely for selection, the organisation can choose people who come closest to matching its requirements, and place them in the jobs to which they are most suited, and which match their interests. Second, the development centre enables the continued development of those chosen. The centre sensitises people to their strengths and development needs, and can be used as the starting-point of a management development programme. The overall aim is to help the organisation ensure that it has people ready to perform its jobs to high levels of competence.

Apart from being a means to choose and develop people, the centres can be part of a strategy to recruit, retain and motivate these competent people (Woodruffe, 1999). The mix of development and assessment centres conveys the organisation's commitment to its people. It chooses people carefully and then invests in their development. Development centres should also help to retain and motivate people by including exercises to get people to think about their interests and aspirations. They can then work in partnership with the organisation to make career moves that match their aspirations and strengths. There should be a better fit or match between what the organisation and its employees need and have to offer each other (Schein, 1978).

To these two ways in which the centres contribute to implementing an HR strategy, a third might be added. The centres provide to the organisation an audit of people's competencies. Plans can be made to fill the areas of general deficit by recruitment of new people or the development of existing staff.

The link to organisational strategy

The HR strategy aims to ensure the organisation has competent people. Not only does this have to be seen as vital by those with power in the organisation. It also begs the question: 'Competent at what?'

Clearly, it could be argued that all would agree that competent people are vital. However, there is a difference between paying lip service to it and being prepared to invest time and money in it as a cause. For development and assessment centres to work and be supported there has to be a belief in the importance of competent people. The HR strategy should be linked to the organisation's strategy to win in its market-place by satisfying its customers. This applies, obviously, to private-sector organisations. Increasingly it also applies in the public sector, which is taking on the same attitude of customer focus. Failing elements of the public sector, such as schools or prisons, are threatened with privatisation as a sanction for their alleged underperformance.

How the organisation wins in its market-place is by being good at what it is meant to be good at – indeed, not just good but world-class. In an era of globalisation, customers can look around the world for many services. Why go to a second-rate supplier when a first-rate one is available? It is in this context that the concept of organisational competencies has particular relevance. These specify what the organisation is particularly good at. For example, Hewlett-Packard are particularly good at making printers, and Nokia have built a similar reputation with mobile telephones. The approach is championed by Hamel and Prahalad (1994), who advocate a business strategy based around core competence leadership. The organisation needs to discern as best it can future opportunities, and build the core competencies to exploit those opportunities. Building core competencies means building them in people.

The concept of core competencies makes clear that the organisation is competing and flourishing because of its people. They become a strategic resource for achieving competitive advantage, and so people are the basis of the business strategy. It may be a cliche, but it is also true that constant change and increased competitiveness have resulted in people being the strategy for success. Bartlett and Ghoshal (1995) are strong advocates of this view. They describe the effect of the contemporary environment as being to 'shift the focus of many firms from allocating capital to managing knowledge and learning as the key strategic task' (p18). Ghoshal and Bartlett (1998) sum up the argument by saying 'in a knowledge-based era, the scarce strategic resource that will allow one company to surpass its competitors is the quality of the people working for it'. Much the same argument is put forward by Pfeffer (1994). He describes how people are 'becoming more important because many other sources of competitive success are less powerful than they once were' (p6). The combination of de-layering and downsizing has added a further twist to the argument, with those who remain in the organisation becoming more important than ever (Meyer and Allen, 1997).

All this might seem a long way from putting an assessment centre together. It is not. The centre is likely to gain far greater support if it is seen explicitly as a way of gaining the people who will enable the organisation to succeed in its market-place and not just as the 'over-the-top toy' of so-called HR perfectionists. It is vital that the leaders of the organisation see the centre in the context of it implementing an HR strategy that is bound to the business strategy.

The starting-point is the organisation's decision on its mission and strategy. This leads to a decision on how the organisation should be structured, and therefore what jobs exist. The requirements for successful performance in each job can then be specified, and the assessment procedure is designed to measure people's competence to perform those jobs. At the same time, the development system is installed to help people increase their competence. This flow is represented in Figure 1 below.

An example is provided by a bank overseas with which I worked. Their mission was to be the dominant market leader. This was to be fulfilled by their being a high-quality, customer-driven and sales-oriented organisation. I worked with them to specify the requirements they had of people, in terms of the competencies that were needed at different levels in the organisation. We designed an assessment process to audit present and prospective staff against those competencies. At the same time, we designed development and training procedures targeted upon those competencies.

As Figure 1 shows, information from the operation of assessment centres should feed back into strategy and organisational design. For example, it might be found that the necessary human resources to match its requirements are not available within the organisation or externally, given its growth targets etc. If this is the case, the organisation must

Figure 1

LINKING HR PROCESSES TO ORGANISATIONAL STRATEGY

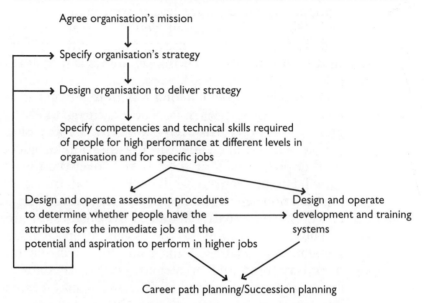

change its needs by redesign or a change of strategy. The growth plans themselves may need to be reviewed, and so the assessment centre will have had an influence upon strategy and will not just be the implementation of strategy.

The centres as part of an HR system

Not only should the assessment and development centres be seen as implementing the HR strategy. They need to be linked in with all the other components of the HR system that are also implementing the strategy. For example, the information from centres will feed back into priorities for training provision. With the bank referred to above, the assessment process found that existing staff generally were weak at marketing and sales. As a result, an urgent programme of training was carried out for all staff.

It is important that the context of assessment centres is thought through in this way, otherwise some of the benefits of the process will not be achieved. For example, some organisations have assessment centres for graduate selection but seem to think of them purely as a way of choosing from amongst applicants. They do not make the maximum use of the information from the centre to lay down the successful applicants' initial development plans. Other organisations have internal centres to which people go purely for the organisation to make immediate choices about them. The choice might be whether they should be promoted or go on a fast-track programme. This type of centre exists without being integrated into the overall HR system. It can all too commonly assess people against a particular list of competencies that are found nowhere else in the HR system. The opportunity for rich information that could be gained from such centres is lost. Properly designed, the centres could be used to determine development plans and, most importantly, to help the organisation plan its future knowing the resources it has available. The information could be used to anticipate future gluts or shortfalls of staff, and be the basis for taking appropriate action.

Assessment centres must be integrated within an overall HR assessment and development system so that the end result is a coherent and integrated system of HR management. An example of such a system is provided by the model in Figure 2. There is a selection centre for graduate intake, which aims to choose people who will become team leaders, and to provide eventually an adequate number of people for the senior management development programme.

Once people are within the organisation, there are assessment centres that are as developmental as possible at the doorway to team leadership and to decide upon a team leader's senior management potential. There is also a full development centre for team leaders to help them continue to develop in that role.

The two internal assessment centres are backed up by a system of training and development. Each internal centre identifies people's strengths as well as areas upon which they should focus for development. The training and development system then takes over, to build upon people's strengths and to work on their development needs. The senior management development programme prepares team leaders who are provisionally seen as joining the pool of senior managers. Part of their preparation will be through their performance of management roles. Overall, assessment centres are bound in with development in meeting the organisation's HR needs. The assessment centres give an accurate indication of people's competencies and provide an impetus to the development programme.

Figure 2 shows how the assessment centres are positioned alongside the HR development system. The internal centres come after some development has taken place, and are also the gateway to further development. Competencies that can be developed easily to a person's level of potential are assessed after some developmental effort has been made. Weaknesses identified at the centre are therefore not merely superficial. This positioning will ensure that the centre is not measuring a simple deficit, which certainly should not intrude on an audit of potential. The only centre at which such deficits might be measured is one that is looking at current readiness to perform the target job.

Locating the assessment centres within an overall model of the HR system ensures consideration of the major policy questions about what will happen after the centre. For example, if the centre is to make a decision about promotion, can people come back a second time? Does there need to be anything other than the passage of time before they return to the same centre? Is the centre the only input to the promotion decision? Questions such as these need to be considered and answered if there is to be coherence to the system.

Integrating the centres with career management and succession planning

The notions of careers and succession planning changed dramatically in the 1990s. The highly structured systems at the start of the decade were replaced by far more fluid processes at the end. In particular, responsibility for careers was placed far more in the hands of the individual whose career it was. The same was true of development. Some organisations appeared to abandon any interest in people's careers.

Figure 2
EXAMPLE OF AN INTEGRATED ASSESSMENT/ DEVELOPMENT PROCESS

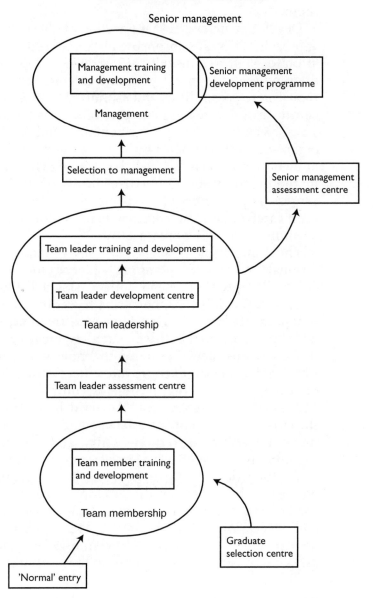

However, others looked to work in partnership with staff. The organisation would provide development opportunities but it was up to the member of staff to make best use of them.

Development centres are well suited to the partnership approach. They are an opportunity provided by the organisation for staff to consider their strengths and weaknesses, to draw up a development plan and to consider for themselves their career possibilities and aspirations. As noted earlier, the centres can be presented as part of a strategy to retain staff. The object is to help people remain employable within the organisation. It is important that this wider context of development centres is presented clearly to participants and others in the organisation. Otherwise, much of the benefit of the centres as promoters of a culture change will be lost. Communicated well, the centres can be an integral part of becoming a learning organisation.

The fluidity of organisations has rendered obsolete traditional succession planning, except for key positions. Generally, people are no longer stacked like aeroplanes waiting to land. Before their time has come, the organisation will probably have changed. However, organisations still have different roles to be filled, such as creating strategy and leading teams, and they need to know whether a person is likely to be able to fill these roles successfully. The emphasis of succession planning is therefore on having 'talent pools', and assessment centres can be used to identify people for these pools. The emphasis is upon identifying potential to move to levels of responsibility, and developing people accordingly. Just such a process was described by Stamp (1989) under the title 'career path appreciation'. Although her methodology is different from the assessment centre approach, the fundamental concept could be used in the assessment centre and succession-planning context. Her concept is that there are particular levels of work within organisations. Under the assessment centre approach, these levels would be associated with particular sets of competencies. The level that people have attained and the level they could attain would be measured by the assessment centre, and the development system would help them realise their potential.

Whereas long-term succession planning focuses on people's ability and wish to succeed to levels of responsibility, the model of short-term succession needs to recognise that jobs are moulded around people just as much as people are developed for jobs (Gratton and Syrett, 1990). For example, a person might want to retain a scientific or professional role as well as taking on managerial responsibility. The need for information about people's wishes can be accommodated in the assessment centre design by including, for example, a measure of people's career anchors (Schein, 1978).

In summary, the succession-planning process is a far more complex and iterative procedure than in the days of predictability. It must be fitted to the current realities facing the organisation, a focus that must be shared by the whole HR system. Nowadays, the reality is change and uncertainty and the need to be responsive. This must be reflected in systems of assessment and development. The assessment must be against the competency dimensions of change rather than of order and predictability, and the development systems must equip people for longer-term change, while also being responsive to their development needs in the shorter term. In some cases, the assessment centre will examine people for particular specific jobs. Increasingly, however, the focus will be to help people prepare for a future level (eg to join a flexible pool of senior managers) and for the change inherent in the particular jobs they might assume.

Choosing the purpose: selection or development

The precise use of the centre will dictate its design. The types of centre range from the traditional selection assessment centre through to a centre for development based upon self- and peer-assessment. Increasingly centres for internal people are said to be for development, a purpose underlined by calling the centre a development centre. However, in some cases, the development centre is simply an old-style assessment centre with a new label. Although some organisations have genuine development centres, many try to do two things at once, namely assessing for grading or promotion and trying to carry out development. This came across very clearly in a survey by Jackson and Yeates (1993) of organisations claiming to have 'development centres'. They say that in many of these there was the aim of identifying people who were ready for promotion or who had high potential. Some centres involved the formal selection of these people. They also note the irony of such 'development' centres, which is that they select for further development the people with the fewest development needs.

Assessment and development do not go well together. Centres that have even an element of selection are bound to be different from those that are used purely for development. In particular, there is no point in calling a centre a 'development centre' if it is clear that a person's performance will be reported upon and might be used against him or her. That centre is going to be seen by participants as essentially to do with selecting or retaining people for a high potential ticket. As Jackson and Yeates (1993) point out, a grapevine will be established, based on what happens to people after the centre. Rightly or wrongly, the assessees will be motivated to outwit the assessors if performance will affect their careers. That is not the frame of mind to confront development needs.

Assessment centres masquerading as development centres are wolves in sheep's clothing. As Ferguson (1991) puts it, 'the term "development centre" covers a multitude of sins'. For example, *Personnel Management* (1990) reported on 'the use of development centres for assessing top executives' at a building society. The report described how 'the result of the exercise was that 18 of the 32 managers eventually left the organisation'.

Organisations must make a clear choice on the primary purpose of a centre. Is it for selection or development? If it is development, then it is vital that the information from the centre does not affect the person's future in the organisation. There is, of course, a great temptation to make use of the development centre information to make decisions about individuals. Succumbing to this temptation clearly turns the centre from one that can rightly be called a development centre into one that is an assessment centre. It would be better to use the centre as a vehicle for development, and to use the information about people to plan rather than to decide. There is nothing obviously wrong with using that information to pencil in people's likely potential, and to use this to alert the organisation to likely over- and underprovision in the future.

Organisations, of course, have a perfect right to use centres to make decisions about promotion or entry to a fast track. They can also make those centres as developmental as possible, but they are not development centres. An example is provided by Tarmac (Woodruffe, 1997). They had to choose people for an executive development programme (EDP). An assessment centre was the fairest way of doing so. It was made as developmental as possible by including some components that were purely for people's development and were not assessed. It also incorporated the chance to receive brief feedback at the end of the first day. An assessor could point out any easily changed behaviour that was marring a person's performance (eg 'Speak less, listen more'). It is nonsensical to exclude someone from the fast track for want of a behaviour that could be changed instantly. People were given as much information as possible before the centre and were given the chance for an extended discussion after the centre to build a development plan. However, the centre never claimed to be a 'development centre'. It was honestly presented as a means of choosing people for a limited number of places on the EDP.

The Tarmac centre was said to be well received by all those who went through it. In general, the reaction an internal selection centre will get seems to me to depend very much on the culture of the organisation and precisely how the centre is being used. What is acceptable, say, for the public service with a tradition of open competition might not be acceptable for middle managers in the private sector. The moment the centre is used to make immediate decisions – even if they can in theory be reversed – then the price of 'failure' can very easily be demoralisation. An organisation should think carefully before it sends its best 10 per cent of young managers to a centre, gives 15 per cent of them 'high-flyer' tickets and leaves the other 85 per cent feeling thoroughly fed up. At the very least, there must be a developmental follow-up to the centre so that the 85 per cent do not give up and see their career as irretrievably blighted.

In deciding whether to have an internal centre that is essentially selective, perceived legitimacy will be an important criterion. In particular, there will be circumstances when an assessment centre is demonstrably fairer than any other system for making decisions about people. Most obviously, this will be the case if the organisation cannot have had sight of the attributes required at the promotion level. For example, in promoting people to team leader positions, the great advantage of the assessment centre is that it enables a preview of how the person would behave in the role. Without a centre the organisation must rely on guesswork. The centre seems likely to be seen as legitimate under these circumstances. On the other hand, a centre to mark a boundary between levels of management might be questioned by people who feel that surely enough is known about their strengths and weaknesses without needing an assessment centre. However, in the public sector, some form of open competition might have to be involved. In that case, the assessment centre is a far better way of deciding than a promotion board. The board cannot possibly be expected to assess candidates fairly or adequately on all the dimensions relevant to the job level. For example, Adler (1990) described how assessment centres had worked towards equality of opportunity in US police forces. In police agencies using an assessment centre, the percentage of eligible women promoted to sergeant was 12.2 per cent, which can be compared with the 4.9 per cent in police departments using traditional promotion systems.

In conclusion, it is vital that a clear decision is taken on the purpose of the centre, and the above points might be borne in mind in making that decision. The purpose of the centre – whether for assessment or development – needs to be thought through. I fear that there are many centres that the organisation would like to be 'development centres' but that are marred. The organisation is not quite able to resist the temptation to use the information for making choices about people. This will compromise their development value and might well be accompanied by a sense of grievance felt by participants. It is likely that the discontent will remain under the surface or be discounted by the 'nobody is owed a living' style of management.

A continuum of assessment centres

Although there is a clear choice between a centre for selection and one for development, the next chapter will emphasise the importance that centres for selection are designed in a way that does not alienate candidates. As such, a good selection centre will be slightly removed from the end point of the continuum of assessment centres, which ranges from the archetypal old-style selection centre to the archetypal development centre. The continuum is summarised in Figure 3.

It can be seen that there are a number of differences between selection and development centres, and that these are inherent in the different purposes of the centres.

Figure 3
A CONTINUUM FROM DEVELOPMENT CENTRES TO SELECTION CENTRES

Purpose	development/career-planning	promotion/development	selection
Label	development centre		selection centre
Philosophy	done by the participant	done with the participant	done to the candidate
Method	self-assessment/peer assessment plus observer's view	assessment with feedback	testing/no feedback
Assessor's role	witness		judge
Includes	self-insight materials		cognitive test
Output	personal development plan	report	selection decision
Information on exercises	open		secret
Feedback given	after each exercise	after centre	not given
Owner of information	participant	participant and organisation	organisation
Duration	two — three days	one — two days	one day

4 CENTRES FOR SELECTION

Achieving the right atmosphere

Assessment centres for selection can be divided into those used for external recruitment and those used for internal selection. The prime example of the former is the graduate assessment centre. Two contrasting examples of internal selection centres are those which are used to identify people for a fast management track and centres for the selection of team leaders from amongst members of the team.

External selection centres

At first sight, assessment centres for external selection might seem simpler to implement and run than those for internal selection. External selection centres carry with them a less obvious need for feedback to participants. There is also less anxiety about the demotivating effects of poor performance at the centre upon those who take part. However, nowadays even centres used for external selection should provide some feedback to participants so that they do not simply feel processed by the organisation. As Herriot (1988) has pointed out, it is vital that organisations do not alienate applicants by making them feel the selection process is purely done *to* them. It needs to be done *with* them, and so the centres should become events for mutual assessment between the organisation and its applicants. The alternative is to risk creating an unfavourable impression with applicants which will be passed on to their colleagues and friends. In turn, these people will be less willing to apply to the organisation. The grapevine operates most obviously with undergraduates, with whom some organisations clearly have a much more favourable image than others because of their selection procedures.

The importance of carrying candidates with you is emphasised at times when there are headlines about the 'talent shortages'. However, even when the headlines carry the opposite story, the importance of treating candidates well cannot be ignored. Whether in a recession or boom, there is always a shortage of the best people. In other words, for the most able it is probably always a seller's market. You cannot afford to be turning them off with an alienating selection procedure. It is this need to keep candidates' loyalty that is one of the arguments for assessment centres. The general user-friendliness of the centres is one of their advantages. Data on the reactions of candidates to different assessment systems generally show the advantageous position of assessment centres. For example, Mabey and Iles (1991) reported that assessment centres were scored highest and personality questionnaires lowest by candidates in terms of both perceived usefulness and fairness as selection techniques.

However, these results will be obtained only by a well-designed centre, and one run with the right attitude. Unfortunately, there are many centres that are badly designed or run by someone with a less than conducive manner. I well remember early in my career attending an apology for an assessment centre by a building society which was run in such a way that I felt just like an object being processed. I certainly did not want to join them after the experience, nor did I particularly feel like having an account with them. This illustrates the danger of a tough 'they can like it or lump it' approach. The risk is that candidates will choose to go to an organisation that treats them better, and take their custom with them.

Even if you think you have got it right, there is still the need to carry out some basic market research and find out candidates' reactions to your procedure. There should always be the opportunity for candidates to provide their reactions to the centre through an anonymous questionnaire. This should cover all aspects of the centre, and can include quite direct contentions such as 'I feel more positive about (the organisation) having gone through the assessment centre.' For example, with a selection procedure I designed, candidates are given an anonymous questionnaire for them to comment upon each aspect of the assessment centre as well as giving overall comments. Happily, most of the feedback has been positive, only one person indicating a lesser likelihood to join the organisation after going through the selection procedure. However, the questionnaire did alert us to a more widely shared feeling of people being unduly rushed in the assessment centre written exercises, and we have done something about that.

For many organisations, the shortage of talented people has shifted the emphasis of selection centres from an accept-reject choice. The new emphasis is upon trying to make the best use of those people who apply. By gaining so much good information on people, the assessment centre can be used not just to select but also to place people, and to work out initial induction and development plans for them. Indeed, some selection centres could be renamed placement centres. A client of mine who was facing difficulties attracting sufficient experienced applicants is now using an assessment centre which includes a career counselling interview. Wherever possible, a fit is achieved between this client's needs and the applicant's interests. Of course, some people will still be deemed unsuitable generally for the organisation, but the tenor of the centre is clearly different from one that has an exclusive role of selecting people.

Internal selection centres

The question of acceptability to the people being assessed is at its most crucial when they are members of the organisation. The assessment is bound to be threatening, but organisations still have to choose people for promotion or identify staff with high potential. Unfortunately, there are many organisations that build up the threat rather than reducing it. They seem to forget some very basic and obvious facts, most notably that people bring emotional needs and reactions to work. In particular, we retain right from the start of our lives the fear of threat and danger. People react to threat in different ways – it might be withdrawal or anger –

but whatever it is, it is clearly not productive. Assessing people internally needs to be done in a very careful and sensitive manner. Yet all too often it is cack-handed, and the end result is people turned off the organisation. Again the robust approach is to say, 'Tough – the world does not owe them a living.' Well, maybe not, but that is hardly the approach to get people working with enthusiasm for you.

Even if there is no intention to adopt a macho approach, there remains the need to be cautious that people do not leave an internal centre feeling they have been 'knocked back' by the experience. Jackson and Yeates (1993) found this to be a rare occurrence, but one that was possible if a participant found him- or herself completely out of depth in an exercise. The impact will be particularly severe if the failure is in front of colleagues, for example during a group exercise.

Assessment centres used for internal selection will definitely need to have a major emphasis on feedback and development planning. The centres should be as developmental as possible, trying to make sure that everyone comes away with some benefit, if only a greater self-understanding and a development plan. For example, Greatrex and Phillips (1989) described how BP stressed that their residential assessment boards were a developmental opportunity for the individual, with full feedback and counselling. This attitude also contributed to the success of the Tarmac centre (Woodruffe, 1997) mentioned earlier.

Generally, it is unwise for an internal centre to be seen as an irrevocable decision-point in a person's career. Assessment centres that are set up in this way build resentment and lose their developmental possibilities. For example, some organisations have centres to which attendance is compulsory and which are used for promotion, performance review, and reward. This type of centre will become an object of fear, and those who have performed less satisfactorily will feel thoroughly demotivated. I believe that it is much better if the centre is used to provide information upon people's current competence and likely potential, but to leave plenty of room for flexibility in the organisation's view of them. The centre should be used to pencil their potential into the organisation's succession plan, and not to make hard and fast pronouncements. My preference is also to separate the centre from an immediate promotion decision, but if the centre has to be used to help make immediate decisions, the participants must be debriefed extremely carefully after the centre. Ideally those who are not seen as ready for promotion will share this perception. Quite definitely, the macho approach to passing and failing internal candidates has highly dysfunctional consequences that few organisations can afford.

This does not mean abandoning any notion of some people being better than others and identifying them. There are clearly advantages to identifying fast-track people. Boehm (1985) describes the benefits of these early-identification programmes as enabling a focus of management development resources on the individuals likely to contribute most to the organisation. They also keep high-potential people motivated and give others an honest account of where they stand so that they can make informed choices about their futures. However, as Boehm also notes, it is crucial that all those not seen as high-flyers remain motivated to perform and develop at their own pace.

I believe that one way to achieve this is to demonstrate that the organisation's view on people's potential is not static; another is to try to make the view at any particular time one that is shared by the person involved. What must be avoided is the assessment centre that is followed up by the 'Private and Confidential' letter, telling people their worth. Indeed, I am not convinced that it is necessary to motivate people by having a highly visible fast-track labelling scheme that people either manage or fail to get on to. The benefits of identifying potential cited by Boehm can still be gained with a more fluid and tentative approach that is set in the context of development.

It can be seen, then, that some of the features that might have been used to distinguish the assessment centre for selection from the development centre no longer hold good. A well-designed and well-implemented assessment centre that is used primarily for selection will have many of the features of a centre used for development. Of course, there will be differences in follow-up and there will be some major differences in design. For example, a developmental centre might well make more use of self-assessments, whereas this will be unrealistic in a selection centre. After all, people cannot be relied upon to vote themselves out of a job, even if it would be wise for them to do so. However, in all cases, a good centre should be a collaborative endeavour between the participants and the organisation. It is something done *with* them rather than *to* them, so that both the organisation and its applicants or staff can reach rational, well-informed decisions about careers. Otherwise, participants are likely to go away feeling 'processed'.

Part of the way around the problem of alienation is to offer something positive to come out of the assessment – namely development. Some development can occur at the centre itself. Having emphasised the need to make a clear choice on the primary purpose of the centre, it remains possible for there to be a developmental component to a centre that is used for selection. The centre might include, for example, sessions on career planning and development, rather than only concerning themselves with assessment.

Achieving the right atmosphere is aimed at ensuring that the centre does not have a negative impact on candidates. Chapter 2 argued that people – including candidates – generally feel positive about assessment centres and are more favourable towards them than to alternatives such as tests. This will be true only if the centre is properly conducted. It has also been noted that internal centres can lead to demotivation. Indeed this was the impetus to development centres.

The impact of assessment was investigated by several people in the 1990s, including Francis-Smythe and Smith (1997). They interviewed 32 participants at the internal assessment centre of a large UK financial services organisation approximately six months after attendance at the centre. Questioning focused upon the impact of the centre on the person's career, the adequacy of the assessment centre process, feedback quality and managerial support. Respondents also completed questionnaires on commitment and involvement.

Not surprisingly, people who had better ratings at the centre perceived it to have a positive career impact and people with poor ratings perceived a negative impact. Less obvious was the finding that those receiving better-quality feedback and those relatively far from middle-management believed the centre had a more positive impact on their careers than did those receiving poorer-quality feedback and those one position away from middle management. The impact of the centre affected people's commitment, involvement and career-planning. A clear conclusion that can be drawn from the study is that good-quality feedback is important in fostering a positive impact and in maintaining commitment, involvement and career-planning. It might also be concluded that it is better for the assessment centre to be staged while people are at a comparatively junior level in the organisation.

5   DEVELOPMENT CENTRES

As Chapter 3 made clear, it is preferable to reserve the use of the term 'development centre' for centres that have *only* a developmental purpose. The moment an element of selection intrudes, I think the term becomes inappropriate. The centre is seen by participants as an assessment centre. The distinction can be seen as based upon the ownership of information. Hall and Norris (1992) use the term development centre if the information is owned by the participant.

In the 1990s a pure developmental goal became the emphasis for many centres, fully justifying their being called development centres. Development centres place emphasis upon participants and observers collaborating to identify the participants' strengths and development needs. They might also agree areas that are less rectifiable weaknesses and that need to be made up for by others in the team.

Development centres tend to focus on management or leadership competencies. However, this is not an unbreakable rule. Beard *et al* (1991) describe a development centre for BT's UK Sales Organisation staff; it gave people a snapshot of themselves in terms of key sales competencies.

Reasons for the growth of development centres

Various forces combined in the growth of development centres. As already noted, one major reason for the change of emphasis of internal centres is the demotivating effects of internal centres that are used with an element of selection. Conversely, there is the motivating effect of being developed. A case study of just such a change of emphasis is provided by Neill's (1989) description of Trent Regional Health Authority's fast-track management development programme. It changed from being based upon a selection centre to being a much more developmental and collaborative event.

Not only is the assessment centre potentially demotivating, it also seems a less worthwhile endeavour than in the past. As mentioned, nowadays, centres can generally only be used for 'pencilling in' people's likely career progression rather than for making enduring decisions. The more tentative nature of the assessment of people is reinforced by the changeability of the template against which they are assessed. It makes less and less sense to give people a seal of approval for the rest of their career. The desired qualities will change as the roles in the organisation changes. Recognising this reduces the impetus to try to measure precisely everyone's potential.

This leads on to the second reason for the change of emphasis. It was the realisation that organisations must develop their people continuously (Wood, 1988). The turbulent and changeable environment in which organisations exist has forced them to emphasise the development of their human resources to meet the ever-changing demands. In addition, these demands themselves have become more exacting with increasing and globalised competition. All this is at the very time that organisations face ever-keener competition with each other for talented people. In general, today's organisations have had to place an increasing emphasis upon developing available resources rather than just being able to pick from a mass of external and internal talent.

A third reason is that organisations are probably less willing nowadays to send people away on courses that are not clearly related to the business needs. They want increasingly to engage in development that is going to affect people's immediate behaviour, as well being obviously relevant to the business. The development centre approach fulfils these specifications well. The focus is on the competencies that the organisation has specified as vital. Furthermore, people can develop these competencies at the centre in exercises that simulate the job itself. On the face of it there is therefore a maximum likelihood that what is learnt at the centre will be transferred back to the work environment. Furthermore, the centre can be used to plan for further development via work-based learning.

A fourth reason for the rise of development centres is that all the above changes have occurred at a time when the competency approach to human resource management has become widespread. This approach ties in very logically to the use of assessment centres, which have always aimed to measure competencies in simulations of the job. It is not a great leap of the imagination to use the same basic approach for development. If the focus is competencies, then development centres are clearly ideally suited to people becoming sensitive to their own level of competence by taking part in exercises that simulate their work. Furthermore, in the more imaginative development centre, they can make a start on developing competencies again in the safety of the simulation exercise.

A fifth reason for the popularity of development centres is that staff themselves demand development. If they do not receive it, they will go elsewhere. A development centre followed up by a personal development plan is a very visible way for organisations to make their contribution. An example is provided by Holbeche (1999), who describes a development centre provided by a financial services organisation. The motivation was the fear that 'the company would lose some of its "star" employees unless some form of development was offered' (p20). The demand by staff has come from the changing psychological contract, which is described vividly by Herriot and Pemberton (1995). Whatever might happen in individual organisations, there is a general perception that organisations are not particularly committed in the employment relationship. Therefore, it is in people's best interests to maintain their wider employability. Paradoxically, development of the ability to leave has to be provided to get people to stay.

A sixth and related reason is that the development centre is a way of showing staff that the organisation is, in fact, committed to them. The development centre becomes part of a strategy to retain people by providing for their employability with their current employer (Woodruffe, 2000). At the same time, the centre also gives people external employability, and this acts as insurance for them against unforeseen events such as a take-over.

Development centre objectives

The obvious objective of a development centre is to help people construct and implement a development plan. However, there are other objectives. One might be for participants to gain a realistic view of their strengths and potential. Development centres place a lot of responsibility in the hands of participants. They empower people not just to carry out development but also to have a realistic self-view. A well-designed development centre might reduce the frustration people feel from failing to advance by promotion. It will do so by getting them to see that promotion is less realistic than the pursuit of lateral moves.

Development centre features

Like an assessment centre, a centre for development still involves assessment of competencies. It also includes participants taking part in exercises that simulate the work for which they are developing. However, the distinguishing feature is that participants gain or increase their awareness of their development needs, and they will probably make some headway in meeting their development needs at the centre itself. For example, they can have feedback and coaching after each exercise, which they can use in subsequent exercises (Griffiths and Allen, 1987). Furthermore, they will normally start to construct a development plan during the centre to be implemented after the centre. The plan will certainly include work-based learning as well, perhaps, as going on competency development workshops.

Having made these points, there are generally fewer hard and fast rules about development centres than about centres for selection. It is up to the centre's designer to think imaginatively about what will be the best design to achieve the developmental aims of the centre. However, the centre would probably drop from the assessment centre 'family' if it was not competency focused, and if it did not include simulation exercises to enable participants to become aware of and address their development needs.

Within those parameters, if a centre is truly for development there can be an enormously liberating effect on its design. One fundamental issue that is present in assessment centres for selection immediately vanishes, and that is the need for some element of secrecy. In a development centre there can be no doubt that the sensible, indeed essential, approach is to be completely open. This means being very clear with participants about the competencies. Indeed, a component that takes place at the start of the centre will probably be an activity that increases participants' knowledge of the competencies and their definitions. There will also be a briefing for them before each exercise on the competencies that will be particularly relevant to that exercise. Equally, at a development centre, there will probably be a more thorough briefing on the exercises themselves, so that participants are clear what is entailed.

There is also much less need at a development centre to be obsessed by a requirement for fairness. At a selection centre, it is usually seen as a prime requirement that the operation and nature of the exercises is even-handed to all candidates. At a development centre, this is less of an issue. If an exercise is in a setting that is less familiar to one participant than another, then the lack of familiarity might itself be recognised as a development need. Beyond that, people will be more accepting of the information that comes out of the exercise. They are less motivated than at a selection centre to attribute poor performance to a fault in the exercise.

The removal of a strict need for fairness also means that, in some exercises, participants can be role-players for each other. In a selection centre, the competitive element and need for as standardised an approach as possible would rule this out, but in a development centre both sides of the role-play can benefit from the exercise.

The above points do not mean that a development centre can be designed sloppily. It is still important that it is a planned event that will provide all participants with an equal chance to develop. If there are role-playing one-to-one exercises, such as a customer one-to-one which participants do in pairs, then both of them should get a chance to play the major role. This will probably mean having two variants for the exercise. Furthermore, the suite of exercises should be of equal use to all participants even if individual exercises are 'fairer' to some than others. Finally, it is still important normally to have a pretty clear timetable for the centre so that you can be sure that participants will be exposed to the developmental experiences that were designed into the centre.

Aside from the removal of paramount concern about fairness and any about secrecy, the designer of the development centre can also think far more flexibly about the role of assessors. Assessors should adopt a coaching role, and it is essential that they put away their assessment centre 'white coats'. To convey this emphasis the word 'assessor' should probably be replaced by 'observer', or something similar. The flavour of the development centre should be collaboration rather than the expert telling the participant about development needs. In addition, the development centre will benefit by the presence of one or more facilitators who are assigned to each participant for the duration of the centre. They build up a relationship of openness and trust, and this relationship might indeed be maintained after the centre.

There will obviously need to be careful consideration about who the observers and facilitators should be. The observers will usually be or include line managers. However, it is not an unbreakable rule. Shuttleworth and Prescott (1991) describe how they used previous participants as coaches and say this was one of their best decisions in the design of their development centre at Pilkingtons. The other role, that of facilitation, is usually carried out by people from the HR function.

There is also room in the development centre for participants to assess themselves and each other. For example, Stevens (1985) reported on a centre that consisted only of the participants and administrators. The exercises were videotaped, and participants could perform their own diagnoses. This is quite a radical design and might be less beneficial in most circumstances than having someone with whom to discuss development messages. However, it illustrates the importance of thinking about the design that suits your circumstances and needs. If the participants are mature enough, or if there is a genuine reason for the private coming to terms with development needs, then this design would seem eminently suitable.

The less radical, indeed common sense, alternative is always to include self-assessment and probably to include peer-assessment. However, this must be handled carefully. If there is peer-assessment then there will need to be a session on feedback skills. If the quality of feedback relates to any of the competencies, there can then also be feedback on the feedback. The risk with peer feedback is probably less that it will be too attacking than that it will be so sensitive that the participant will come to doubt that there are any development needs at all. There will be a need to encourage honesty and to think carefully about how to timetable the feedback. In particular, should you start or finish with the observer's feedback? Probably over the course of the centre you will include both possibilities, if only for variety, and there are no hard and fast rules over which is better.

If the observer's feedback comes first, the self- and peer-feedback might be seen as superfluous. If the observer's feedback comes at the end, the observer can carefully integrate it at the time with the other feedback. On the other hand, there might be occasions when the observer does not want a particular message to get diluted, and so it might be put across before the self- and peer-assessment.

The running of the exercises can be treated in a more flexible fashion at a development centre. For example, it might be appropriate to interrupt an exercise and draw to a participant's attention the observation that he or she is or is not exhibiting the competent behaviours that were to be the focus of the exercise. Similarly, although the timetable should not be abandoned, there is room for an exercise to run on if people are benefiting from it.

The development centre should get away from the examination tone that might apply to the centre for selection. For example, the instructions for written exercises might soften the demand that people complete the exercise within a strict time limit. Rather than saying 'You must complete this in-tray in an hour and a half', the instruction might be 'People normally complete the in-tray in an hour and a half. However, you can take a little longer if you feel you need it.' The time a person requires and the reason for that requirement can then become part of the developmental message of the centre.

Exercises should still be simulations of the job for which you are trying to increase competence. This might be the person's current job, or you might be helping development for a future job. If the developmental message is to be received it is important that people can see that their development needs have been identified in settings that are highly relevant to the target job. The same consideration will maximise the likelihood that behaviour that is developed at the centre will be transferred to the job. For example, if a person's job involves dealing with customers, then an exercise that simulates the precise type of customer contact would seem to carry the maximum impact in terms of developmental messages. Furthermore, competent behaviour learnt at the centre can be transferred directly back to the work setting. Neither outcome would seem as likely if the person is 'playing a part' that is not played in the target job.

A central feature of the development centre will be its output: a development plan. It might be most beneficial if this plan is refined during the course of the centre. A possible approach is for participants to arrive with some idea of their development needs expressed in terms of competencies they want particularly to target at the centre and afterwards. These would be discussed with facilitators at the beginning of the centre. Before the first exercise, the facilitator and participant could discuss how the participant might behave so as to perform with greater competence on the target competencies. After that exercise it might be apparent that the participant has indeed made a start on addressing the original development needs, but another need might have been made apparent by the exercise. The development plan would therefore be updated after the first exercise, and so on through the centre. At the end of all the exercises, the participant would then have an updated and more refined notion of where his or her development needs lie. The participant would then work with the facilitator to decide how to address these needs. As noted earlier, the possibilities include attending a workshop as well as engaging in work-based learning.

Line-manager involvement

It is important that line managers have a sense of involvement and ownership over the process. This might be achieved by involving a sample of them in the design of the centre, including the identification of the competencies and design of the exercises. It is also important to brief the line manager carefully on the nature and purpose of the centre before one of their staff takes part in it. They might also be asked to help prepare a participant for the centre by carrying out a pre-centre discussion of development needs. In addition, the line manager will almost certainly be involved after the centre in agreeing the development plan with a participant.

Ferguson (1991) stresses the importance that the line managers have a sense of ownership over the development plan. They will be the sponsors of the work-based learning. They need to be involved at an early stage, ideally before the centre. They might also be invited to the centre on the last day and collaborate with the participant in drafting the development plan.

A partnership approach

The various differences that have been discussed in the design and operation of a development centre in contrast to a selection centre should elicit a corresponding change in the approach of participants. They can behave quite naturally and declare and discuss their development needs. They should feel no sense of threat from the centre, and certainly there should be no feeling of competition. Defensiveness should also be removed. Participants are not being forced to accept each and every item of feedback from their peers and observers. Instead, they are being asked to approach the experience of the centre in an adult way, and if they know a particular piece of feedback is at odds with how they normally behave then it is up to them to decide to discard it. The centre is placing responsibility for their development firmly in their hands, while demonstrating the organisation's commitment to facilitating their development by providing the centre itself. Certainly participants should have an overall feeling that the centre is being done with or indeed by them rather than to them. However, none of these points are guaranteed, and it would certainly be wise to include at the end an opportunity for the participants to give feedback on the centre and its operation.

In conclusion, hopefully this chapter has conveyed the broad thrust of a development centre. It is important not to lay down too many hard and fast laws about such centres, and it might be appropriate to depart from some of the generalisations that I have made. The key purpose is to design a centre that achieves the maximum developmental impact for participants, and to think with maximum flexibility towards achieving this aim. However, one point upon which there can be certainty is that the developmental impact will be greatly diluted if participants feel that what happens at the centre will have some impact on career decisions that the organisation makes about them. Common sense tells us that this is bound to make participants feel far more constrained in their behaviour and far more likely to pick up on such points as the fairness of exercises.

6   DECIDING TO HAVE A CENTRE

The opening chapter presented the 'headline' news that development and assessment centres work and sell themselves. This needs to be examined in greater detail so that you can satisfy yourself and others that the centre is the right way to spend your budget. After all, there are plenty of other ways both to choose people and to develop them. This chapter considers the published evidence for the validity of development and assessment centres. It also describes the economic case that can be made for them with the aid of a technique called utility analysis. Finally, it considers the arguments against their introduction.

Validity is broadly defined as how well the centre does what it is meant to do. Depending upon the centre's purpose, the issue might be whether it is valid as a way of choosing high-performing people or whether it works as a catalyst for development. The evidence that has been published on validity concentrates upon the traditional type of centre being used for selection. There is far less published evidence on development centres.

The validity of assessment centres

The indices against which assessment centres have been validated are many and varied, but they fall into the two main categories of current performance in the job and performance over time in a career. For some jobs, current performance might be readily quantifiable. For example, salespeople can be measured in terms of performance against targets.

However, for many jobs the criterion is less clear cut and ratings of performance by a superior against the job competencies have to be relied upon. The second criterion is performance over time. This is frequently measured in terms of ratings of potential by supervisors, and so it is really dealing with expected performance. However, in some cases performance over time is measured in terms of promotion or salary.

The studies on validity could be taken one by one. There will inevitably be variations between them, though, and some of the evidence will be negative. For example, Pynes and Bernardin (1989) report a correlation coefficient of 0.2 between assessment centre ratings for US police officer entrants and their subsequent job performance. Correlation coefficients can vary between zero (absolutely no relationship between the variables) and one (a perfect relationship). Just to complicate matters for non-statisticians, the correlation coefficient has to be squared to find out how much of one variable is predicted by the other. In the case of Pynes and Bernardin's study, the answer is just 4 per cent. They conclude that 'the results do not justify the high cost of this particular assessment center' (p833). Garavan and Morley (1998) are equally negative. They declare that 'there are grounds for suggesting that assessment centres are an elaborate charade' (p217). They base the conclusion on a study of the graduate assessment centre of a bank in Ireland. They found a small negative correlation between performance at the centre and subsequent appraisals of the performance of successful candidates. As they recognise, the problem is as likely to be due to the performance appraisal process as to the assessment centre, and their conclusion might be seen to err on the side of pessimism. Against this negative evidence might be placed more positive studies, such as that by Chan (1996). He reported a very high correlation (0.70) between an assessment centre's views on promotability, which were kept secret, and subsequent promotion board decisions. The assessment centre was a better predictor of promotion board decisions than supervisor ratings.

One reaction to fluctuations in the evidence is to look for explanations in the methodology of the different studies. For example, it seems highly contentious to take supervisor ratings as correct and the basis on which to dismiss the assessment centre. Another reaction is to say that the positive evidence at least shows what can be achieved with a well-designed centre. Negative evidence might just cast doubt on the particular centre upon which the evidence was obtained. It does not undermine the assessment centre approach. For example, Pynes and Bernardin admit that their measure of performance suffered from most ratings being near the middle of the scale, and their assessment centre ratings had the problem of being on only a three-point scale with 55 per cent of people gaining a '3'. In such circumstances a high correlation between assessment centre scores and performance would be hard to obtain. The fluctuations in validity led Dukes (1996) to conclude that 'good results cost money and require an obsessional degree of care at every stage' (p2). They will be obtained only if the centre conforms to best practice. As if to confirm this opinion, Aitchison and Wigfield (1999) reported how the validity of a centre was transformed by modifying it to conform to best practice. The correlation between the centre and performance was raised from 0.06 to 0.47 by ensuring the proper measurement of the competencies.

A different reaction to fluctuating evidence is to take an overview of the validities of a number of individual assessment centres and to find out how valid assessment centres are in general. This is the approach taken by the advocates of a methodology known as meta-analysis. It is an approach championed by Hunter *et al* (1982). The variations in validity between individual assessment centres are put down to the different errors and quirks that will always be present in studies. A number of meta-analyses have now been published that deal either exclusively with assessment centres or that compare assessment centres with other methods of prediction. Schmitt *et al* (1984) carried out a comparative study. They surveyed validity studies published in *Personnel Psychology* and the *Journal of Applied Psychology*. They found validity coefficients on assessment centres that had been used to predict a range of criteria, including ratings of people's performance and status change. Assessment centres were superior to all other methods of predicting performance ratings, with a mean coefficient of 0.43. They were also among the best predictors of status change, with a mean coefficient of 0.41. Taking all the criteria together, Schmitt *et al* report that assessment centres were the most valid predictors (the mean validity coefficient was 0.41), along with evaluations by peers and supervisors. Personality measures were the worst predictors, with a mean validity of 0.15.

Quite similar statistics for assessment centres came from a study by Gaugler *et al* (1987). They carried out a meta-analysis of validation studies of assessment centres containing a total of 107 validity coefficients. The overall validity coefficient was 0.37, the best coefficient being obtained when the centres were used to predict ratings of management potential (0.53). The coefficients with performance were 0.36 for overall performance and 0.33 for performance on the individual competency dimensions used at the centre.

The point appears to be made, and there is no need to quote study after study. The published evidence leads even the sceptic to state that 'given the predictive validities consistently reported in reviews we would have to conclude that indeed assessment centers do work' (Klimosky and Brickner 1987, p244). This is the broad conclusion that is built upon in the salesperson's argument for assessment centres, which tends to launch into superlatives. In fact the validity correlations that have been described imply a far from perfect prediction of performance. Furthermore, there are people who reach rather different conclusions than that drawn by Klimosky and Brickner. In particular, Schmidt and Hunter (1998) seem determined to advance the cause of cognitive tests over assessment centres. They reviewed the results of various meta-analyses of the validities of different personnel measures in predicting job performance. They conclude that work sample tests were just superior to cognitive tests of general mental ability (GMA), with validities of 0.54 and 0.51 respectively. For assessment centres, they used the Gaugler *et al* validity of 0.37. They say that, in comparison with GMA, assessment centres are 'much more expensive and have less validity' (p264). This conclusion seems questionable and odd. As Schmidt and Hunter acknowledge, assessment centres frequently include a GMA test. Their argument must be that the test alone is more valid than the test plus the simulations. It seems strange not to question the implication that the other exercises have a negative effect on validity. It is an especially odd implication, since the simulations provide measures of cognitive ability 'in action', as well as giving an indication of people's 'emotional intelligence'. Schmidt and Hunter appear to be arguing against the entire bandwagon who say that emotional intelligence is far more important than cognitive intelligence for job success.

Schmidt and Hunter could also acknowledge that a meta-analysis includes studies of assessment centres that range from the good to the bad. The meta-statistic plays down the power of a properly designed centre. On the other hand, the cognitive tests are likely to be of a more uniform quality. Another result from their meta-analysis gives a strong clue to good assessment centre design and to the resulting power of the centre. This hint comes from the high validity of work-samples. Assessment centres should be designed as closely as possible to replicate the actual work that people will be carrying out. As Wood (1994) explains, this reduces to a minimum the span of the inference between performance in the 'test' and performance in a job. Clearly, managerial work cannot be sampled in the same way as bricklaying, because it is less well defined. Nevertheless, the assessment centre should be designed to be as close as possible to a work sample. The assessment centre should not contain a series of 'games' that appear to require the competencies. As Blanksby and Iles (1990) conclude, 'all the research evidence shows that centres need to be designed for the organisation/job in question' (p42). If this is done, there is good reason to suppose that Schmidt and Hunter's work-sample statistic of 0.54 will be a better estimate of the validity of an assessment centre than the Gaugler *et al* overall figure of 0.37.

In summary, it can be concluded that there is strong evidence for the validity of a well-designed assessment centre. However, this evidence must be tempered by the need to separate the validity of the centre as a measure of competencies from its validity as a predictor of performance. The centre's validity as a measure of competencies does not guarantee its validity as a predictor of success. After all, the competencies might not be those required for success. Conversely a centre can be successful as a way of choosing people, but its success might not be because it operates in the way intended by its designers (ie via the measurement of particular competencies). It might still achieve predictive validity but in some other way, for example by measuring a person's overall fit to the organisation.

These somewhat intractable issues are considered in the final chapter. They mean that validity coefficients do not provide an unquestionable basis for using an assessment centre. However, what is far less open to debate is the face validity of an assessment centre. The emotional arguments in favour of assessment centres have been introduced in the second chapter in considering their seductiveness. Quite simply, they are an extremely plausible way of finding out about people's strengths and weaknesses on the dimensions of relevance to the target job and, once they are under way, assessment centres that are well designed will act as their own ambassadors. They sell themselves to line managers and participants. As Stevens (1985) found, the attitude of users is that the cost of the centre 'is minimal compared with the cost of not using them' (p28).

Assessment centres and development

As noted, assessment centres are frequently designed to have as much developmental impact as possible. Evidence that they might be succeeding in this objective comes from Higgs (1996), who reports an analysis of assessment centres at six UK financial services organisations. He says that attending a centre had its strongest impact on the personal insight of participants. He also describes the centres as stimulating self-development. He concludes that 'an assessment centre does provide a useful development tool' (p5).

The validity of development centres

The validation of development centres can cover either the centre itself or the centre together with the implementation of the development plan. Taken alone, development centres have relied to some degree on their face validity. There is not a great deal of hard evidence on the development value of the centre itself. As Carrick and Williams (1999) observe, their developmental value is assumed but largely untested.

What about the validity of the centre as part of a package that includes implementation of a development plan? There is some evidence provided by Engelbrecht and Fischer (1995). In a careful study that compared those who went to a development centre and those waiting to go, Engelbrecht and Fischer demonstrated that the development centre followed by on-the-job development had an impact upon all the competencies they studied except synthesis and judgement. The competencies that developed were action orientation, task structuring, development, empathy, managing information and probing. The lack of development of the cognitive competencies is not surprising in hindsight. It does, however, suggest a limit to what can be expected from a centre and from development generally.

Jones and Whitmore (1995) compared the promotion rates of people who had and had not been to a development centre. They found that the promotion rates were broadly similar. For those who attended the centre, 'overall the percentage of developmental recommendations followed did relate to promotion' (p385). When Jones and Whitmore looked at this in more detail they found that promotion was particularly related to development concerning career motivation and working with others.

The evidence is, then, somewhat equivocal. There is a need for more empirical studies to show that development has taken place following a centre and that this development is tied to improved job performance. However, there is inferential evidence of the value of centres for development. For example Schmitt *et al* (1986) demonstrated that attending the centre would help the person gain an accurate self-perception. People's self-perceptions after the centre altered from their pre-centre self-perception for five of eight dimensions. The alteration was in line with their performance at the centre as seen by the assessors (whose reports had not been disclosed to the participants). Having an accurate self-perception must be a first step to development planning, even if it does not guarantee the development will take place.

Estimating the benefit with utility analysis

Before making the considerable investment in the design and running of a centre you may well want to estimate the financial benefits. In order to do this the methodology of utility analysis can be applied. It looks at the monetary gains from substituting a more valid personnel procedure to replace a less valid one. In the case of selection, the gains come from the organisation recruiting people who are on average higher performers than would be recruited by a less valid procedure. This increase in average performance will yield a gain in output if the same number of people are recruited. Alternatively, it will allow a reduction in the payroll by requiring a smaller number of higher performers to do the volume of work that was previously carried out by average performers. Utility analysis was developed in the 1980s by Schmidt and by Hunter (eg Hunter and Schmidt, 1983; Schmidt *et al*, 1986). They built on earlier contributions by Brogden (1949), Cronbach and Glesser (1965) and Dunnette (1966). It is a quite complex procedure but, in the case of selection, the analysis is based upon a knowledge of the accuracy of different methods of selection and of how much people's performance can vary in a job depending upon their ability to perform it. For some jobs, it might be that everyone will perform equally satisfactorily and so the expense of any selection procedure is hard to justify. For other jobs, there will be a wide and readily apparent variation between the high and low performer. The greater the potential variation in performance, the more point there is in investing in an accurate procedure for choosing between applicants. The analysis calculates the financial benefit of a more accurate procedure that raises the average level of performance of people. The variation in performance can be put into monetary terms quite easily for some jobs. For example, the variation between salespeople is directly calculable in terms of the sales each of them makes. However, for many jobs, including managerial jobs, the direct measurement of performance in monetary terms is less easy. Schmidt *et al* (1979) provided a practical method for estimating the variation in such cases. The method yields a range of figures depending upon the job. The range reported by

Schmidt and Hunter (1983) was from 42 per cent to 60 per cent of salary. To be conservative, they put their rule-of-thumb estimate in monetary terms for the variation between high and low performers as 40 per cent of salary for the job.

Apart from the variation in performance, it is also necessary to know the selection ratio (the number of applicants for each post). There is no point in having an elaborate selection procedure if all applicants must be hired. Finally, there has to be an estimate of the accuracy of different procedures. One way of obtaining this estimate is to hire groups of people using different procedures and to determine the differences in performance between the groups. Such studies are rare but three were reported by Schmidt *et al* (1986). These studies showed that the use of cognitive tests in selection would raise the output of US public-sector employees by just under 10 per cent or would allow the workforce to be reduced by just under 9 per cent.

Clearly, it is far from easy to conduct this kind of experiment. It means installing the new procedure and then waiting some time before people's performance can be measured. This is obviously not a great help if the objective is to decide whether to install the new procedure in the first place! In such cases, the validities of different procedures are estimated from meta-analyses. It has been seen in the above section that the meta-analytic estimate of the assessment centre's validity might be put at around 0.40. For comparison, the figure generally quoted for the interview is about 0.2 (0.19 was quoted by Reilly and Chao, 1982). Knowing these figures, it is possible to work out the benefit from the assessment centre. For example, suppose an organisation is choosing 10 people from 50 applicants and is considering using an assessment centre instead of a simple interview. Suppose also that these people will each be paid £25,000 in their first year. The rule-of-thumb variation between high and low performance is 40 per cent of £25,000, ie £10,000. The utility of the interview over random selection for each person hired is this figure multiplied by the validity of the interview (0.20) multiplied by the figure from statistical tables that takes into account the selection ratio. For a selection ratio of 1:5, this figure is 1.40. The utility of the interview over choosing people at

random is therefore £2,800 for each perso[n]
are used in the calculation of the utility
centre over random selection, except th[at]
efficient is now 0.40. This gives a utility [of]
assessment centre yields a gain of £2,800 [... for]
people the gain is £28,000. This is a ga[in ...]
Against this must be set the initial costs and greater ongoing
expense of the assessment centre as opposed to the interview.
However, when the gain is finally added over the length of
the person's employment, the net gains become very high.
Assuming a length of service of eight years and that the
assessment centre costs £5,000 for each appointment, and
assuming also that the interview costs nothing, the saving is:
(8 [years] × £28,000 − 10 [people] × £5,000), ie £174,000. If
service were only three years, the saving would be £34,000.
As noted above the saving will either be in terms of needing
fewer staff to do the same job (an argument which applies
more with managerial and administrative work) or in the
greater productivity of the same number of staff (which will
apply more, for example, with sales personnel).

The above estimate would be altered under more sophisticated approaches to utility analysis that take account of such
variables as discount rates and taxes that affect other investment decisions (Boudreau, 1983a, 1983b; Cronshaw and
Alexander, 1985). However, whatever the detailed amendments it is clear that using more valid procedures such as an
assessment centre produces an economic benefit over using
inferior methods. Indeed the figures that come from utility
analysis tend to stagger people by their size. To give a published example, Feltham (1988b) estimated that using the
Civil Service assessment centre (the CSSB) instead of an interview to select batches of 70 administrators saves the UK
taxpayer at least £1.8 million for each batch.

In summary, assessment centres have empirical evidence
on their side, and this evidence can be turned into an estimate
of financial returns. As has been seen, such an estimate generally shows that an assessment centre will save a great deal
of money if it is substituted for less predictive methods of
selection. However, all this analytical evidence is far less
important to a decision on whether or not to have a centre

than the way it is extrapolated by those who advocate centres or ignored by those who are not convinced. In other words, I think that the analytical arguments are far less influential than the more emotional arguments based around face validity. Equally, the most powerful barriers to assessment centres might well be based around culture and vested interests. The arguments against them together with counter-arguments must now be considered.

Barriers to acceptance

Insufficient benefit

Development and assessment centres are complex to design. They are also time-consuming and resource-intensive to administer. There will clearly be many situations where nobody other than a complete zealot would claim they are warranted. For choosing people, it might well be more appropriate to use a structured interview (Wright et al, 1989) and tests of aptitude and ability rather than an assessment centre. This will be the case, for example, in hiring lower-level trainees. However, there will be other situations when these are not convincing rivals to assessment centres for external selection. They might be used as part of the centre but do not bear close examination as an alternative to it. For external people, the obvious justification for assessment centres is that there is no other opportunity of viewing all the competencies, particularly the emotional intelligence competencies that are important for the job.

The problem is that, even when they would be thoroughly worthwhile, the organisation's thinking about human resource issues must be sophisticated enough for the assessment centre approach to be seen as an appropriate rather than an exaggerated response. In particular, the assessment centre approach must be seen as worthwhile and valid by senior management. They are going to have to put in time in identifying the competencies and to commit their staff to designing the exercises, being trained and acting as assessors. In addition, if the centre is for internal people the managers must release the participants from their everyday work. Until there is a degree of sophistication, the advantages of assessment centres over other methods will not be appreciated. The highly visible direct costs of the centre will be more persuasive than the much less visible and unappreciated opportunity cost of not having it.

The same thinking applies to development centres. The project needs explaining carefully and to be seen as part of the implementation of a strategy to win in the market by developing and retaining highly competent people. Otherwise the benefits will not be seen to justify the cost.

External selection adequate without centre

The cheapest alternative to an assessment centre is not to have any assessment. It might be believed that the organisation can get away with hiring people on a short-term contract and renewing it or not, depending upon whether people make the grade. This is the inheritor of the old approach of taking people on probation and firing those who do not make the grade. In other words, the short contract or the probation period is the assessment. On the face of it, this seems quite a clean and honest approach. The short-term nature of the contract is there for all to see. There is no need to fire people. Their contract ends.

This might suit organisations in some sectors for some positions. However, in most sectors, it is not a suitable alternative to answer the bulk of their recruitment needs. For example, it is not a viable way for large organisations to fill their graduate vacancies. Apart from anything else, the short-term contract will lead to their getting a decreased quality and quantity of applicant. Furthermore, people who are found to be unsuitable are not free. It costs money to recruit them, they are paid during their stay and there is the opportunity cost of not having someone good in the post. As Schmidt and Hunter (1998) note, there is the possibility that these minimally screened probationary workers will perform poorly which, in turn, can lead to 'serious economic losses' (p268).

An alternative to the short-term contract is a pre-employment training scheme. Burke (1997) reports how the textile company, Courtaulds, operates such a scheme. Potential employees spend approximately 100 hours over a three-month period on a course in which they are assessed for team leadership and team membership. If it is structured appropriately, this type of event could be seen as an extended assessment centre. Clearly, the difficulty will normally be in finding candidates who are prepared to go along with it.

Aside from these alternatives that involve trying people out, there are the various other ways of selecting people to consider. Quite rightly, people will ask whether there is a simpler way of finding out about people's competence than by using an assessment centre. Generally, line managers' reservations about assessment centres hinge around their having great faith in the existing methods of assessment ('What's wrong with the interview or a 30-item personality "test", graphology or whatever?'). Many will be convinced that these methods are almost 100 per cent accurate, and so the benefits from an assessment centre will be seen as too small to justify the cost. The limitations to the alternatives are not fully appreciated.

One of these alternatives is to rely upon the right technical qualification or experience as a guarantee of competence, coupled (probably) with a quick interview. Of course, this might be adequate for some jobs, especially those that depend largely on technical expertise. However, for many jobs the non-technical requirements such as interpersonal skills need to be assessed carefully. For example, computer systems analysts need both technical and interpersonal competence if they are to work successfully, and an assessment centre exercise would reveal clearly how they interact with their clients. In more managerial jobs, relying on experience suffers from two problems. Most obviously the person might have failed to benefit from the experience and develop competence. Secondly, whilst it is dangerous to overplay the uniqueness of organisations, competence in one organisation does not mean competence in another. The culture might well be different, giving a different emphasis to the competency dimensions that are important for success.

The greatest competitor to any innovation in assessment will be the interview. In many cases, this will be poorly structured, based around what the particular interviewer feels are appropriate questions for the candidate. Despite the research evidence against it, many people have an implicit belief in the interview's utility, probably because they themselves carry out interviewing. They believe they get it right most of the time. In fact, there is a body of evidence against the interview as the sole means of selection, certainly in its unstructured format. Common sense also tells us that for many higher level jobs it cannot be expected to yield evidence on all the competency dimensions of importance. The interview might get at some of the competencies, for example self-confidence. However, the interview is quite obviously not suited to getting at other competency dimensions, such as organisation and co-operativeness. Such competency dimensions as these are better observed via an assessment centre exercise. So, interviews lack the logic and the empirical evidence that assessment centres enjoy.

On the other hand, structured interviews have a more favourable body of evidence behind them. Indeed, McDaniel et al (1994) estimate a correlation of 0.24 (before various corrections) between interview ratings and subsequent performance. The result is from a meta-analysis of a range of studies involving various interview formats. Evaluating this evidence is made difficult because some people compare structured interviews favourably with assessment centres when their definition of a structured interview turns out to be a mini-assessment centre. For example, Lowry (1994) reports a structured interview for a US police service that involved a role-play, a written report and an interview based around the role-play and written report. He describes this as less costly and generally as valid as an assessment centre. However, it could be said that Lowry is simply comparing a full assessment centre with a reduced version. Certainly it is more than a structured interview, albeit not quite an assessment centre as defined in the *Guidelines* (Task Force, 1989 and Appendix A). His article does however, raise the very real question of what constitutes the base package needed for an assessment centre to get near its maximum effectiveness. There is little sense in adding exercise after exercise if the marginal gain in validity is barely noticeable.

Is the structured interview alone a substitute for the assessment centre? It is a vast improvement on the unstructured version, because it represents a systematic attempt to measure the competencies. However, it still seems to suffer from the problem that it is clearly not the best way to measure all the competencies. Not only is it hard to imagine the structured interview giving the quality of insight into a person's strengths and weaknesses that an assessment centre offers, it is also unlikely to be as acceptable a method. Candidates are likely to leave the interview with less of a feeling that they have had the best opportunity to demonstrate their capabilities.

As another alternative, tests of aptitude and ability are an obvious cheaper alternative to an assessment centre. They have a good track record as predictors of success (Schmidt and Hunter, 1981; 1998) and will often be appropriate for inclusion in the selection procedure. Of particular relevance are cognitive tests, such as those of reasoning ability. But for higher-level jobs they should normally be an adjunct to the assessment centre rather than a rival of it. Although the qualities the test measures might be very similar to one or two of the competencies needed for the job (especially analysis and solution-finding) the assessment centre is still required to measure the remaining competencies. Furthermore, as Frederiksen (1986) points out, the simulation exercises measure a much broader conception of intelligence than the test does. For a start, real-life problems do not come in a multiple choice format. Even if the test measures a quality that is thought to lie behind many of the job competency dimensions, the link between the source dimension and the performance dimensions might well not be proven or strong. Certainly, it will not extend to all the competencies. There is also the issue of acceptability to applicants. Just giving people tests carries the message that applicants are there to be processed as efficiently as possible. Nowadays, many organisations are trying to give the message that they welcome applicants and that the selection procedure will be more of a mutual exchange of information. In addition, in the unlikely event of tests and inventories being used on their own (ie without any face-to-face component to the selection procedure, particularly an interview), there is the risk of making a gross error of selection. On the other hand, the assessment centre is a quite conservative procedure and unlikely to let through anyone who will turn out to be a complete non-starter (Dobson and Williams, 1989).

Another potential alternative to an assessment centre is an inventory of personality. It might appear to give a sophisticated measure of the same competency dimensions that the assessment centre would address. However, behind the apparent sophistication it is important to remember that all it can actually do is ask people to report on their own behaviour and preferences. The inventory should be chosen carefully to get at the relevant competency dimensions, but unfortunately inventories are installed all too frequently without a proper analysis of the competency dimensions required for successful performance. The invitingly labelled personality dimensions are all seen as important whether or not they are actually related to success. If the inventory's use is based on a proper job analysis, it may well be found that its coverage of the competency dimensions is incomplete. There is also still a great leap between a self-report of behaviour and how the person actually behaves in a specific job. Assessment centres give a direct preview of behaviour, if in a somewhat contrived situation. Personality inventories have to rely on the hope that the way in which people report their general past behaviour indicates the way in which they are going to behave in future in a particular job. The issue of generality is not entirely avoided by inventories that get people to report on their behaviour at work in general, rather than on their whole life. The problem is that there is a low cross-situational consistency in behaviour. This phenomenon undermines prediction from reports on situations in general to what a person will do in a particular job and organisation.

Many personality researchers nowadays emphasise that behaviour is an interaction between the person and the particular situation they are in. They look at personality as mediating between the person and the situation. Mischel (Mischel and Shoda, 1995) is particularly associated with this approach. He describes how individuals build up their own ways of reading the features of situations and their own ways of responding to those features. Situations with different features will be responded to differently. Assessment centres get much closer to simulating the actual situations in which the person will be working. Following Mischel, we might reasonably expect variability even across these situations. For example, a person might find a group exercise threatening but a role-play less so. The assessment centre therefore gives the opportunity for both a richer description of people, and it gets much closer than a personality inventory to ensuring that any generalisations about people are based upon the particular situations they will be in at work.

Apart from their focus on the general, there is the obvious difficulty of people faking measures within the personality/ interest realm or just presenting a self-deluded view of themselves. This cannot be avoided by so-called lie scales. The scales incorporate the test designer's view of implausibility and the items are often obvious; and if the scale suggests someone is too good to be true, what does one do then? Is it a case for automatic rejection or for ignoring the inventory results?

Perhaps these various problems explain why personality instruments do not have empirical evidence on their side. They are not good predictors of performance (Schmitt *et al*, 1984). In addition they are not accepted readily by applicants as a proper alternative to simulation exercises. Certainly, I have anecdotal evidence that undergraduate applicants resent them, and this view is endorsed by Iles and Robertson (1989).

The closest alternative to the assessment centre is a situational test. This asks people what they would do in situations that are described in the test. Good and bad answers are predetermined. Weekley and Jones (1999) studied such a test in the retail industry. They found the test results were better related to job performance than either cognitive ability or experience. Particularly favourable evidence for situational tests, presented in interview format, was obtained by McDaniel *et al* (1994) in their meta-analysis. This suggested that situational interviews had a higher correlation (0.27) with job performance than the behavioural interview (0.21) that concentrates on actual situations in the candidate's past.

The problem is that situational tests seem more applicable

for experienced than inexperienced candidates. Weekley and
Jones found an association between performance on them
and experience. By their nature the tests cannot be transparent, but people without work experience are likely to
indulge in wild guesswork in producing their hypothetical
answers to hypothetical situations.

Internal assessment adequate without centre

There will be occasions when the apparent fairness of the
assessment centre makes it desirable that it is used as
the gateway to promotion. The main alternative is an assessment by the line manager, probably via the appraisal system.
Line managers will often be idiosyncratic in their ratings and
may well focus on those competency dimensions that they
value personally. For some managers these may be the interpersonal dimensions, whilst for others they will be the
cognitive dimensions. If appraisal is used, some people may
feel their prospects are blighted by a boss who does not like
them. Others will complain of a boss who uses the appraisal
process more accurately than the lenient bosses their colleagues enjoy. In contrast, the assessment centre will be seen
as fairer when career decisions are being made. Everyone is
assessed in the same exercises using a small team of highly
trained assessors.

The disadvantage of using the centre for promotion is that
it will become an object of fear and demotivate those who
fail. However, this might be outweighed by its demonstrable
fairness. Certainly, exactly the same downside will be carried
by the other alternatives to the line manager's appraisal, such
as an interview, tests or personality inventories. They will be
just as feared as the centre but do not enjoy its compensating
validity.

Austin (1986, p6) observes that assessment centres will be
an 'unnecessary and expensive luxury' if senior executives
meet three conditions. They should have all the necessary
information that is needed to make promotion decisions,
understand that there are different criteria for success at different levels in the organisation, and be able to monitor and
assess employees against these changing criteria. Meeting

these conditions is a tall order. The conditions also emphasise that assessment centres are particularly useful when they focus on a job or job level that has different requirements from those of the participants' present job or job level. For example, the assessment centre is ideal for identifying potential team leaders amongst members of the team. Team members do not usually have a chance to demonstrate leadership attributes. Conversely, assessment centres will seem less justified if the attributes are highly visible in the person's current job, and if there is confidence in the appraisal process.

Development systems adequate

The main outputs of the development centre are a personal development plan and the enthusiasm to implement it. How else might these outputs be achieved? The appraisal process might be seen as an alternative to a development centre. The advantage of the development centre is that it can focus on the future. The exercises are in settings that the person will face in higher-level jobs, and the competency dimensions are those that apply to such jobs. In this way, the centre contrasts with appraisal that focuses upon past behaviour. Even if the main concern is immediate development needs, these are likely to be identified much more accurately by the development centre approach, and in a way that will be owned by the person concerned. The centre will have taken people away from their jobs to focus intensively upon development needs as well as career aspirations, and the feedback can be carried out in a way that will result in people owning their development plans. Personality inventories might also be seen as an alternative method to encourage development. However, they would be much better seen as an adjunct to development centre exercises than as a rival. Filling out the inventory will not have nearly the same impact upon people as taking part in simulation exercises. Even in the adjunct role, there is the danger that people hold the notion of a 'personality test' in awe. Feedback must be sensitive and tentative, and certainly not the highly dogmatic approach with phrases like 'The test says . . .'. This makes participants assume that having a particular disposition is not open to change, which is hardly a message to encourage development.

The main rival to development centres is probably the 360-degree feedback process. However, as Goodge (1997) notes, the limitation to this is if the person is changing job or the job is changing. In such cases feedback on present performance will be 'only a partial indicator of new job performance' (p14). There is also the issue that 360-degree feedback is by untrained observers. Nevertheless, if the person is developing in their current job, and if proper resources are given to facilitating the feedback, this can clearly be a powerful alternative to a development centre. It can also be a more acceptable alternative to senior people. It is individual and the timing of the feedback meetings can be scheduled to suit the person.

The power of 360-degree feedback can, of course, be harnessed by the development centre. People can bring their feedback to the centre, discuss it with a facilitator and use it to decide some of the competencies they will try to develop at and after the centre.

Expense

Centres have highly visible direct and indirect costs. From a survey of US organisations, Spychalski *et al* (1997) estimated the average cost per candidate at $1,700 (approximately £1,000).

The cost might include consultancy fees for the centre's design, as well costs for hotels, stationery, etc for running the centre. More important will be the indirect cost in terms of managers' and participants' time. Beard and Lee (1990) describe the design costs as a 'small element in the cost structure' (p61). They draw attention to the cost of time spent in briefing participants and their managers, in training observers at the centre and in both observers' and participants' attendance at the centre.

Imada *et al* (1985) found in an international survey that 'by far the most consistent obstacle to implementing an assessment centre is the economic issue' (p62). The Roffey Park survey (Holbeche and Glynn, 1999) produced much the same results. Cost, both of time and resources, was an issue both for assessment and development centres.

The organisation might feel that it simply cannot afford these costs, especially as the loss from not having the assessment centre is only that staff are less effective. They are not totally ineffective. With or without a centre, the work still gets done, and the costs of not having the centre are hidden. On the other hand, the development and running costs of having a centre are all too apparent. In these circumstances, rather than using utility analysis to demonstrate 'telephone number' savings, it might be more persuasive to tailor the approach so that the actual costs of the centre are less threatening. For example, I had to design an assessment centre for an organisation that had been using a panel interview. The centre was to cost no more in time than the interviewing procedure, which was based upon a board of three people that saw six candidates a day. I was able to design a one-day centre that still saw six people and used three assessors, but now they saw the candidates in a variety of settings across six hours, rather than in one setting for 40 minutes. Indeed, even the time to interview each candidate was longer.

Too small an organisation

An organisation might be seen as being too small for an assessment centre. It might be that the organisation has too few people at any level for it to be seen as worthwhile to have an assessment centre. To enjoy the benefits of a centre, such an organisation might focus on the generic competency dimensions across a set of jobs rather than emphasising the specifics of each job. The use of off-the-shelf exercises might also be investigated, although Chapter 9 advises caution with this option.

Loss of power

An assessment centre may be seen to be taking away the power of decision and patronage from some line managers, or from 'local barons', and putting it in the hands of the assessors. It is therefore important to ensure that the assessors represent a cross section of the organisation. It may also be appropriate to leave line managers with the final choice, based on the profiles from the assessment centre.

A development centre may also threaten local managers. It will analyse people's strengths and development needs, and part of their development might well include movement to other jobs. This will prove unpopular with local managers when they lose their 'stars' to other parts of the organisation. So, to sell the concept, it is clearly vital to carry along those with power by selling them the benefits, and ensuring that they will still feel in charge of the new system by helping to design and operate it. Certainly, the centre must not be seen as a way of the human resource department reining in more and more of the decision-making from them.

Biding time

The old adage holds good, that it is better to be told to introduce the HR enhancements by the chief executive rather than to be battling against a cynical board of directors. A top-driven approach is always more satisfactory, and it is certainly not going to be productive to try to introduce a centre with top-level resistance. Centres take up a lot of time in their design and – more importantly – they are resource-intensive to run. The initiative simply will not survive against the opposition of key stakeholders in the organisation. Until the need is underlined to senior management by some problem, all of the arguments for the centre will be seen as academic. The status quo will feel all right and not be disrupted by intellectual argument. The champion of development or assessment centres will have to wait for a favourable opportunity to sell the centre as the solution to an obvious need. Maybe the opportunity will be a set of people let in through the interview who turn out to be unsatisfactory, or maybe it will be difficulty filling posts with experienced people so that the organisation has to turn to trainees with no real track record. Maybe it will simply be that competitors are using assessment centres, and so a decision is taken to try them out.

7 PROJECT MANAGEMENT

Gaining commitment

Once it has been agreed to design the centre, it is important to gain and keep people's commitment. This means involvement and communication. It is important to involve people in the design of the centre and to make its purpose clear throughout the organisation.

Communication

Communication is needed before any work is done to design the centre. Otherwise, rumours will abound. This is particularly important with development centres and internal assessment centres. The major stages of design should be outlined and the major purpose of the centre should be made quite clear. As Lee and Beard (1993) point out, poor communication will easily result in apprehension among would-be participants. It is particularly easy for poor communication to destroy a development centre before it is even designed. Unless they are told otherwise quite unambiguously, people will readily see it as having an agenda that includes making decisions about their fate as well as helping their development. Therefore, attention must be paid to the precise wording of any announcement, because an unfortunate impression at this stage will be hard to dislodge. For example, a development centre will be undermined if people going to it are called candidates rather than participants.

Once all the work is done, there will need to be a briefing document for the whole organisation so that everyone is clear about the new system. The document need not be lengthy, but it should cover a brief introduction to the development or assessment centre process. It will describe how the centre has been designed to look at participants in terms of the competency dimensions that mark out successful performers at the job or job level. It should be explained that the centre uses job simulations, and that these exercises are observed by trained people. The briefing should also explain the role of the centre in the HR system, and why it is being used. It will also need to describe who the potential participants are and who the assessors will be.

The communication is also important in managing expectations, particularly for a development centre. It is vital to be clear about what can be expected after the centre. Certainly, it cannot propel everyone to the top of a flat organisation. Equally, the organisation might have no intention of providing other than on-the-job development. This needs to be clear at the start. It will be too late if it is only thought about once the first participants have been to a centre. The issue seems to be recognised in organisations. The Industrial Society survey (1996) found that raising 'expectations that the organisation may not be able to meet' (p20) was the biggest concern about development centres among its respondents.

Involvement

The main means of involving line managers will be by getting them to take part in the job analysis and in the exercise design. People from across the organisation should be included, not just a group of HR trusties. It might be worthwhile to do some groundwork that is unnecessary from a technical point of view but that gets maximum involvement. For example, in determining the competency dimensions, representatives from all interested departments should be interviewed, and any job analysis questionnaire that is developed should be sent to as many people as possible. In two recent assignments, we sent the job analysis questionnaire to all managers in the organisations concerned, which meant 400 people in one case and 1,200 in another. The costs in terms of paper and of data entry were far outweighed by the benefit of being able to say that everyone was included in the analysis.

Line managers should be involved in the design of the ercises and asked to act as assessors. Once they have been volved in the centre's design they will be its ambassadors. Any doubters should be won over by involving them in this way. It is very important that all interested parts of the organisation are included. If this means more people than can be used for the exercise design, the remaining people should be brought in as assessors. This may mean having more assessors than are needed, but that is preferable to letting some parts of the organisation feel they do not own the centre. Giving a sense of ownership to line managers results in the centres passing the consultancy test of their being acceptable as a method of selection and for initiating development. It involves line managers and gives them the same belief that some of them have with the interview. The difference, of course, is that for assessment centres the belief is well founded. The centres pass the technical test of being a good way of finding out about people's strengths and weaknesses. The first step in this technical aspect of assessment centres is to specify the dimensions upon which they must focus. This is the subject of the next chapter.

To summarise, it is vital that the centre is owned by the organisation and that it is not seen as an HR enterprise. This means involvement and communication. It also means the centre's designer exercising the consultancy skills of listening and adapting to suit the needs of the line managers and participants. It is therefore better to avoid having too fixed an idea at the outset of how the centre is going to be.

Project stages

Designing and running an assessment centre is a fairly complex but logical project. It consists of a series of interlinked stages and substages, as shown in Figure 4.

Once the project has been set up, the main stages are the job analysis, the design of the centre itself and, if necessary, of the development system. There will then need to be the training of assessors and role-players. After the centre has run a few times, the first validation should be carried out. There should also be an examination of the results in terms of general areas of strength and weakness for the organisation. The remainder of this book goes through these stages of the assessment centre project.

Project personnel

The people involved in the assessment centre project will usually be as follows:

- ❏ the co-ordinator
- ❏ steering group
- ❏ project team
- ❏ exercise material teams
- ❏ assessor/observer group
- ❏ role-players.

The co-ordinator

This person will usually be the 'champion' of the assessment centre initiative. He or she is most likely to come from the management development function of the organisation.

Steering group

The co-ordinator probably needs to involve a small number of key people to oversee the project. They should be senior people who are the 'customers' of the centre. They will be in a position to endorse the project at its major stages. These are: deciding the competencies; agreeing the centre's format, the budget and the assessors; agreeing policy on whether the primary purpose of the centre is selection or development, and on who should be invited to attend the centre and what happens afterwards; and agreeing the development programme.

Project team

They will carry out the detailed work with the co-ordinator. The team may well be just one other person who will help with the competency analysis, the design of exercises and so on, and will usually come from the management development

Figure 4

STAGES TO THE INTRODUCTION OF AN ASSESSMENT CENTRE

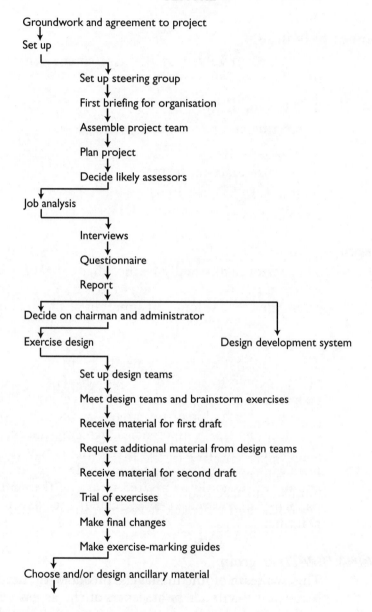

Figure 4 (continued)

Design rating forms

Choose role-players

Flesh out role-players' briefs

Role-player training

Choose first participants

Briefing to participants

Briefing to participants' managers

Assessor training

Run first centre

Make final changes

Validation of the centre

function. Having such a team is strictly speaking optional, because the co-ordinator might perform these tasks alone.

Exercise material teams

These will be teams of line managers who will work with the co-ordinator to provide ideas and material for the exercises. They will have been picked to be representative across the organisation. They are needed to ensure that the exercises have a high face validity. This is achieved by the material being representative of the real work of the organisation. In today's busy times it is important not to place too much of a burden on these teams. Their primary role is to provide exercise ideas and material. It is up to the project team to shape it into exercises.

Assessor/observer group

This is a team of line managers, probably including the design teams, who will act as assessors at the assessment centre or observers at the development centre. A fuller discussion is contained in Chapter 12.

Role-players

They will be required for any one-to-one exercises; again, there is a fuller discussion in Chapter 12.

It can be seen that getting to the stage of having a centre involves a considerable number of people and a good deal of co-ordination.

Project timetable

A rough timetable for the project is shown in Figure 5.

If a competency analysis is required, it can be seen that about four months will be required between deciding to have a centre and the first one being run. If the competencies are already installed, approximately two months will be needed.

Using consultants

It might be decided to call in a consultant to work on the design of the centre, especially if there is a lack of experience within the organisation. The argument is well-put by Finkle (1976, p882):

> As tempting as it may appear, the ready availability of group exercises is, in and of itself, hardly a case for a 'do-it- yourself' approach to assessment centers any more than the availability of scalpel and suture recommends a 'do-it-yourself' approach to brain surgery.

Perhaps consultants will be engaged only for particular stages in the design. For example, it will be better for someone who really is not sure about the process of analysing the competencies to seek consultancy advice. However, the same person may feel more confident in the process of exercise design. I hope that this book will help buyers know whether they are speaking to someone who really does have expertise. Beyond that, it is good advice to ask for references of organisations with whom the consultant has worked, and to check that the people who will actually be operating the assignment have substantial experience. The well-known risk is to be sold the project by the person with experience only to find that the operating consultant is the latest addition to the

Figure 5
A GANTT CHART OF THE PROJECT

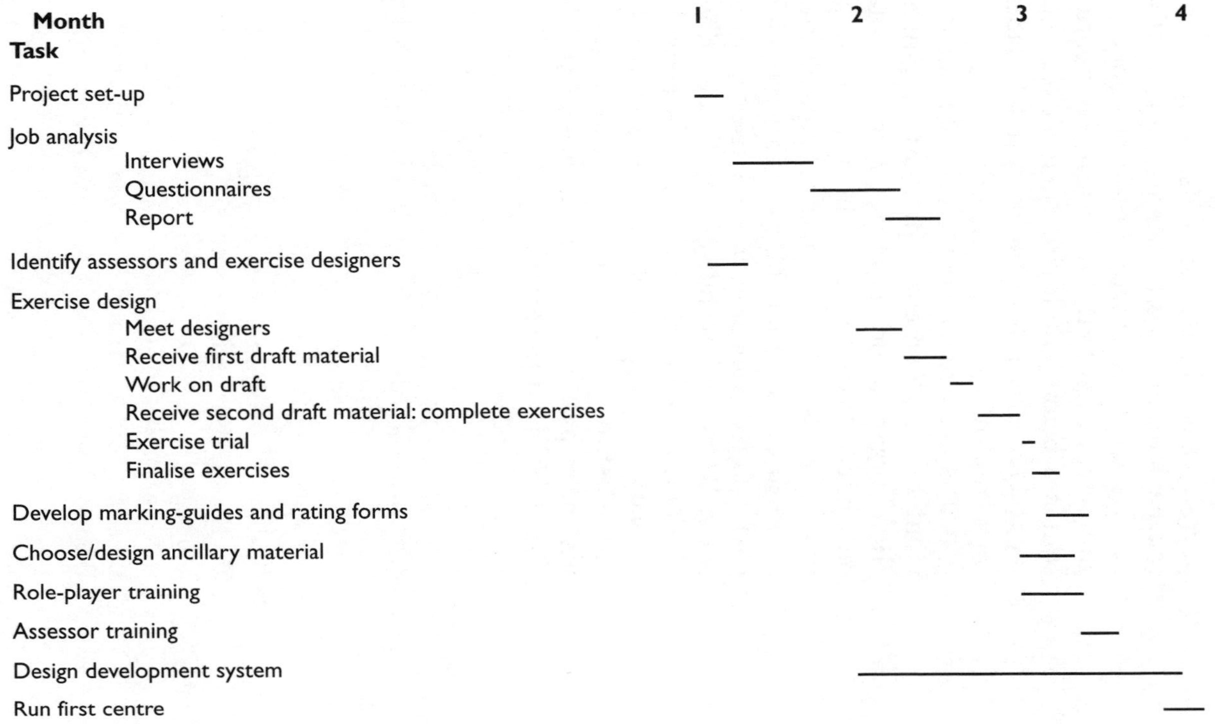

Month	1	2	3	4
Task				

Project set-up

Job analysis
- Interviews
- Questionnaires
- Report

Identify assessors and exercise designers

Exercise design
- Meet designers
- Receive first draft material
- Work on draft
- Receive second draft material: complete exercises
- Exercise trial
- Finalise exercises

Develop marking-guides and rating forms

Choose/design ancillary material

Role-player training

Assessor training

Design development system

Run first centre

payroll. It would also be advisable to ask to see examples of the consultants' work. For example, if they are to do the analysis of the competencies, it is a good idea to be shown a competency list that the consultants regard as being of a high standard before employing them. They should certainly not try to create awe with the esoterically labelled methodology they employ.

If it is decided to use consultants, the design of an assessment or development centre still requires input from the client organisation. It is not a project that can simply be outsourced in its entirety. The internal co-ordinator will need to take on the role of an internal consultant. The relationship between the internal and external consultant will be critical to the project's success. It requires trust and openness on both sides. Wylie and Woodruffe (1994) describe their experience of working as internal and external consultants respectively at NatWest. They draw attention to the importance to the relationship of the external consultant being genuinely willing to pass on skills, if that is wanted, rather than keeping them shrouded in secrecy.

8 THE COMPETENCY ANALYSIS

The starting-point of the development or assessment centre project is to get a clear and accurate specification of what the centre is measuring. The word 'competencies' has become the accepted label for what a development or assessment centre measures, and getting the list of competencies right is arguably the most crucial part of the centre's design. It was Boyatzis' (1982) book *The Competent Manager* that triggered the popularity of the term 'competency' so that it became obligatory for the serious consultant in the late 1980s. Nowadays, many organisations have a list of competencies. There are also several books on the subject (eg Spencer and Spencer, 1993; Whiddett and Hollyforde, 1999), together with a quarterly journal, *Competency*.

Unfortunately, there are also plenty of examples of competency frameworks that would serve as a poor basis of an assessment or development centre. One can only shudder on reading Walsh's (1998) report of the organisation said to have 300–400 broad competencies. It is impossible to imagine how they cope.

If the list is wrong, people are being looked at against the wrong requirements, and there will be incessant problems in the design, development and operation of the centre. Indeed, the competency list is the hub of the whole assessment and development system. It should drive not just the assessment centre but also appraisal, training and development (eg Treadwell, 1989). In addition, the recruitment and pre-selection system should be based on the competency dimensions revealed by job analysis. The list dictates the application form and the preliminary selection procedure. It can also exert an influence before pre-selection. For example, a recruitment advertising agency should be able to make use of the job analysis in framing an advertisement to appeal to people with the required qualities. In short, it can be appreciated that time and resources put in at this stage will pay off. Conversely, any shortcomings in the competency analysis will rebound on all subsequent assessment and development initiatives.

Unfortunately, the potential for such shortcomings is legion. Fundamentally, it is far from simple to get a clear definition of what a competency is. Secondly, there are a number of points that need to be considered in carrying out the competency analysis. Both these matters will be considered in this chapter, which will close with a discussion of some issues surrounding competencies.

Defining a competency

Boyatzis may have made competencies popular. Unfortunately, there was not an accompanying agreement either on what competencies were or on how to specify the competency lists. Boyatzis defined competency broadly as 'an underlying characteristic of a person'. It could be 'a motive, trait, skill, aspect of one's self-image or social role, or a body of knowledge which he or she uses'. Likewise, Hornby and Thomas (1989) define competencies as 'the knowledge, skills, and qualities of effective managers/leaders' (p53). In contrast to competencies defined in these ways, Dulewicz (1989) notes that the dimensions assessed at assessment centres are clusters of behaviours. However, as he says, these 'have now been called "competencies" although they are not directly related to Boyatzis' model' (p56). It is important for the person doing a competency analysis to find a way through this apparent confusion. Otherwise, the analysis is bound to lack a clear and coherent focus. The analyst is not sure exactly what is to be identified and so cannot discriminate between useful and not so useful information given by people being questioned about the job. Any lack of clarity will also be a problem when the centre is developed, because there is no clear model of the relation between the different types of variable that might be measured at the centre. For example, one long list of competencies might include behaviours (eg behaving with sensitivity); their presumed causes (eg emotional stability), and their consequences (eg good staff management). The general confusion was partly created by Boyatzis himself. His definition quoted above seems to cover pretty well anything, but avoids getting to the heart of what the common denominator of all these things is. It raises the question of whether Professor Randell (1989) of Bradford University is correct in describing a competency as just a 'trendy name' for 'nothing more, nor less, than glorious human skills'.

Competencies and areas of competence

The words 'competence' and 'competency' are interchangeable. They have been used in two different ways. The first is to refer to an ability to do something. This is the dictionary definition. So from the dictionary we could say 'he has the competence generally to manage', or more specifically 'she has the competence to interpret a balance sheet'. The second use of the word is to define what gives rise to that overall ability (eg incisiveness). In this second sense, the word 'competency' refers to one of the sets of behaviours that the person must display in order to perform the tasks and functions of a job with competence. Each competency is a discrete dimension of behaviour. Furthermore, it is a dimension of behaviour that is relevant to performance in the job. Examples of competencies in this second sense are contained in Table 1. The table shows three of the competencies required by the UK's Government Information and Communication Service (GICS), whose members are responsible for government press office and publicity work. Each competency is relevant to some or all aspects of GICS work and, overall, the competencies enable GICS members to be competent to perform a range of jobs and tasks, including:

❑ briefing a minister before a media appearance
❑ commissioning a television advertisement
❑ editing a government magazine
❑ devising a publicity campaign.

Table 1

EXAMPLES OF GICS COMPETENCIES

RAPPORT – The skill to develop and maintain relationships
Being able to talk to people of all levels; getting others to talk; forming good working relationships; seeing the situation from the others' view; adapting to the other person; building on others' ideas; helping others in crises; keeping others/seniors informed.

REASONING – The ability to assimilate issues and provide practical solutions
Maintaining an open mind; analysing a client's real needs; getting to the crux of a problem or argument; extracting the relevant information from verbal and numerical data; seeing overall context of work; thinking through a problem and translating it into practical terms; generating practical ideas for a solution; evaluating solutions by gauging outcomes of action; looking beyond the obvious.

SELF-CONFIDENCE – The ability to assert him/herself
Standing own ground; sustaining an argument; not being overawed by seniors; questioning and probing; showing tenacity; taking charge of events; being able to take snap judgements; acting on own initiative in situations.

There are, then, two uses of the word competence(y), as follows:

❑ First, it can be used to refer to areas of work or roles at which the person is competent (eg devising publicity campaigns). This is the job-related and dictionary sense of the word. For clarity, I propose to term these 'areas of competence'.

❑ Second, it is used to refer to the dimensions of behaviour that lie behind competent performance. This is the person-related sense for which I will reserve the word 'competency'.

An example of a list of competencies, which I believe is a reasonably good approximation to a list of generic management competencies, is contained in Table 2 below.

It can be seen that the competencies are clusters of behaviours. Their headings, such as self-confidence and incisiveness, aim to capture the essence of each cluster. The areas of competence and the competencies themselves should be in separate lists. The areas of competence need not be presented to assessors, but will be used by the project team to ensure

Table 2
AN EXAMPLE COMPETENCY LIST

Breadth of awareness to be well informed
Develops and maintains networks and formal channels of communication, within the organisation and with the outside world; keeps abreast of relevant local, national and international political and economic developments; monitors competitor activity; has a general awareness of what should be happening and what progress is being made.

Incisiveness to have a clear understanding
Gets a clear overview of an issue; grasps information accurately; relates pieces of information; identifies causal relationships; gets to the heart of a problem; identifies the most productive lines of enquiry; appreciates all the variables affecting an issue; identifies limitations to information; adapts thinking in the light of new information; tolerates and handles conflicting/ambiguous information and ideas.

Imagination to find ways forward
Generates options; evaluates options by examining the positive and negative results if they were put into effect; anticipates effects of options on others; foresees others' reactions; demonstrates initiative and common sense.

Organisation to work productively
Identifies priorities; thinks back from deadline; identifies elements of tasks; schedules elements; anticipates resource needs; allocates resources to tasks; sets objectives for staff; manages own and others' time.

Drive to achieve results
Is prepared to compromise to achieve a result; installs solution within timeframe; innovates or adapts existing procedures to ensure a result; takes on problems; suffers personal inconvenience to ensure problems are solved; comes forward with ideas; sets challenging targets; sets out to win new business; sets own objectives; recognises areas for self-development; acquires new skills and capabilities; accepts new challenges.

Self-confidence to lead the way
Expresses and conveys a belief in own ability; is prepared to take and support decisions; stands up to seniors; is willing to take calculated risks; admits to areas of inexpertise.

Sensitivity to identify others' viewpoints
Listens to others' viewpoints; adapts to other people; takes account of others' needs; sees situation from others' viewpoints; empathises; is aware of others' expectations.

Co-operativeness to work with other people
Involves others in own area and ideas; keeps others informed; makes use of available support services; utilises skills of team members; is open to others' ideas and suggestions.

Patience to win in the long term
Sticks to a strategic plan; does not get side-tracked; sacrifices the present for the future; bides time when conditions are not favourable.

the exercises include the main areas of competence. The competencies and the areas of competence can be related to each other in the form of a grid such as that in Table 3.

Unfortunately, the distinction between areas of competence and competencies is not always carefully maintained by people who put together competency lists or frameworks. They produce muddled research with final lists that contain both types of variable jumbled together. Such a list cannot be used satisfactorily, for example, to assess people. Any particular behaviour will be evidence both of the competency and of the area of competence. Those making the assessment become confused and double mark any given behaviour. For example, a list might contain both sensitivity (a competency) and people development (an area of competence). If someone exhibits the behaviour 'refrains from interfering unnecessarily with subordinates' work', assessors want to credit the competency of sensitivity, but they also want to give credit to the people development area of competence. This duplication helps give rise to a halo effect whereby marks get generalised across competencies. Furthermore, designing development workshops for each competency is made well-nigh impossible because the same content will surface in more than one workshop. For example, if sensitivity (a competency) and people development (an area of competence) are in the same competency list, the content of workshops to develop them will inevitably overlap.

Competencies and traits, motives, dispositions and other psychological variables

It can be seen from the examples in Table 2 and elsewhere that words other than 'competency' might be used to refer to these dimensions of behaviour. They are, after all, many of the things Boyatzis said they could be – underlying characteristics, traits, motives, etc. What is the point of another word? I have suggested (Woodruffe, 1991) that one main reason for the new word is that it offered a fresh start, a chance to get away from the muddle of traits and motives. At the outset, it could be defined as a dimension of behaviour. That, of course is all that a trait or motive is. However, most people

Table 3
GRID RELATING COMPETENCIES TO OUTPUTS

Output / Competency	Strategic thinking	Problem-solving	Persuasion	Staff management	Training and development	Customer service	Business development
Breadth of awareness	×	×					
Incisiveness	×	×	×	×	×		
Imagination	×	×	×	×	×	×	×
Organisation		×		×	×	×	×
Drive		×	×	×	×	×	×
Self-confidence	×	×	×	×	×	×	×
Sensitivity		×	×	×	×	×	×
Co-operativeness		×	×	×	×	×	
Patience	×		×	×	×	×	

see motives and traits as having explanatory rather than just descriptive power. In everyday language we say a particular person is self-confident because she has self-confidence. However, it is only known she has self-confidence because she behaves self-confidently (Mischel, 1968, 1973), and so we are caught in a circular argument. In fact the person behaves in a self-confident way not because of a trait, but because she has a string of successes behind her which allows her to face each new challenge in a confident way. The trait of self-confidence is merely a description of behaviour. It is not an explanation.

Unfortunately, the fresh start was instantly lost when Boyatzis bequeathed on competencies all the confusion that surrounded traits, motives, etc by noting that competencies could be defined in terms of these variables. Perhaps Boyatzis assumed too much psychological knowledge on the part of his readers when he gave his definition. It led many away from the fact that, although the competency might be a trait, it is still, at heart, only a convenient summary label for people's behaviour. The potential confusion is compounded by the use of the term 'soft competencies' or 'soft skills' to refer to such qualities as creativity and sensitivity. Soft competencies are contrasted by those who make the distinction with what are seen as more directly observable qualities, like planning and organising. The distinction was made, for example, by Jacobs (1989), who went on to claim that the soft qualities could not be measured by assessment centres but were of increasing importance to organisations in times of rapid change. The soft and any other competencies are only summaries of behaviour. People behave creatively (ie they produce original ideas to solve problems, etc) and so we know they have creativity. People behave sensitively (ie they take account of other's needs, etc) and so we know they have sensitivity. In the same way, people are only known to have what Boyatzis calls 'efficiency orientation', because they behave in the various ways used to indicate their efficiency. In summary, competencies and traits are both descriptions of behaviour. They are effectively the same, and neither offers an explanation of behaviour.

Competencies and technical skills

Apart from the behavioural competency dimensions, the job analysis might also reveal specific 'technical' skills and knowledge and abilities that are required for the job. Calling these competencies seems likely only to muddle the definition of a competency again, and it seems better to use a separate label. These knowledge skills and abilities apply particularly to jobs with a professional component, for example the job of a solicitor. Many of the behavioural competencies in Table 2 will be necessary to perform satisfactorily as a solicitor. In addition, there are the specific technical/professional skills and knowledge such as knowing the law of tort and how to draw up a will. This professional knowledge is likely to be the result of, and perhaps can only be assessed by checking the possession of, particular levels of experience and qualification. However, it is important to note that what is really required to be a good solicitor is both the professional skill and behavioural competence. It will be important to build this information on professional requirements into a selection assessment centre by including an interview that focuses upon people's experience, together, perhaps, with a review of a portfolio of their work if it is appropriate (eg for a creative job). A model relating the variables that can be examined at the centre, and which might be uncovered by the job analysis, is presented in Figure 6.

Specifying the competencies

This book does not attempt to cover job analysis in detail. The various techniques are dealt with by many textbooks on personnel management. However, there are a number of specific points to be made in connection with the analysis for a development or assessment centre. These points revolve around the fact that the primary objective is to design, within an integrated management development system, processes for assessing people's levels of competence and for developing their competence.

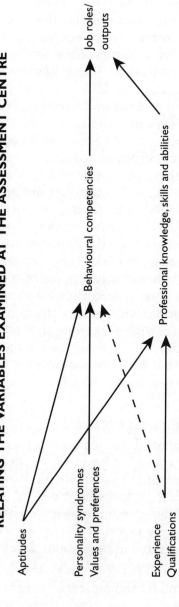

Figure 6

RELATING THE VARIABLES EXAMINED AT THE ASSESSMENT CENTRE

Job roles/
outputs

Behavioural competencies

Professional knowledge, skills and abilities

Aptitudes

Personality syndromes
Values and preferences

Experience
Qualifications

Different approaches for areas of competence and competencies

Maintaining the distinction between areas of competence and competencies is nowhere more important than in the quite different ways in which the two should be analysed. Areas of competence are derived by a methodology that is based on the analysis of job functions, known as functional analysis. It proceeds by asking what job holders do, ie what they must be competent at. For example, the Manpower Services Commission (MSC) (1987) in their 'Standards of performance for administrative business and commercial staff' derived 47 'statements of competence in a task, job or occupation', an example being 'file documents and open new files within an established filing system'. Areas of competence can be broken down to a level that is quite specific, as shown in this example.

On the other hand, analysis of person-related competencies proceeds in the opposite direction. It starts from specific behaviours and groups these under the competencies. Whatever the precise techniques (eg repertory grid analysis) used to assist the identification of competencies the goal is to cluster into dimensions the behaviours that differentiate the high performer. The label for a dimension is simply the best wording to capture the common denominator of the behavioural indicators. For example, one cluster of behaviours might be:

Identifies priorities
Thinks back from the deadline
Identifies elements of task
Anticipates resource requirements
Allocates resources to tasks
Manages own and others' time.

It might be decided that 'organisation' best captures this cluster. The process is from the indicators to the label and not vice versa. The title is only the best summary that can be found for the cluster of behaviours. The order is not finding the dimensions and then defining them in terms of behaviours. Indeed, the title for the dimension can be unhelpful as it leads people to flesh out the dimension in their own ways. It is, of course, unrealistic, but it would be advantageous to cut the title and just give the dimension an index number followed by the indicators. It is the behaviours, not the title, that assessors must learn and focus upon, and which participants must develop.

Focus on the future

One problem in deriving the competency lists is the danger of becoming bound to a particular methodology. It might be thought that job analysis has to be done in a particular way, for example via the repertory grid or the critical incidents technique. Worse, these techniques might be seen as producing guaranteed results. They appear to yield the royal road to competency analysis, but it can turn out to be a royal cul-de-sac. A major danger is of producing lists based more on history than on the future. This can easily happen from using a simple version of the repertory grid or critical incident techniques of interviewing. As Dulewicz (1989) observes, the grid must include 'a definition of the current manager who is likely to be successful in the environment envisaged for the future'. He continues, 'involvement of top management in the final stages of discussion . . . is also imperative' (p59).

The need for an orientation to the future makes very questionable competency lists that are based exclusively on comparing current high and low performers. Such lists risk specifying the competencies up to today rather than those from tomorrow. Unless there is also a stage of checking out that 'have been' characteristics are also the 'will be' ones, the analysis might only be of historical interest. This is particularly important in the conditions of rapid change that organisations face nowadays.

The level of analysis

The job analysis will need to identify the competencies that differentiate the high performer from others in the job or job level. The list used for the centre should not include dimensions or behaviours that are so mundane that everyone possesses them at the level of focus. The job analysis will also need to recognise the distinction between centres that are to measure readiness to perform a job tomorrow, and those that focus upon potential. If the focus is upon potential, the analysis should not include behaviours that everybody can be expected to learn between the time of the centre and being ready for the job. Such behaviours do not discriminate between people in terms of their potential. However, these behaviours might be included if the centre is to measure readiness to perform the job tomorrow, if only to point up immediate training needs.

Seeing the wood for the trees

It is important to focus on the level of generality that is appropriate to designing the centre. It is easy to get obsessed with detail, but an analysis carried out to uncover the micro-skills of a job is very different from one carried out to design an assessment and management development procedure. It is pointless making distinctions between competency dimensions which are so fine that they might be intellectually satisfying but which assessors will never be able to follow. To take a simple example, report-writing and e-mail writing can be combined under written communication, and speaking at meetings and speaking one-to-one can both come under oral communication.

The trick is not to become too general. For example, it might seem sensible to combine oral and written communication under the umbrella of communication skills. The risk is that the list will be so general that a competency dimension could be assessed at a given level for very different reasons. The umbrella dimension of communication skills runs just such a risk. Some people are excellent at writing and not so good at oral communication (for example, the caricature don). For others, the opposite applies. A related example of an umbrella competence is the dimension labelled 'personal factors' that appears in the lists of some organisations. It is difficult to assess people on such a general title. A person can be strong on one personal factor (integrity was a sub-component in one list) yet weak on another (career ambition was another sub-component in this same list). The competency dimensions must, therefore, steer a middle ground between making unnecessary distinctions and being too general to be useful.

Visible dimensions

The end-goal of the job analysis is to have a set of competency dimensions against which people can be observed. Hypothetical psychological variables are inappropriate to such a list. For example, one organisation had a list which included the dimension of self-monitoring. Assessors simply did not understand what it meant, let alone how they were to observe it.

The advice to keep to visible dimensions was borne out in a study by Shore et al (1992). They found that more observable dimensions (such as 'most active in business discussions') were more valid than dimensions requiring greater inferential judgement (such as 'can work with least direction').

Simple and brief

The number of competency dimensions must be kept within bounds. Gaugler and Thornton (1989) demonstrated that the accuracy with which assessors classified and rated people declined as the number of dimensions was increased. Indeed, Gaugler and Thornton argue for having just three to six dimensions because this is the maximum number that people can make use of in reaching decisions. In their support, Russell (1985) demonstrated that assessors' ratings on 18 dimensions could be grouped into just four factors, the most important of which were interpersonal skills and problem-solving skills. This research should be borne in mind if there is a temptation to produce a long list of dimensions.

The number, in practice, probably needs to be greater than Gaugler and Thornton's recommendation, especially if the purpose of the centre is not just to make a decision but also to give developmental feedback. Probably 12 to 15 competency dimensions is the most that can be used in the centre before the list becomes unwieldy, and between eight and ten is the ideal number. This contrasts with Walsh's (1998) report that lists of between 21 and 30 competencies are common among the UK's FTSE-100 companies. It is to be hoped that they use no more than half their lists for any particular centre. The numbers Walsh reports are far too great for assessment purposes. Assessors cannot possibly distinguish between and rate all these dimensions, and the system is likely to fall into disrepute and disuse.

User-friendly

It is important that the system of competencies and areas of competence is easy to understand. There should be a clear model so that people can see how they fit together. Furthermore, the system should be put across as far as possible in plain English. Even the word 'competencies' might be unnecessary for assessors. All that assessors really want is a list of what they are supposed to be assessing. The more complex the system becomes, the more confused they will get. All that they need to focus upon is the behavioural competency dimensions and the specific knowledge, skills, and 'technical' abilities for the job.

Do reinvent the wheel

Undoubtedly there are generic management competency dimensions. Spencer and Spencer (1993) devote several chapters of their book to their estimate of generic competencies. Their views are compiled in Table 4.

This list is not applicable in its entirety to any particular job. As the authors say *'The Generic Dictionary Scales Are Applicable to All Jobs – and None Precisely'* (p23). Other lists that might be compared are those presented by major organisations during 1998 and 1999 in the journals *Competency* and *People Management*. The summary lists are in Table 5.

Without passing judgement on the merits of these various lists, clearly there is much overlap, which supports Dulewicz's (1989) belief in generic competencies. However, there are organisation-specific competencies and, most important, there is the problem of choosing between competencies in a

Table 4

GENERIC COMPETENCIES DISCUSSED BY SPENCER AND SPENCER (1993)

Achievement and action
  Achievement orientation
  Concern for order, quality, and accuracy
  Initiative
  Information-seeking

Helping and human service
  Interpersonal understanding
  Customer service orientation

The impact and influence cluster
  Impact and influence
  Organisational awareness
  Relationship-building

Managerial
  Developing others
  Directiveness: assertiveness and use of positional power
  Teamwork and co-operation
  Team leadership

Cognitive
  Analytical thinking
  Conceptual thinking
  Technical/professional/managerial expertise

Personal effectiveness
  Self-control
  Self-confidence
  Flexibility
  Organisational commitment

Adapted from L. M. Spencer and S. M. Spencer, *Competence at Work*, New York, John Wiley, 1993.

generic list. The drawback to generic lists is that they will be seen as applicable in their entirety. In this way, they are rather like personality descriptions, which people accept readily, whether they are actually based on the person's own inventory or on another's. To make the choices, and ensure the inclusion of important competencies that are specific to the organisation, I believe that it is important to go through a process of obtaining a list tailored to the particular organisation. It is difficult just to make minor adaptations to a provided list and I recommend starting with a fresh sheet to derive a list that really does fit the particular level of job

Table 5
EXAMPLES OF COMPETENCY LISTS

Company	ABB	IBM	KPMG	Motorola	Xerox
Author	(Competency, 1999b)	(Competency, 1999a)	(Competency, 1999c)	(Adams, 1998)	(Maclachlan, 1998)
	Innovation/creativity Teamworking skills Customer focus Communication skills Flexibility Quality of work Development of others Professional knowledge/ skills Leadership Accepting responsibility	Customer insight Breakthrough thinking Drive to achieve Team leadership Straight talk Teamwork Decisiveness and decision-making Building organisational capability Personal dedication A passion for the business	**Client responsiveness** Relationship-building Professional judgement **Business skills** Commerciality Business development **Management** Task management Team skills **Personal effectiveness** Drive and commitment to results Resilience **Social skills** Communication skills Social confidence **Thinking skills** Analytical thinking Proactive thinking **People Development**	Relevant background Business awareness Logic/analytical thinking Planning and prioritising Creativity and initiative Communication skills Teamworking Leadership Confidence under pressure Quality, motivation and working conditions	Strategic thinking Strategic implementation Customer-driven approach Inspiring a shared vision Decision-making Quick study Managing operational performance Staffing for high performance Developing organisational talent Delegation and empowerment Managing teamwork Cross-functional teamwork Leading innovation Driving for business results Use of 'Leadership through quality' Openness to change Interpersonal empathy and understanding Personal drive Personal strength and maturity Personal consistency Environment and industry perspective Business and financial perspective Overall technical knowledge

Published in *Competency and People Management*.

in the particular organisation. Certainly, it is not to be recommended that an organisation simply adopts a list of generic competencies. There are inevitably differences as well as similarities between the competencies required for different organisations. These differences arise, for example, from the different business conditions they face (Gerstein and Reisman, 1983).

The process of having a tailor-made list has the second major benefit, which is that the list is owned by the organisation. Organisations like BP (Greatrex and Phillips, 1989) and Royal Insurance (Walkley, 1988) make it very clear that their competencies are personal to them, even if it is only the language of the indicators. For example, for Royal Insurance, Walkley describes how it was important that 'the jargon used was acceptable to non-personnel staff and also helped to share ownership of the concept across the organisation' (p17). Similarly, as Greatrex and Phillips (1989) observed, the names of the 11 competencies produced for BP 'could be the universal requirements of any competent manager'. However, the 'crucial point' is that 'the behaviours listed within the clusters are cultural artefacts of the BP organisation and expressed in terms of the language of the organisation' (p8). It is most important that organisations go to the effort of gaining a list over which they feel a sense of ownership. A generic list might, however, be used as a check on the organisation's own research.

Carrying out the analysis

There is no one way of deriving the list of competency dimensions or carrying out the rest of the job analysis. A theme of this book is the need to think flexibly around the particular situation that is faced, and adopt the most appropriate approach. However, the job analysis almost certainly will include interviews. A typical way of getting at the competencies is to carry out interviews with managers of the target job, job holders, and maybe subordinates and 'customers' of the job. For example, to analyse the job of managers in a bank who each handle a group of customers (relationship managers), one batch of interviews would be with those to whom the managers report. The focus would be what differentiates a good manager both now and under future plans for the bank. Relationship managers themselves would be interviewed to find out what they believe are the important behaviours that distinguish high from average performance. Members of their team could add further light to what makes a good manager, and interviewing customers of the bank would also be most revealing, but it is rarely part of a job analysis.

Aside from what distinguishes high and low performers in terms of behaviours, the analysis must find out about the job itself. With job holders especially, interviews will find out what they do in their job and the typical situations they face. To help people describe their jobs, it can be helpful to ask them to keep a diary for a week and fill in each half day what they have been doing. At the end of the week, they would add any other aspects of the job not covered. The diary can be used to help identify the major types of situation in the job, as well as the major outputs and roles. For example, the list might include one-to-one meetings with customers, fellow managers, and staff, as well as group negotiations, and dealing alone with paperwork. This information can be used to start deciding the exercises that should be designed to simulate their work.

It is best to start with one-to-one interviews in a job analysis. However, after about 10 to 15 interviews with any particular type of respondent (eg managers of the job, job holders, etc) the information tends to become repetitive. At this point, it can be more productive to collate the notes from the single interviews, and then to interview pairs or groups of people to check out the information. The pairs or groups might be used to draw out any differences that are suspected between different categories of job. For example, differences might be suspected between departments or between head office and field offices.

In interviews, especially with the managers of the job, it is crucial to focus on expected changes in the job and its requirements. For example, banking has clearly changed to a much more proactive, sales- and customer-oriented, and risk-acceptant profile, from a profile that was pretty well the opposite. If the job analyst a few years back had concentrated on the job as it was and not as it was about to be, the centre would quickly have been assessing against an historical template. The need to incorporate the future means that people responsible for the organisation's strategy must be interviewed. Incorporating the views of these people not only adds crucial information to the analysis, but it also involves them psychologically in the project.

In carrying out any of the interviews, I do not believe in feeling compelled to use a particular methodology, for example the repertory grid technique or the critical incidents technique. These are means to an end, and they might not be productive, especially when senior people are interviewed. The end-goal is to find out where these people see the organisation going and what the competency requirements will be, given that scenario. How the end-goal is achieved needs to be adapted to suit the situation.

Having carried out all the interviews, the next task is to derive a preliminary list of competency dimensions. Whatever specific technique of interviewing was used, the majority of interviews will have included eliciting the positive and negative behaviours that differentiate levels of performance. These behaviours must now be grouped into the competency dimensions. There are various ways of going about this. The first is to cut out obvious duplicate statements of behaviour, and then present the rest in the form of a job analysis questionnaire. The responses to the questionnaire are analysed to yield the competency dimensions. The statistical process, known as factor analysis, in essence shows which behaviours cluster together. Each cluster is a competency. The questionnaire is inevitably going to be rather long. Little is lost by grouping small numbers of the items into obvious sub-dimensions, and analysing these. Either way, the analysis will be of people's self-ratings on the competency dimensions or behaviours. It should not be of their ratings of the importance of the behaviours for successful job performance. The reason is that quite disparate behaviours (eg focusing on deadlines, treating customers politely) might be equally important for competent performance. If the ratings for importance were factor analysed, behaviours at the various levels of importance would group together into their factors but they would not be dimensions upon which people could be assessed meaningfully.

After the statistical analysis, the groupings of indicators that appear under each empirical factor should be inspected to make sure that they appear to be psychologically homogenous and yet distinct from the other groupings or competency dimensions. The factors should be rational and intuitively sensible. It is important to be very well versed in the procedure being used, which should be seen as an assistant not a master. The list from statistical analysis should be adjusted so that it works in practice. The computer results do not have to be followed slavishly, however counter-intuitive they may be.

In all, it is vital to remember the purpose of the analysis. It is to derive a list of competency dimensions that will drive the assessment and development process. Assessors must be able to understand it, and management development staff must be able to design their systems around it. A particular problem with lists derived by statistical analysis is competency dimensions that jumble up quite disparate indicators. An example is the dimension entitled 'direction', which is made up of the following behaviours:

> Being able to tell others what they must do and confront performance problems; to plan, organise, schedule, delegate and follow up.

These are quite clearly very different indicators that do not group logically under one dimension. There are aspects of self-confidence, and of organising ability. The risk with jumbled competency dimensions is that assessors will become confused. For example if they see a participant confront a performance problem, they will want to give credit to the dimension of self-confidence as well as having to credit the participant's direction. It is vital that the final list is coherent enough to bear close examination by a cynic.

Apart from ensuring homogeneity within competency dimensions, it is important to make sure that the distinctions between dimensions that the statistical analysis has made can also be made by assessors. For example, a job analysis

I carried out distinguished between self-confidence and assertiveness. I am sure that these are separate dimensions and that someone could be highly self-confident but not very assertive, and vice versa. However, assessors found the distinction hard to assimilate, and, in retrospect, it might have been better not to make it.

The final draft list of competency dimensions from the interviews and questionnaire will need to be ratified by the senior policy-makers within the organisation who should, once again, make sure that the future requirements of the organisation are covered.

Once the final list of competency dimensions has been obtained, it can be helpful to group them under broader headings. For example, a recent job analysis I carried out clustered the dimensions under the headings of information management, self-management, and people management. Similarly, BP cluster their dimensions under achievement orientation, people orientation, judgement, and situational flexibility.

Adding levels

The process that has been described will yield the set of competencies that are relevant for the particular development or assessment centre. Each competency will be specified at the level needed for the job upon which the centre is targeted. If the job is that of director, then 'imagination to find ways forward' will be concerned with strategic thinking. On the other hand, if the job is that of team leader, the same competency will be expressed at the level of finding solutions to the day-to-day problems referred by team members.

It can be seen that to go a step further and build a competency framework that applies throughout the organisation requires the adding of levels for each competency. The levels will come from the original interviews and can then be checked by focus groups and by the questionnaire.

However, for any particular centre, it is important to take only the levels of the competencies required for the job under consideration. It is not particularly useful to be able to tell the directors that they only have the imagination applicable for team leading. Conversely, you are unlikely even to be able to tell team leaders that they have the imagination needed by directors because the team leader workshop will not deal with strategic thinking.

In short, you do not need to build a competency framework that covers the entire organisation for any particular centre. If you already have such a framework, you need to choose the competencies and levels that apply to the job targeted by the centre.

The areas of competence

The job analysis questionnaire will be used to get further information on the job itself as well as on the competencies. It will be used to finalise the list of areas of competence or roles that the job involves. Frequently, the analysis will be covering a grouping of jobs which it makes sense to deal with generically, but which have only some roles in common and some that are different. This will be particularly true when the target is a job level, such as middle management, rather than a narrowly defined job. For example, some specific jobs at a job level will include business development as a role, whereas others will not. The analysis can uncover the actual similarities and differences between jobs. This will be useful information for participants in carrying out the career planning that will be a major follow-up to an internal centre.

Think critically about methodologies

It is easy to be beguiled by a particular methodology, and to lose sight of what it is doing fundamentally. For example, it is important to beware of techniques that rely too much on managers' views of psychology. Some approaches to job analysis get managers to relate competencies to areas of competence. This can result merely in a statement of the obvious. It is the job of the expert to challenge and question conventional wisdom. For example, if two of the competencies are analytical skills and interpersonal skills, and two of the areas of competence are problem-solving and coaching staff, most people will see analytical skills as required for problem-solving and interpersonal skill as required for coaching staff. However, this pooling of conventional views might miss the fact that analytical skills are also required just as much as interpersonal skills if managers are to succeed in their coaching role. This might not be obvious from a pooling of conventional wisdom.

No amount of apparently sophisticated statistical analysis can change the status of the data that goes into the analysis. The old adage of 'garbage in garbage out' applies. It is important to step back and examine the fundamentals of the technique to ensure that it cannot be accused of 'garbage in'.

Constant review

It is vital that a list of competencies is flexible and able to reflect changes in the organisation's direction. The list must reflect the best estimate of what the future will require of people, and it must be kept under review. It should be kept under review as the definition of a high performer varies. For example, David Duffield, group personnel manager of National Westminster, said in an interview with Crabb (1989) 'We have done a lot of work . . .on the skills and competences which are very important in the bank . . . And we're constantly looking ahead to see how these things are likely to change' (p37). Similarly, Greatrex and Phillips (1989) talk of BP recognising the importance of checking their model and its validity 'about every two years to ensure it still reflects the company's needs' (p39).

Issues around competencies

Using competencies and areas of competence in HR management

As noted at the start of this chapter, competencies and areas of competence, kept separate, should drive a major part of the HR system. Dealing first with person-related competencies, an example of their power comes from BP (Robertson, 1990), which derived its competencies from its vision and values and then used them in many of its HR initiatives and in its culture change. Indeed, competencies should be the common language of the human resource system, allowing the organisation to match the human resources it has against the resources it needs. They are the dimensions against which people should be assessed for readiness or potential to move into jobs, and against which people should be appraised. They are also the dimensions upon which people should be developed.

Exactly such a comprehensive use of competencies is being made by the Government Information and Communication Service (GICS). The original research on their competency list was carried out in 1988 and since then competencies have been updated on a regular basis. Competencies were put to immediate use in an assessment centre for new recruits as well as in writing copy for recruitment advertisements, re-designing the application form, and shortlisting applicants. Later, a supplementary appraisal form was designed for GICS members and the competencies have been used to help devise a sophisticated promotion procedure. To back up the assessment of competencies, a set of behavioural workshops was instituted to help people develop. People coming to the workshop analyse and agree the behaviours that are desirable to carry out their jobs to a high standard, and then practise those behaviours in the context of their jobs. For example, to develop rapport, officers agree the specific behaviours that enable them to 'see the situation from the other's view', and they then practise these behaviours in a role-play of a typical piece of GICS work for which this behaviour is important. This is where the areas of competence come in. By specifying them, the competency is assessed and developed within the actual area of work the person must carry out. In the GICS example, rapport is needed among other occasions in briefing a minister. On the other hand, in an investment bank it might be required in a meeting with the board of a multinational client. Specifying the areas of competence ensures that assessment and development is relevant. GICS do not practise rapport at meetings with multinational boards, and investment bankers do not practise briefing ministers before media appearances.

It is important to note the different roles for areas of competence and competencies. In particular, areas of competence are much less useful than competencies for developmental feedback to participants. For example, Colloff and Goodge's

(1990) description of British Rail's 'competences model' shows that it deals with areas of competence, including:

Improving: Making things efficient, problem-free

If someone is not good at 'improving' they need to know why. As the list stands all that can be said is that they fail to make things efficient, problem-free. But why? What are they doing wrong? How can they improve? The answer will lie in a combination of the competencies they need to acquire.

It is essential to know what determines competencies when using them both in selection and development. If a particular competency is hard to improve then you can be less forgiving of a deficiency spotted at selection, and obviously less optimistic about development than if it is easy to improve.

Looking at a competency list, general comments about development can be made. For some competencies, particularly in the cognitive area, it is reasonable to suggest that the possibilities for development will be quite limited. Apart from such general observations, the exact determinant of a particular person's level of competency will depend upon that person. For example, what causes one person's lack of self-confidence will be different from what causes another's. Without going into all the possibilities, it is probably a job for the competent psychologist to advise on what has contributed to a particular person's level on each competency and to suggest the most productive programme for competency development.

While the heart of the job analysis is the behavioural dimensions that distinguish performance, the job analyst might, of course, also be concerned to discuss the causes of behaviour. These might be looked at in the centre. However, they will not be examined via the centre exercises. For example, the cause of a lack of self-confident behaviour might be a deep unresolved internal conflict. Alternatively, maybe it is a spouse who undermines the person's self-confidence. In fact, all manner of psychological variables as well as training and experience might lie behind the behaviour, but these cannot be observed directly at the centre. The cause of these behaviours can only be revealed by in-depth psychological interviews. Finding out the reason the person does or does not behave in a particular way matters because it will suggest the ease or difficulty of development.

Management Charter Initiative

The distinction between areas of competence and competencies was well made by the Management Charter Initiative (MCI) (1990) and it is a distinction they continue to maintain (Management Charter Initiative, 1999). The current version (MCI, 1999, and see Appendix B for weblink) presents seven 'key roles' such as 'manage people'. Each role has several 'units of competence' such as 'C5: Develop productive working relationships'. Each unit has 'elements' such as 'C5.1: Develop the trust and support of colleagues and team members'. To be accredited, the elements must be performed to National Standards of Competence. Effective performance requires people to have the required 'personal competencies' such as 'acting assertively' and 'communication'.

It seems fair to say that the emphasis of the Management Charter Initiative (MCI) is to define a set of generic national standards for the areas of competence (the elements of the units of the roles). MCI aims to develop them, and indeed to assess them nationally. However, the lists of areas of competence in the MCI Standards are inherently far harder to agree than a list of personal competencies. The areas of competence dealt with by the standards will vary much more between jobs and organisations than the list of personal competencies, and perhaps this is why the lists of standards are so long. Arguably, the current list is quite unwieldy. The risk is that the person who achieves the MCI standards will not need a good number of them in a particular managerial job, and that he or she will need additional areas of competence not covered in the MCI list.

Categorising competencies

Boyatzis distinguishes between threshold and performance competencies. Threshold competencies are basic requirements to carry out the job, but do not differentiate between high and low performers. On the other hand, performance competencies do differentiate between levels of performance. A problem with the distinction between threshold and performance competencies is that it is really a matter of degree, rather than of category. Normally a competency will tend towards threshold or performance rather than being absolutely one or the other. People should be assessed on all competencies relevant to the job and there should be the opportunity to develop all of them.

The difficulty with dividing competencies into threshold and performance is also inherent in other categories. For example, competencies might be differentiated in terms of importance, being given labels such as core and peripheral. The danger in practice is that organisations will concentrate exclusively on those that were labelled 'core'. Less important becomes unimportant. It is anyway not generally possible to assess the importance of each individual competency. Competency lists usually need to be taken as a whole. The competencies balance each other. For example, a list might include both self-confidence and sensitivity. Both are required in equal measure. A very sensitive person who is not self-confident would be a push-over. A very self-confident person who is not sensitive runs the risk of being seen as lacking rapport.

Competencies and equal opportunities

A concern with competencies is that they represent a white male definition of success. This could occur quite easily if only white male managers were interviewed or observed in the process of defining competencies. With respect to gender, it is argued that males and females have different routes to successful performance. They use different competencies but both are successful. For example, Clements (1994) describes how men tend to be more transactional and attribute their power to their position. Women are more transformational or interactive and attribute their power to personal characteristics. If men define the competencies, the result will be a list of qualities that reinforce the masculine corporate culture.

Clearly, the risk is a real one. However, the issue is complicated. Many competency lists lay heavy emphasis on the very qualities that are said to be feminine. Organisations want the more transformational, interactive person. They are the qualities of emotional intelligence. As Hutchison *et al* (1998) point out, the 'feminine' quality of consideration or interpersonal orientation has for a long time been paired with the 'masculine' quality of initiating structure or task orientation in specifying leadership behaviours. However, they note that 'both male and female managers believe that successful managers possess the same traits as those ascribed to men in general' (p172) while subordinates tend to reserve favourable evaluations for leaders who conform to their respective gender roles.

The pragmatic advice is to be sure that you scrutinise the competency list to make sure that it is not simply the prejudices of the current elite in the organisation.

Rejecting competencies

Some people reject the competency approach altogether, ridiculing it as trying to build an identi-kit manager. Mangham (eg 1990) is particularly associated with this criticism. Mangham says that among other things the competency lists fail to take account of the person's fit within the culture of the organisation. For example, Mangham said that people with a bank's competencies would not necessarily be good university administrators because they are not sympathetic to the university culture. The argument is hard to follow. The university administrator's competencies would be different from those at the bank precisely because each set would reflect the culture of the organisation. Of course, there is more to being a good manager than a set of competencies. However, they are a large part of the recipe.

Nevertheless, Mangham has been joined by several others who accuse competencies of leading to a sinister cloning of people. For example, Buckingham (1999) argues that long lists of behavioural competencies can only suppress individuality. 'The greatest managers', we are told, 'reject this approach' and concentrate on people's talent. Buckingham illustrated his article with examples of talent such as a love of crossword puzzles and the ability to remember names as well as the panache of various sports stars. Being of absolutely no interest to most employers, these very examples show that each organisation must specify what it means by talent. Defining talent can be seen as being entirely in line with – and not opposed to – defining competencies. What about people's individuality? A good list of competencies will not 'grind down each person's idiosyncrasies', as Buckingham luridly put it. If the idiosyncrasy is irrelevant to performance it will not appear in the list. Talent is scarce enough, without adding unnecessary extras.

Others suggest that competencies ignore values. For example, Brittain and Ryder (1999) remark that assessment centres produce people who perform against the competencies but who are not seen as right for the role. They suggest that assessment centres need to examine whether 'the candidate can deliver the goods in a way that is consistent with the organisation's values *and* aligns to the competencies' (p51). This does not seem wholly convincing. The behaviours represented in competencies are not value-free. They should reflect what makes up successful performance in the organisation, including, for example, such value-based items as behaving with honesty and integrity.

It is also possible to get side-tracked by a mystery ingredient such as charisma that makes some people absolute stars. Management developers cannot give up because there happen to be a few charismatic people at the top of a few organisations. We have to improve the overall competence of the estimated two million people in the UK involved in management, and not be transfixed because they will not all be media stars.

In short, competencies seem to me to be common sense. They simply specify what is needed for the person and therefore the organisation to be successful. If they are not specified explicitly, managers will still choose people according to some criteria. The problem is that these criteria will be implicit and reflect the prejudices of each individual, rather than being a list agreed through a process of consultation.

9 THE EXERCISES

The grid of exercises

The simulation exercises are the heart of a development or assessment centre. The job analysis will have revealed the typical and representative situations faced by people in the job (eg customer meetings). It will also have made clear what are the main outputs (eg customer relations; business development) in these situations. The exercises are set within the organisation and aim to simulate these situations and require the same outputs. For example, there might be a one-to-one exercise with a customer that gets the participant to maintain the relationship with the customer and to try to expand the business with the customer.

To perform effectively in an exercise, the participant will have to use a selection of the competencies revealed by the job analysis. In this way, the exercise design and job analysis cross-validate each other. If the job analysis competencies are correct and the exercises are well designed as simulations of the job, then it will be possible to see the competencies in people's performance of the exercises. If the competencies cannot be observed in the exercises then either the exercises or the job analysis are wrong.

The choice of exercises should depend solely upon the findings of the job analysis, coupled with practical constraint. An exercise should not be included just because it is usually found in assessment centres. For example, leaderless group discussions and in-trays are usual in assessment centres, but if they do not simulate the target job or job level they should not be part of the centre. They will give access to irrelevant competency dimensions, and deny access to the relevant. Conversely, a novel type of exercise certainly should be included if it is practical and would be a good simulation of the job.

For example, in an assessment centre I helped to design to choose supervisors for an engineering company, each participant was given six apprentices who had to be instructed on a method of working to make a simple piece of equipment. The participants then had to supervise the apprentices actually making the equipment. It worked very well as an exercise, and was certainly much better than a leaderless group discussion, which would not have been relevant.

The mix of exercises must bear in mind the eventual timetable and the available resources in terms of assessors and role-players. For example, there will be great difficulties if the centre consists of a series of one-to-one role-plays. Unless there is one role-player and assessor per candidate, participants who are not taking part in a role-play must be occupied with some other activity. This might well be possible in a development centre. The time could be used, for example, to get people to consider their own performance in the last exercise, perhaps including a group discussion of the issues raised. The time might also be used for individual consideration of career aspirations, etc. However, if the centre is to be used for selection, the time will be less easy to use, and it is usual to have one or more written exercises that can be run in parallel with the one-to-one exercises.

The full set of exercises should fit together in a workable timetable, simulate key aspects of the job, and give an adequate measure of the competency dimensions that are critical to the job. There is debate about the ability of assessors to assess individual dimensions as opposed to assessing overall exercise performance (see Chapter 17). However, at this design stage, care should be taken to ensure that the dimensions are properly represented across the suite of exercises. Then, even if assessors only give an overall score for each exercise, that score should represent the different dimensions.

To ensure that the competency dimensions are properly covered, it is usual to have a grid of dimensions against exercises, and check off which dimensions will be shown by each exercise. Fine-tuning of exercises is possible to bring out under-represented dimensions. An example of a grid of competency dimensions by exercises is presented in Table 6.

All competency dimensions should be measured at least twice, and preferably three times. If some dimensions are clearly more important to the job, and therefore to anyone's suitability for the job, then it must be measured three times, and a fourth time would be an advantage.

Types of exercise

Written exercises

The written exercises are simulations of the type of written work that might be undertaken by the target-level job holder. They are not abstract tests of psychological abilities. Apart from their validity, they have the practical advantage that they are completed by the participants on their own, and so they are a great help to timetabling. Their disadvantage is that too many such exercises become dull for the participants. Within the category of written exercises, there are the following specific types of exercise:

In-trays

The most famous written exercise is the in-tray, which simulates the typical pile of papers that might confront a job holder on return from a business trip, holiday, etc. Items should be targeted upon particular competencies, and it should be made clear to participants that the in-tray is not simply a test of delegation. If the person delegates, then there will be difficulty in getting any useful information from the exercise upon most of the competencies it was meant to measure. Suppose the item that should have revealed the person's analytical skills is delegated, no conclusion is possible about analytical skills.

The ability to set priorities can be measured via the in-tray by collecting the participants' out-trays every 15 or 30 minutes, and time-stamping each collection. This is much better than getting people to write out priorities on a sheet. The sheet alerts them to the need to set priorities, and it

Table 6

EXAMPLE OF A GRID OF COMPETENCIES BY ASSESSMENT TECHNIQUES

	Group Neg'n	Group Problem	In-Tray	Analysis	Sub 1 to 1	Interview
Breadth of awareness to be well-informed Develops and maintains networks and formal channels of communication, within the organisation and with the outside world; keeps abreast of relevant local, national and international political and economic developments; monitors competitor activity; has a general awareness of what should be happening and what progress is being made.		X	X	X		X
Incisiveness to have a clear understanding Gets a clear overview of an issue; grasps information accurately; relates pieces of information; identifies causal relationships; gets to the heart of a problem; identifies the most productive lines of enquiry; appreciates all the variables affecting an issue; identifies limitations to information; adapts thinking in the light of new information; tolerates and handles conflicting/ambiguous information and ideas.		X	X	X		
Imagination to find ways forward Generates options; evaluates options by examining the positive and negative results if they were put into effect; anticipates effects of options on others; foresees others' reactions; demonstrates initiative and common sense.	X		X	X	X	
Organisation to work productively Identifies priorities; thinks back from deadline; identifies elements of tasks; schedules elements; anticipates resource needs; allocates resources to tasks; sets objectives for staff, manages own and others' time.		X	X	X	X	
Drive to achieve results Is prepared to compromise to achieve a result; installs solution within timeframe; innovates or adapts existing procedures to ensure a result; takes on problems; suffers personal inconvenience to ensure problems are solved; comes forward with ideas; sets challenging targets; sets out to win new business; sets own objectives; recognises areas for self-development; acquires new skills and capabilities; accepts new challenges.		X	X		X	X
Self-confidence to lead the way Expresses and conveys a belief in own ability; is prepared to take and support decisions; stands up to seniors; is willing to take calculated risks; admits to areas of inexpertise.	X	X	X		X	
Sensitivity to identify others' viewpoints Listens to others' viewpoints; adapts to other people; takes account of others' needs; sees situation from others' viewpoints; empathises; is aware of others' expectations.	X		X	X	X	X
Co-operativeness to work with other people Involves others in own area and ideas; keeps others informed; makes use of available support services; utilises skills of team members; is open to others' ideas and suggestions.		X	X		X	X
Patience to win in the long term Sticks to a strategic plan; does not get side-tracked; sacrifices the present for the future; bides time when conditions are not favourable.	X		X	X		X

remains unknown whether they would actually carry out work in the priority order they have indicated.

In-trays can test interpersonal competencies as well as cognitive competencies, such as analysis. For example, the in-tray might require the participant to write a memo showing self-confidence and a letter requiring sensitivity. Therrien and Fischer (1978) demonstrated the validity of assessing empathy using a paper and pencil method rather than a one-to-one role-play. They constructed a series of statements that were either spoken by role-players in a one-to-one exercise, or presented to participants in written form requiring a written response. The two types of presentation elicited very similar responses from participants. The finding could be used to justify including in an in-tray items that measure interpersonal skills. However, I do not think it should be the basis of a major departure from the overall approach of having direct simulation exercises. It is important to have participants perform in oral as well as written simulations of the job.

Otherwise, the assessment centre could end up as a series of written tests. These might pass the technical objective of measuring the dimensions, but fail the consultancy objective of acceptability to participants.

Nowadays, the in-tray might be completed and can be partly presented to people by computer. The in-tray can include simulated e-mails. The only limitations to this are the practical ones of the availability of equipment and of ensuring that all the participants are familiar with the software.

It is also important that the possibility of the computer interface does not cause the principles of good exercise design to be lost sight of.

Analytical exercises

The second well-used type of written exercise involves the participant doing a piece of analytical work. Such exercises are especially susceptible to the problem of favouring people from a particular department or with a particular background. For example, in a bank's assessment centre it would be unfair to have an analytical exercise that would be easier for people with a background in reviewing loan applications. The exercise must involve an issue that is even-handed to all participants.

As with the in-tray, nowadays the analytical exercise might be completed on a word-processor and make use of spread-sheets. The only limitations are practical ones.

Written components to interactive exercises.

There might also be a written component to the interactive exercises. For example, participants might be asked to write up the outcomes of the group discussion, or write a file note on the results of a one-to-one role-play. This can be valuable in that it provides concrete evidence of the person's cognitive competencies in the interactive exercises, and removes any ambiguity about whether someone might have been extremely good at, for example, breadth of awareness, but said very little because of a lack of self-confidence.

One-to-one exercises

These exercises involve role-players who will play, for example, the customer or team-member while the participant plays the part of the target-level job holder. For example, in one institution with which I worked, being able to deal with highly confident seniors was an important part of the job under consideration. We therefore had a role-play exercise in which the participant had to negotiate with a bombastic senior. In other organisations, maybe the meetings are with outside contractors, government agencies, etc. The exercise might be essentially one of fact-finding and decision-making, or of negotiation. The choice of the setting and roles or outputs will depend upon the job analysis.

The disadvantage of one-to-one exercises is the need for role-players. They add to the resources needed for the centre, and the exercises are time-consuming to run. However, they add realism to the centre, and this might well make their costs worthwhile.

One way of avoiding having a role-player is to use video vignettes. They are described by Tol Bedford (1987). The vignettes present participants with the videotaped lead-up to a situation (for example an argument between employees) to which the participant (acting as the supervisor) must make an oral response. The same approach is explored by Weekley and Jones (1997). They describe it as a form of situational testing. The approach seems a good way of preserving fidelity, while ensuring that participants are presented with a consistent 'situation'. However, in isolation, it loses the richness of the full interactive exercises. The video is perhaps best used as the lead-in to a full one-to-one exercise, rather than a substitute for it.

There might be a temptation to get another participant to do the role-player's job, but this will be very questionable if there is any element of competition to the centre. However, it is a possibility in a development centre. In such cases, everyone should be allowed to take the role of the job holder so that they feel they have had the chance to derive equal benefit from the centre.

Group exercises

The group exercises should replicate the key types of group with which people in the job will be involved. The major options are a problem-solving and a negotiating group. Negotiating group exercises give each participant a role. A good example of this type of group exercise is provided by IBM, and described by Cascio (1982). IBM's negotiation exercise got each participant to champion a candidate for promotion. They make a brief presentation of their candidate and then lead the group discussion. It is particularly important only to have a negotiating group if it is relevant to the job. If it is decided to have this type of exercise, it is very important that the briefs given to each participant are approximately even in terms of the weight of the arguments they contain. This is easier said than done.

By way of contrast, problem-solving group exercises might involve all the participants working from a common brief. Again, as described by Cascio (1982), IBM's problem-solving exercise asked the participants to work together as a group to operate a manufacturing company, without their being given any assigned roles.

In the problem-solving exercise one can either have no one assigned as the leader, or leadership might be rotated. The leaderless format carries the particular difficulty that whoever emerges as leader will depend upon the other group members. A reasonably strong person will appear weak if all the others are very strong. I think that it is far better to revolve the leadership role, so that each person can be assessed in the role. For example, each participant might have their own problem, which they introduce to the group, lead the group discussion, and then sum up. I also advocate having a very light-touch chairperson (probably the centre's administrator or chairperson) who ensures that nobody completely dominates the discussion, and who draws in any obvious non-participants. This resolves whether a non-contributor is saying nothing because they have nothing to say or because they lack the self-confidence to say something that is quite valuable.

Even with this chairing control, the group exercise suffers the drawback of being the least standardised of the assessment centre exercises. Candidates are responding to each other's behaviour and this is not laid down in advance. This problem leads Brittain and Ryder (1999) to advocate having the group consist of one candidate together with 'stooges' who behave in a relatively scripted manner. Clearly, this solves the issue of standardisation, but raises problems with timetabling and resources.

Innovations in exercise design

The obvious innovation in exercise design is to introduce into the centre the various elements of technology that are found at work. If participants have a computer link they can make use of an intranet, databases, even the Internet to formulate their responses to exercises. Aside from such possibilities, Jansen (1997) presents a clever idea for assessing adaptability. It is to present an in-tray on two occasions and measure the degree to which the person has learnt from the first administration.

At a more technical level, Hakstian and Scratchley (1997) present a method for getting people to self-score in-tray responses, thereby saving a great deal of assessor time (around 1.5 to 2 hours). The method was for people to complete the in-tray in the normal way. They are then asked to review a list of actions for each item, checking the items that they have already covered in their answers and choosing a maximum of three new 'action elements'. In checking off the actions already covered, participants on whom the method was trialed reported that they felt it in their interests to be honest so that they could choose the alternative actions in a straightforward way.

The self-report is scored objectively and Hakstian and Scratchley found the scores using this version were more reliable than the scores from the traditional in-tray administration and scoring. The main finding was that the self-report score based on actions taken in completing the in-tray and on the additional follow-up actions was 'tapping precisely the same constructs' (p624) as the traditional scores. They also found 'a similar pattern of predictor-criterion correlations between the self-report and traditionally scored forms' (p625). Their conclusion is that 'with care and attention to detail, the In-Basket technique can be adapted to the self-report format' (p628).

Exercise production

Exercises can be produced internally by the HR department. This avoids depending upon the co-operation of others, but it has the major disadvantage of failing to involve the line. The result might be that they lack a sense of ownership in the centre. The alternative is to set up teams of line managers to assist in the design of the exercises, along with the HR co-ordinator. Unless there is a particular reason against it, I would advocate strongly this alternative. The line managers can help to provide the detailed material necessary for exercise design and will serve as assessors at the assessment centre or observers at the development centre. They should be carried along from the start of the exercise design.

The production will start with the HR co-ordinator deciding which line managers to involve as designers. I have found it helpful then to get exercise designers together as a group at the start of the exercise design phase. This allows any worries they might have to be discussed and tackled at the outset. There should then be a second group meeting of exercise designers, at which ideas for the exercises are generated.

I would advise having teams of two exercise designers for each exercise. By the end of the meeting it should be possible to visualise the different exercises in sufficient detail to generate the preliminary grid of exercises against competency dimensions.

Design meetings

Each design team must meet with the co-ordinator to sort out the detail of their individual exercise. About two hours will be required for these meetings, after which it may be necessary to ask the designers to provide some extra material for the exercise. This will mean differing amounts of work depending upon the exercise. The written exercises are probably the hardest, together with a group negotiation exercise. One-to-one exercises are generally more straightforward to design, as are group problem-solving exercises.

Nowadays it is not generally realistic to expect line managers to devote a great deal of time to the detail of writing exercises. The co-ordinator will need to do the bulk of the work because line managers do not usually have time to do more than provide the unedited material. However, the co-ordinator might be fortunate enough to find some line managers who are able to give more time to the project. In that case, they might work as a team with the co-ordinator in writing the exercises.

Exercise writing

In writing the exercises the goals are to have proper simulations of the target job, to use the correct format, to elicit the competency dimensions, to be fair, and to ensure that different levels of competence on the dimensions can be graded. Each of these is considered in turn.

Proper simulations. The exercises should be clear simulations of the target-level job within the organisation. This will ensure that their content relates to the job, and it will help them be predictive. It will also help to gain their acceptance by assessors and participants. As examples, a team member one-to-one exercise might get the participant to discuss with the role-player an inadequate piece of work by the role-player; a customer one-to-one might simulate the initial meeting with a prospective customer, etc.

This approach contrasts sharply with having exercises that appear to show the competency dimensions but which do not try to simulate the target-level job. For example Rothwell (1985b) describes the inclusion of management games in the exercises, and gives as examples 'the well-known "Mast" exercise using Lego blocks, or the "Shipwreck" or "Desert Survival" game' (p94). She goes on to comment that open-air exercises are 'more appropriate for graduate trainees or first line managers. Nevertheless, indoor versions of them for senior managers, using cardboard boxes and paper clips can provide useful diagnostic and self-development exercises' (p94). An example of this type of exercise being used for graduate selection by a commercial organisation was described by Hagedorn (1989). The organisation was described as having a two-day assessment centre. The second day 'was like one of those army survival courses where teams had to work out how to get a bomb and all their equipment across a six-foot-high electric fence in 45 minutes or cross a ditch full of piranhas'.

I do not favour this type of exercise for a number of reasons. One pessimistic reason for having good simulations is that assessors are not particularly good at assessing the competency dimensions they are supposed to be assessing, as Chapter 17 will discuss. They tend to lapse into assessing overall performance. If they are assessing performance in a direct simulation of the job, the assessment is still likely to predict job performance (Herriot, 1988). On the other hand performance with Lego or piranha-filled ditches is most unlikely to bear any obvious relation to job performance. A second problem is that these exercises do not give a preview of the job to applicants, nor do they demonstrate the relevance of the centre to internal participants. Thirdly, it is far easier to ridicule the relevance of performance at the centre if it is in a non-simulation. Anyone who does poorly can reject the whole basis of the assessment.

Goodge (1995) examined the effect of realism on development centres. He confirmed that centres that lack realism suffer from a lack of credibility with participants. The feedback from such centres is largely ignored. It seems clear that development centres should contain tailor-made job-related exercises if the feedback is to have an impact.

Format. The exercises should not be written as if they were examinations. Instead, they should place the participant in a situation, such as being a manager preparing to meet a customer or subordinate, etc. The written exercises will consist of the set of papers for the participant, together with instructions to the administrator, for example, on the times to give out additional papers, and collect out-trays. One-to-one exercises consist of the set of papers for the participant, together with the additional brief for role-players. Group exercises are made up of the set of papers for participants, together with notes to guide the chairperson if one is involved in the exercise. The participants' papers for the group exercise will frequently consist of some papers that are common to all of them, and some that are unique to each of them. An example of one person's brief in a fairly simple group problem-solving exercise is contained in Table 7.

Eliciting dimensions. There should be sufficient evidence on all of the participants for assessors to judge their strength on each of the competency dimensions targeted by the exercise. It is best to think through different ways that people might undertake the exercise, and decide whether it gives good evidence of the target dimensions. The grid of competencies by exercises might require revision as the exercise design progresses.

The goal of eliciting adequate evidence is more elusive than it might appear at first sight. A common pitfall is that the exercise may not oblige participants to reveal their strength on the competency dimension. It might be optional in the exercise whether the person demonstrates it or not. As noted already, the problem comes to the fore in group exercises. Such an exercise might take the form of all participants having a common brief that they are left to get on with,

Table 7
EXAMPLE OF A GROUP PROBLEM-SOLVING BRIEF

The example is a hypothetical exercise for a retailer. The *competitor* who is mentioned would be the name of an actual competitor.

Area Managers' Meeting Exercise

Instructions

1. Time Limit: 1 hour 30 minutes

2. You are the six area managers from the North-West Region. The areas are:
   - Merseyside
   - Manchester
   - Cumbria
   - Peak District
   - North Wales
   - Pennine

You will be the participants at the quarterly area managers' meeting to be held in FIFTEEN minutes' time. Each of you has a problem to be discussed at the meeting. When it is the turn for your problem to be discussed you should present it briefly, lead a discussion of it, and sum up at the end of the discussion. The meeting will then move on to the next manager's problem.

3. The exercise is in three parts.

   The first part lasts FIFTEEN minutes and is for you to read and familiarise yourself with your brief.

   The second part lasts ONE hour and involves each of you presenting your problem to the others in the group, and leading a discussion of it for TEN minutes. The discussion will be chaired by the Regional Manager, who is well known for taking a back seat at this kind of meeting. Normally, she just asks people to take their turn in leading the group, and will enforce the ten-minute time-limit strictly.

   The third part lasts FIFTEEN minutes. You will be asked to write a report on the discussion of your problem which can be e-mailed to your Assistant Manager, before you leave on a one-week business visit to an exhibition in Vienna.

Area Managers' Meeting Exercise

Manchester area instructions
You are the Manchester area manager.
   You have FIFTEEN minutes to read, analyse and make notes on your problem as stated below, so that you are ready to brief the other managers on it and lead a discussion of it. Your problem will take up TEN minutes of the meeting.
   The problem that you face in the Manchester area is the very severe competition from *a competitor* who has opened up just down the road from you (see attached map). With a combination of *the competitor's* special offers and marketing drive, the competition is having a noticeable impact on your monthly figures, as shown on the attached sheets. An analysis of the competitor's products and prices compared with ours is also attached.
   You need to get ideas from your fellow-managers for a local marketing campaign, or for some other response to the competition that is in line with company policy.

Area Managers' Meeting Exercise

Part Three instructions
You have to leave in FIFTEEN minutes for a one-week visit to an exhibition in Vienna. Before you leave, you should write an e-mail to your Assistant Manager that summarises the results of the discussion of your problem for him or her.

observed only by the assessors. If the exercise was meant to measure analytical ability and someone says nothing, it is completely unclear whether it shows a lack of analytical ability, a lack of self-confidence or simply that all possible bright ideas have been produced by the others in the group.

In many cases, this issue can be overcome by distorting the exercise. For example, as noted already, participants could have their own problems that are brought to the group for discussion. The instructions might call upon them to sum-marise their problem and then to lead the group discussion. They might also be asked to summarise the results of the discussion at the end of the exercise, perhaps in a memo to their boss. It is thereby possible to be much more confident in the exercise as a measure of, say, analytical ability than if the people just took part in the discussion itself.

The same problem occurs in an in-tray with instructions that enable some items to be missed. The missing items do not mean the person is weak on the competency dimensions they were meant to measure. Instructions need to be worded carefully to minimise the dilemma. The goal is that an item could have been omitted only if the participant was weak on the target competency dimension. No evidence should be negative evidence.

Participants must be left in no doubt about what they are supposed and obliged to do. I sometimes use the indicators of the competency dimension in wording an item to ensure a dimension is measured. For example, 'solution-finding' might be the target dimension for an in-tray item, and one of its indicators is 'generates and evaluates options for solving the problem'. The instructions for the item could be embedded in a memo from the person's boss which concludes with 'Please let me have your thoughts on our options and state the pros and cons of each option.'

To check whether an exercise succeeds in eliciting the dimensions as planned, it is best to visualise the exercise being completed by participants. If it is questionable whether a particular dimension is measured, it might well be possible to change the exercise to bring the dimension out. It might be achieved by making the instructions or contents of the exercise clearer and more specific. However, there will be some exercises that cannot be altered to reveal one of the original target dimensions. It will then be a matter of determining whether any of the other exercises can be adapted to measure the dimension instead.

Fairness. The issue of fairness concerns whether some people have a better chance than others with the exercises for some reason independent of their strength on the competency dimensions. A simple example of unfairness is if the exercise contains in-house jargon that some participants will know and others will not. Avoiding jargon is especially important for selection exercises used with internal and external candidates. For example, the civil service uses the word 'minute' to refer to their equivalent of a memo. Clearly 'minute' would not be understood by external candidates, and it would put them at a disadvantage. The same goes for the various acronyms in use in all organisations. This is basic common sense.

Just as obvious, but harder to solve is the exercise that puts someone from a particular background or department at a major advantage. For example, an in-tray for general managers might contain a set of accountancy papers, which have to be analysed and form the basis of a report. If knowledge of accountancy itself is not critical to the target job, someone with an accountancy background would be at an obviously unfair advantage. There is no quick and simple solution to this problem: The papers would have to be omitted, and replaced by new ones that are more evenhanded. With a centre for external people the equivalent problem is the exercise that favours particular degree subjects or particular work experience.

A problem for internal centres is that the members of the department an exercise is set in could be seen as having an advantage. This is especially true if the exercise is based upon genuine material from that department. The problem is less acute for a development centre. Observers can take people's backgrounds into account when they give feedback, and participants will not feel so threatened by issues of fairness. On the other hand, it is particularly aggravated if the centre is used for internal promotion.

The best solution is to continue to set the exercises within the organisation but to make sure that the specific material is simplified and can be grasped without specialist knowledge. For example, the one-to-one exercise might be a meeting with a team member or with a customer. The background papers will be made up and will not put anyone at an advantage.

Total fairness is impossible and, as a goal, it is self-defeating. For example, a customer-meeting exercise might be said to favour those who regularly meet customers as part of their job and a group negotiation favours those who have to negotiate regularly. They are advantaged, if only by feeling more comfortable with the exercise. They are on home ground. Rather than trying to eradicate totally this type of unfairness, a solution would be to give some additional experience to those with a particular disadvantage. For example, someone who has never interviewed a customer could be allowed to practise a customer interview before the centre.

A tempting way out is to set the exercise in some mythical organisation. Adams (1987) recommends that assessment centres for existing staff should have exercises set outside the organisation so that the scenario is equally unfamiliar for all participants. For example, it is clearly appropriate for a bank manager's assessment centre to have an exercise that involves meeting a customer, but the exercise could be said to be unfair on people without experience of customer interviews (eg people who work in one of the support departments). A way out of the problem might be thought to be provided by setting the centre in some other organisation. To emphasise the customer care, perhaps a store would be a good setting. The customer meeting would now be between the store manager and a customer.

The problem is that the exercise is still unfair on people with no experience of customer meetings, and it also carries new difficulties. First, the externalised exercise forces participants to rely only upon their general knowledge and common sense. This makes the measurement of some of the dimensions quite problematic. For example, if flexibility is a target competency dimension, a less imaginative participant might appear not to be flexible simply because the options to show flexibility are unknown in the unfamiliar setting. On the other hand, the participant who goes in for flights of fancy might appear very flexible.

The use of the external setting was adopted by Novotel in an assessment centre described by Littlefield (1995). The centre was set in a fictional recruitment agency. In so doing, the centre presented people with what was described as 'analogous material', which is familiar situations in unfamiliar settings. The reason Novotel took this approach was to stop people relying on their technical skills in tackling exercises. It is not entirely clear what is meant by technical skills and it seems a less persuasive argument than trying to make the centre as close as possible to a work sample, which dictates an in-house setting.

However, Keenan (1997) takes issue with those graduate recruitment centres that make use of exercises based within the organisation. He argues that graduates lack, for example, the 'concept of the marketing function or how it fits into the organisation' (p517) and they cannot be asked to assume the role of the marketing manager. He suggests putting graduates on their 'home ground' by having exercises set in a university environment. I can only say that setting the exercises in the organisation has never seemed to me to present graduates with a problem. It is important that they are properly briefed and that the exercise is stripped of esoteric 'organisation-speak'. It is also important that the exercises are tried out and that the comments of candidates are solicited. Setting the exercises in a university loses all the public relations advantage of being able to sell your particular organisation. More generally, external exercises prevent the centre giving a clear preview of the job and organisation to participants, and this might have been an important objective. Sacrificing it can lose an important recruitment by-product of the centre if it is being used for selection. It also lessens the point-to-point correspondence between the exercises and the job.

Setting the exercise in a hypothetical organisation disrupts the faith that assessment centre performance will be a preview to actual performance. Behaviour at the centre will be much more a matter of making the best of an uncertain and unfamiliar world. If it is a development centre, the simulation of an actual job within the organisation will have much more impact on participants than performance on an exercise in a mythical organisation. The external exercise means that participants can say they did not do well because they knew nothing about the setting.

Internal exercises also have more credibility and impact on assessors, and the organisation as a whole. For example, it will be much easier for the decriers of the assessment centre initiative in a bank to ridicule an assessors' report if it is all based upon performance in running a store.

Locating exercises outside the organisation also means that role-players have to place heavy reliance upon their general knowledge and play-acting. For example, an exercise might revolve around a career development meeting with a team member. Role-players know a great deal about the career opportunities, etc in their own organisation. However, if the interview is set in another organisation, role-players will have to rely much more on common sense, general knowledge and extemporising. In a similar way, setting the exercise outside the organisation makes life very much harder for assessors, who will not be viewing the exercises as experts. They will have to fall back on common sense and conjecture.

The design of the exercises will also be much harder if they are set outside the organisation. If the exercises are internal, it is reasonably easy to take material that exists within the organisation (eg reports, appraisal documents, etc) and adapt it. For example, a subordinate appraisal exercise can use the actual appraisal form; the in-tray can be based on actual documents. This will not be possible in an external setting.

Difficulty level. The exercises should be appropriate to the general level of intellect and experience of the participants. The average participant should not be patronised by exercises that are too easy, nor bemused by those that are too difficult. The exercises should discriminate between people, and neither be so easy that everyone does well nor so difficult that everyone does badly.

Whether the difficulty level is right will be revealed clearly when the exercises are tried out on a test run. Some exercises will be too difficult or too easy. It is usually possible to simplify an exercise that is too difficult, perhaps just by cutting back on the volume of material in the exercise. On the other hand an exercise that is too easy might have to be abandoned. A recent example from my experience was an exercise in which the participant was meant to assemble and assimilate a number of different pieces of information and put these into a well-argued case to head office for additional office space. However, once the exercise was written it was clear that all the participant could be expected to do was copy out or precis the background information – or go in for flights of fancy. It was not an exercise at all really, and would only divide participants according to how much they let their imagination run riot.

Such difficulties might only become obvious once the exercise is written, and a new exercise has to be found. However, it is preferable not to lose the goodwill of the line managers who have provided the idea by abandoning the exercise completely. In the office space example, I made the exercise into an in-tray item, so the manager was not left feeling that the time on the exercise had been completely wasted.

Graded responses. It is important that the exercise does not turn on one critical insight. For example, I was once involved with an analytical exercise which participants had to tackle in a particular way. If they used the correct logic, then they did well. If they did not use it, they did very badly. This carried three problems. First the trick could be passed on; second, those failing to know the trick appeared equally weak; third, people who did badly appeared equally weak on all the dimensions: There was nothing to mark. The exercise should draw out the full range of differences between people across all the dimensions it is measuring. It should not divide people into good and bad.

Harmonising the exercises

Once they have been drafted, the co-ordinator will need to produce the exercises as a suite, and standardise the presentation of instructions, typeface, etc, so that the end result is professional.

Standardisation of the format of opening instructions will cover the timing of the exercise, and the number of sections.

The instructions should be clear and tell participants exactly what the setting is, and what they are meant to do. An example from an in-tray is contained in Table 8.

Integrating the exercises

A development or assessment centre can have much more impact if the exercises are linked together in an integrated centre. One form that the integration might take is to get the participant always to assume that he or she is the same fictional character, for example, a particular manager. There might be some issues that are common across the exercises. As an example, the centre might be based around the acquisition of another organisation by the participant's organisation. One of the written exercises might concern the marketing plan for the new larger organisation; one of the role-plays might be with a member of staff of the acquired organisation who is worried about their prospects. As another example, the centre might be for a bank's relationship managers and feature a manager who has transferred to a new region. It transpires from the customer one-to-one and the team member one-to-one that one of the team is underperforming. These two role-plays might occur as 'interruptions' to the written exercise that contains material relevant to the role-plays. Furthermore, the role-plays might provide information that helps the participant complete the written exercise.

Integration of exercises is a definite bonus but it is by no means essential. The centre should not be distorted around this goal. Integration helps convey realism to the development or assessment centre. It replicates the manager going about the various settings that will normally be encountered. Linking exercises also carries the practical benefit of not having to present candidates with lengthy background information at the start of each exercise. Care is needed, however, to ensure that, with the linkages, somebody who has done badly on one exercise is still able to do well on later exercises. If this is not so, the later exercises are made redundant.

Table 8
EXAMPLES OF TRADITIONAL IN-TRAY INSTRUCTIONS

In-Tray Exercise

Instructions

1. Time limit: ONE hour 30 minutes

2. Your stationery consists of:
   - company headed paper
   - e-mail forms
   - plain A4 paper for reports
   - fax transmission paper
   - a pad of forms for writing outgoing telephone messages – the messages you would make if you had a telephone available.

3. Please use a separate sheet of paper for your response to each item and write:
   - the item number
   - your response to the item. Your response might be:
     - an e-mail or letter. In this case you must write out the e-mail or letter itself. You should not just say you intend to write it.
     - a telephone call. In this case you must indicate the points you would wish to make in the call.
     - a fax. In this case you should write out the fax ready for transmission.
     - a decision to delegate the item or leave it until later. If you delegate an item you must give clear instructions to the person to whom you are delegating on how you wish him or her to handle it. We want to find out how you would tackle the items so that we can get a complete view of your strengths. This is not a test of the amount you can delegate.

4. Although the exercise deals with fictitious people and events, you should refer, where appropriate, to actual people and events in this organisation and elsewhere.

Background

Today is Tuesday 4 January, and it is 8.45am. Your name is Jon Chandler. You are Manager of the Edinburgh office, which employs 25 people as shown on the attached organisation chart.

You have been away from the office since Christmas Eve, on holiday in Australia. You only got back last night, and have had no contact with anyone from the office since the start of your holiday. You left your Assistant Manager, Helen Palmer, in charge during your absence. The Christmas period is normally quiet, and you consider Helen a very capable person.

The attached is the in-tray that greets you on your arrival. A messenger calls by your office every half hour from 9.00am to collect outgoing mail, faxes, and messages, and to make deliveries of post and messages.

Trial of exercises

The co-ordinator should take the original designers through the final versions of the exercises so that the designers feel ownership of the exercises. The exercises are then ready to be tried out on a group of people who are at the same level in the organisation as the people who will go through the centre. The group should be made up of a mix of people in terms of performance.

The trial day should start with the co-ordinator stressing that it is a test of the exercises and not of the trial group. It should be made clear that their views and comments are wanted. The trial of each exercise should concentrate particularly upon:

❑ clarity of instructions

❑ whether the time limit on the exercise is right – the exercises should all be run for their stated times, so that an idea of the realism of the time limits is obtained

❑ whether it is at the right level of difficulty.

The trial run of the group exercises and one-to-one exercises should be videotaped. The recording is essential for assessor training. In making videos of group exercises, I have found it best to zoom in on two participants, and they will be the ones that assessors concentrate upon in practising their observation and recording skills. These two people should be chosen as likely to differ in their levels of competence. At least one person should be expected to do a reasonable amount of talking during the exercise. Both should speak clearly so that assessors will be able to practise making notes from the videotape.

Timetable for the trial

It is best to test out one of the group exercises first, as it will act as an ice-breaker. The trial can then move to the one-to-one exercises. I usually run through each of these exercises twice, making video recordings. Role-players will be needed for these exercises. An obvious choice for the role-players at this stage is the exercise designers, as they are closest to the exercise, and it will involve them in the trial process. Next, there are the written exercises. If there are two written exercises, it is sufficient for half of the trial group to do one of the written exercises and half to do the other. Finally, a second group exercise can be tried out and videotaped. Whatever the precise timetable, the trial will usually be accomplished within a day. It is important to take good notes of any problems that are evident in the exercises, and a little time should be left after each exercise for a discussion with the designers and the trial group.

Final version

The co-ordinator should make the changes that are considered beneficial in the light of the trial. This is the time to put the finishing touches to the exercises and to get them ready for the assessor training. In their final version, it is very helpful to use a colour coding to distinguish between papers for participants, role-players, and assessors.

Marking-guides

Once the exercises have been designed, it is necessary to decide upon any marking-guides that will be used for assessor training. My view is that anything too detailed is a hostage to fortune because all the possible responses to an exercise will never be anticipated. I prefer to ensure that assessors really understand the competency dimensions and the behavioural indicators so that they can interpret, in terms of the dimensions, the actual behaviour of participants, whether or not it might have been anticipated in a marking-guide. For example, with a one-to-one exercise, it is impossible to cover every possible way the conversation might unfold. It is better to make sure the assessors can classify correctly and rate whatever actually transpires. Some exercise designers advocate producing a 'behavioural framework' for each exercise. These contain the positive and negative behaviours that participants might produce for each competency in a given exercise. The difficulty is that some assessors lapse into using these as 'tick sheets', which runs the risk of any unanticipated behaviours being unnoticed.

Similar arguments apply to model answers to written exercises. A model answer carries the danger that assessors will downgrade an equally acceptable but unanticipated alternative to the model. Indeed, the risk is that assessors become so tied to the model answer that they will overlook a brilliant answer. However, with written exercises, it is a very good idea to indicate to assessors the dimensions that each part of the exercise is targeting. For example, each in-tray item should be focused on one or more dimensions, and these should be made clear to assessors. This is good discipline anyway, as it provides a check that the dimensions are addressed properly. The assessors will be in no doubt what they are to mark for each part of the exercise. It can also be beneficial to provide assessors with a guide to the linkages and issues in the exercise. This will make their job easier in reminding themselves about the intricacies of the exercise at each centre.

There are also particular portions of exercises for which guidance about the answer will be helpful. One obvious example is to give the correct answer to any computations that have to be carried out. Another would be if the subordinate exercise includes a rough and ready report the subordinate has written. Clearly, it will be a good idea for assessors to have an annotated copy so that they know some of the problems in the report that the participant should spot.

My general reluctance to have model answers might appear to build an unreliability into the marking. For example, it has been demonstrated by Smith and Tarpey (1987) that the more specific the guidelines to written exercises, the greater the agreement on marking among assessors. This is hardly surprising, and, as Smith and Tarpey note, the danger with highly specific guides is that assessors cease to see their input as being of value, and lose their commitment to the exercise. It is an interesting dilemma, and I come down on the side of maintaining the assessor's motivation and his or her ability to recognise a maverick but high-quality answer.

Assessment centre exercise forms

There are a number of different forms required for a centre. With the exception of observation sheets, I would advise against producing any of these forms until the exercise design is complete. It might well be that the dimensions addressed in particular exercises change during the design process. Each change will require these forms to be amended.

Observation sheets

These are simply for assessors to note the proceedings of one-to-one and group exercises. An example of each type of form is contained in Figures 7 and 8.

Rating forms

Rating forms are needed to accompany each of the exercises. The forms should give the positive indicators of the competency dimensions, and reproduce the rating scale. The objective is constantly to remind assessors of the scale they should be using. The forms should also have ample space for assessors to present the positive and negative evidence for the dimension. One possibility is to have a separate rating sheet for each dimension. It gives the space for evidence, and it is easy, in practice, for the administrator to make up the relevant batches of sheets for each exercise.

However, sheets for specific exercises, with several competency dimensions on each sheet, are generally more appropriate. After all, the detailed evidence is on observation sheets (or written out by the participants in the written exercises). Assessors are not going to fill a sheet of A4 with evidence on each dimension. An example is contained in Table 9.

Ratings grid

A grid upon which ratings can be entered as the exercises are marked is also required. This grid will be the focus for discussion at the assessors' meeting, and an example is contained in Table 10.

Figure 7

EXAMPLE OF A GROUP EXERCISE BEHAVIOURAL OBSERVATION AND RECORDING FORM

Assessor: ....

Participant A: .... Participant B: ....

Date: ....

Time	Record on participant A:	Comment	Record on participant B:

Continuation sheet

Time	Record on participant A:	Comment	Record on participant B:

Figure 8

EXAMPLE OF A ONE-TO-ONE EXERCISE BEHAVIOURAL OBSERVATION AND RECORDING FORM

Exercise: ....   Assessor: ....

Participant: ....   Date: ....

Time	Record

Table 9

EXAMPLE OF A RATING SHEET FOR AN EXERCISE

GROUP NEGOTIATION RATING SHEET	Positive Evidence	Negative Evidence	Rating
Incisiveness to have a clear understanding Gets a clear overview of an issue; grasps information accurately; relates pieces of information; identifies causal relationships; gets to the heart of a problem; identifies the most productive lines of enquiry; appreciates all the variables affecting an issue; identifies limitations to information; adapts thinking in the light of new information; tolerates and handles conflicting/ambiguous information and ideas.			
Imagination to find ways forward Generates options; evaluates options by examining the positive and negative results if they were put into effect; anticipates effects of options on others; foresees others' reactions; demonstrates initiative and common sense.			
Self-confidence to lead the way Expresses and conveys a belief in own ability; is prepared to take and support decisions; stands up to seniors; is willing to take calculated risks; admits to areas of inexpertise.			
Sensitivity to identify others' viewpoints Listens to others' viewpoints; adapts to other people; takes account of others' needs; sees situation from others' viewpoints; empathises; is aware of others' expectations.			
Patience to win in the long term Sticks to a strategic plan; does not get side-tracked; sacrifices the present for the future; bides time when conditions are not favourable.			

Showed multiple clear evidence of a high level of competence in the dimension and no substantial negative evidence — 5
Showed clear evidence of competence in the dimension and little negative evidence — 4
Showed more positive evidence of competence in the dimension than negative evidence — 3
Showed sufficient negative evidence to be judged lacking in competence in the dimension — 2
Showed multiple clear evidence of lack of competence in the dimension and no substantial positive evidence — 1

Table 10

EXAMPLE OF A GRID FOR RATINGS

Assessment Centre Grid   Name _____   Number _____

Measure / Dimension	Group negotiation	Group problem-solving	In-tray	Analytical	Subordinate one-to-one	Interview	RESULT
Breadth of awareness	■				■		1 2 3 4 5
Incisiveness					■	■	1 2 3 4 5
Imagination		■				■	1 2 3 4 5
Organisation	■					■	1 2 3 4 5
Drive				■			1 2 3 4 5
Self-confidence				■		■	1 2 3 4 5
Sensitivity		■		■		■	1 2 3 4 5
Co-operativeness	■	■			■		1 2 3 4 5
Patience							1 2 3 4 5
ASSESSOR							
FINAL RESULT							

Off-the-shelf and customised exercises

Off-the-shelf exercises

Apart from designing your own exercises, there is a ready availability of off-the-shelf exercises. They are presented in a catalogue that might be part of a computer package of exercise material. You, with the aid of the catalogue, choose the exercises that best match your requirements. This might appear the modern way, particularly if a computer package is involved. Certainly, it is cheaper than designing your own exercises. Unfortunately, you get what you pay for. It seems perverse that organisations are prepared to jeopardise the integrity of, for example, their graduate recruitment programme for the sake of less than one year's salary of one of these graduates.

Using off-the-shelf exercises carries all the problems of external exercises, together with some additional drawbacks. The most crucial is that the exercises are not specifically designed with the organisation's competency dimensions in mind. That means going through the off-the-shelf catalogue and trying to choose a set of exercises that best addresses the dimensions. The obvious problem is that the competency dimensions are being fitted to the exercises rather than the other way around.

You might, of course, go one stage further and adopt generic competency dimensions. Then you use the computer package to provide a catalogue of competencies as well as the catalogue of matched exercises. Without wishing to be a killjoy, this is not nearly as elegant a solution as it sounds. Choosing competencies from a catalogue is a well-nigh impossible task. Suddenly, they all seem useful. Furthermore, you miss the language of your own organisation. You also miss the buy-in of line managers. It is difficult to imagine the HR director sitting down with the board and going through a competency catalogue to decide which ones they will have for next year.

You also miss having exercises set within your own organisation. They tell potential recruits at an assessment centre nothing about you and they turn a development centre into a set of management games. Off-the-shelf exercises can never target the particular job or job level of a particular organisation. They do not simulate the target job, and so they cannot be said to preview how the person would behave in the job. How someone behaves in the setting of the off-the-shelf exercise might be very different from how they would behave in the target job. Of course, off-the-shelf exercises might well simulate some aspects of managerial jobs that are generic across organisations. However, other aspects are most likely to be missing.

An additional problem occurs if assessors lapse into marking the overall quality of participants in the exercise rather than succeeding in marking the specific individual dimensions. This is common in assessment centres. With off-the-shelf exercises, the marks will be less predictive of job performance to the extent that the exercises are not a genuine preview of the job. The likelihood of this being so is exaggerated by the fact that off-the-shelf exercises can be used with little job analytical justification. An in-tray or group exercise might be irrelevant to the target job but is included simply because most organisations have them, or because of limitations to the publisher's range of exercises.

Having off-the-shelf exercises also means that assessors come to them completely cold, having had no part in the exercise design phase. This means they lack ownership of the exercises and they will lack an understanding of them. This definitely will make life difficult at the assessor training. Furthermore, in many organisations it is thought to be wise to have two or more different versions of each of the exercises. The different versions are parallel in terms of having the same format, measuring the same competencies, taking the same time, etc. The need for parallel versions is particularly strong for a centre that is promotional or quasi-developmental. Parallel versions overcome the worry that the exercise will have leaked out, putting some at least at an unfair advantage. As Adams (1987) notes, parallel versions are 'infinitely easier to design when the exercise was initially tailor-made' (p2). For example, one organisation I worked with now has four versions of each exercise, with my input coming predominantly with the first set. The organisation has become expert at assessment centre exercise design! If they had gone down the off-the-shelf route, they would have long since passed the break-even point where off-the-shelf would have been more expensive than the tailor-made version.

The advantages of off-the-shelf exercises are that they can be obtained immediately, and with no development cost. In addition, there will have been some testing of the exercises, and groundwork put into their development. However, buyers should not be thrown by talk of exercises having had such research that they possess in-built psychometric properties. It is wrong to conclude that an off-the-shelf exercise carries guaranteed conformity to a normal distribution curve, as well as reliability and validity. These properties will depend upon the participants and on the assessor training. Indeed, as Bray (1985), who is a founding figure in assessment centres, notes, the assessment centre method embodies a break from traditional psychometry and its elementalism.

Customised exercises

A halfway stage between off-the-shelf and tailor-made is customised exercises. These are supplied by consultants who take a basic exercise and customise it to the client organisation. The customisation must be more than simply inserting the name of the client organisation on a word processor! It should give a genuine simulation of work at the job or job level in the organisation, and this might mean some considerable rewriting. For example, in a customer one-to-one exercise, the basic character sketches of the people involved could be generic, but the detail should be from the client organisation.

Similarly, the in-tray should have items that fit into the organisation, and are not so generic as to be meaningless to the organisation. Finally, for some exercises, customisation is not an option. An analytical exercise with its background papers is either tailor-made or off-the-shelf. There is not a halfway stage. If customisation is to be thorough it will require a good deal of work. It will be cheaper than having consultants design tailor-made exercises by themselves, but it could be more expensive than working collaboratively with consultants on exercise design.

A different type of customisation might be carried out if

you buy an off-the-shelf exercise and adapt it to your organisation. Ballantyne and Povah (1995) make clear that this raises legal issues that you might not have imagined, centring on copyright. They suggest you ask the original publisher for permission if you wish to make changes to their material.

External centres

A final option is to send people away to a centre that is run by a consultancy. For example, Skapinker (1989a) describes his experience of one such centre. On the one hand, this carries the benefits of being able to 'sub-contract a time-consuming procedure, and gain the added advantage of objectivity and independence which outsiders appear to give' (Rothwell, 1985a, p80). The downside is that the exercises are not tailored to the organisation and there will be no real sense of ownership of the process by the organisation. Nevertheless, if there are very few people to be assessed, this might be a cost-effective alternative.

10 NON-EXERCISE MATERIAL

The exercises are the heart of the centre. However, there is a range of other material that might be included. The primary issue is the usefulness of the information that the material would provide. It is all too easy to gather information just for the sake of it. The two major uses of additional material are to add value to the assessors' meeting, and to contribute to career counselling and development planning. If the additional information is to be useful at the assessors' meeting for making decisions there must be an overall framework or model for combining it with the exercise information. Otherwise, there is a risk of gathering the additional information and using it in different ways depending upon the participant, or not using it at all. Blinkhorn (1986) describes how an audit in one company revealed that assessors based their decisions almost exclusively upon the components of the centre in which they had been involved, largely ignoring components for which they had been presented with marks, such as psychological tests and written exercises. One solution must be to involve assessors in all the components of the centre. Another is to ensure there is a framework for integrating information. This alternative has the advantage that the additional information need be shared with assessors only after they have completed their assessments. This timing avoids their being influenced by and distorting their ratings around the extraneous material.

Interviews

There will probably be several competency dimensions for which the interview might be felt to give reliable information in addition to that provided by assessment centre exercises.

For example, one of the competences might be 'breadth of awareness', which might be measured at an interview by suitable questions on current and economic affairs. The interview might also be used to try to find out about the competence 'resilience to pressure', by asking about pressured situations that the person has faced in the past. The key is to confine the interview to measuring those competency dimensions that it is likely to measure well, and to make sure that it is carried out systematically. The dimensions and the possible lines of questioning should be specified beforehand; responses should be recorded and rated on the same scale as that used for the exercises.

The interview will also be used in an external centre to find out about the person's experience and qualifications. It should have been decided in advance what experience and qualifications are necessary and desirable, so that people can be assessed on these as for any other dimension. A separate interview will also often be used at external centres for the purpose of public relations and career counselling. It would be most odd for a candidate to come to an organisation and for nobody from the organisation to sit down outside the context of the exercises and talk with him or her.

Ratings by self and others

Self-assessment

Self-assessment will be most appropriate for a development centre. Self-assessment gets participants to think about themselves in terms of the competency dimensions. It can reveal to them where their areas of strength and development need lie, and it can certainly be a vital preparation for the developmental feedback from the observer. The self-assessment might be at the start of the centre, at its conclusion, or after each exercise.

Self-assessment seems less appropriate for an assessment centre. People cannot be relied upon to select themselves out of a potential job, even if that would be a more rational alternative than taking a job that is unsuitable. Reilly and

Chao (1982) considered self-assessment among various alternative selection procedures, and concluded from a survey of the small body of research they could find that it 'cannot be recommended as a promising alternative' (p33).

Clapham (1998) compared assessors' ratings and self-assessment and found mean self-ratings to be generally higher than assessors' ratings. She also found a fairly low correlation (0.18) between the two types of rating. Again, this leads one to question the use of self-ratings at an assessment centre. They would appear to commit candidates to views that will be in conflict with assessors'.

Somewhat more positive evidence for self-assessment in assessment centres comes from Shore et al (1992). They found self-evaluations of assessment centre performance to be 'significantly associated' with measures of conceptually similar dimensions obtained by cognitive tests and personality inventories. They make the helpful suggestion that self-evaluation should focus on people's relative strengths rather than their overall standing on each dimension.

Peer assessment

Peer assessment takes place at the centre and is contrasted with 360-degree feedback, which might be collected before a development centre. Peer assessment can be the basis for valuable feedback in a developmental centre. For example, knowing how participants viewed each other's contribution at a group exercise would be useful additional feedback. In the case of selection, peer assessment can be useful as an additional source of information for assessors. Indeed, Reilly and Chao (1982) found it to be a good alternative selection procedure, with validities quite similar to assessment centre exercises. Likewise, Shore et al (1992) found 'fairly strong evidence' for the validity of peer assessments. Indeed, they found peers were the most able to predict subsequent job advancement. However, for internal candidates at a selection centre, there is a major problem of acceptability. Peer ratings could be the start of some terrible grudges. In addition, people have been shown to be better at peer rating those perceived as similar than dissimilar to themselves (Fox et al, 1989).

This could imply that the practice might discriminate against people from minorities at the assessment centre.

Line managers' ratings

Internal centres might well include the line manager's rating of the participant on the competency dimensions. Quite apart from being valuable information, including line managers' ratings has the major side-benefit of ensuring they feel involved in the process. It also allows analysis of the relation between the ratings given by line managers' and those by assessors, participants and peers.

360-degree feedback

The use of 360-degree feedback increased enormously in the 1990s and seems to have reached a critical mass of acceptability. 360-degree feedback and the development centre process can benefit each other. Such feedback is an extremely helpful way for someone to gain insights on their strengths and development needs. As such, it can be a key input to a development centre. Bringing the feedback to the development centre gives the participant the chance to consider it carefully and with the help of the facilitator. It can be the basis for the participant deciding to try and approach the exercise 'situations' differently in the safe environment of the centre. For example, if someone has been given the feedback that they are a poor listener, the development centre is a chance to try out listening skills.

Rating forms

If it is decided to have self, peer, or line manager ratings, or 360-degree feedback, the appropriate forms will have to be designed. The precise design of these forms will depend upon their uses, but they should all be targeted upon the same competency dimensions that are examined in the exercises. The dimensions should be clearly defined, with space given for comment. In addition, self-rating forms that are to be completed before the centre should contain a section to allow people to indicate the opportunity they have had to display the dimension in their work so far. The line manager should also be able to indicate the opportunity that the participant has had to demonstrate each competency. Both the line managers and participants might summarise their view of the participant on each competency with a numerical rating. On the other hand, if the centre is developmental, I think that it is better not to have a numerical rating on the peer's rating form. It introduces an awkwardness into the feedback by peers, and could be used by the participant to argue with a rating given by an observer.

Tests and inventories

The choice of whether to include any psychometric tests and personality inventories, attitude measures, etc, will again depend on the use to which the information will be put. At an assessment centre, one possibility is that it will be combined with the exercise information at the assessors' meeting. Indeed, some centres consist largely of such measures. A test or inventory for use at the assessors' meeting must be relevant to one or more of the target competency dimensions. This necessity is easily and frequently lost sight of. It is felt that a measure of, say, numerical ability or of a set of personality characteristics must be relevant and so they are used because what they measure appears to be of interest. In fact, the qualities may have nothing to do with successful performance in the target job. The correct approach is to choose tests and inventories that are expected to add to information about the competency dimensions. Ideally, there should also be a check to determine whether people's scores on the test or inventory actually relate to performance on the competency dimensions. This is a statistical check that will confirm and refine the model of the relationship between the construct measured in the test and the competency.

A test of ability will probably be included if it is thought to measure a dimension that lies behind the competency dimension. The test dimension reveals the person's potential to acquire the competency. For example, a cognitive ability test can be seen as revealing the potential to be competent at analysis. It is important that organisations choose a test that is appropriate to the centre and its participants. Jackson and

Yeates (1993) found in their survey of organisational practice that several organisations were using very brief tests of the type that would be more appropriate for pre-screening. Such tests will not be sufficiently reliable for use with the relatively small number of people who have all succeeded in getting to the assessment centre stage of selection and who are all therefore toward the top of the range of ability.

A personality inventory that is to be useful for the assessors' meeting must also be related to the competencies. Otherwise it will be unclear how the information it provides is to be used at the meeting. The problem is that the personality information does not really add to the information from the assessment centre exercises. It is important to remember that the personality measure is actually a self-report of behaviour. It only measures a disposition inasmuch as repeatedly behaving in a particular way suggests the person is disposed to behave that way. However, a self-report of a general disposition seems to be of far less interest and value than a person's actual behaviour in the specific and relevant situations of the assessment centre exercises. In short, I am not certain that even a good measure of personality adds value to the assessors' meeting. It seems to me most unlikely that conclusions from the centre would be modified by information from the inventory.

On the other hand, the additional information of the inventory can be used for the feedback and career counselling and development sessions at a development centre. It might help participants to reach an understanding of themselves and their performance. For example, a participant's values might not be congruent with, say, a managerial career.

Different types of personality inventory appear appropriate for the assessors' meeting and for feedback. Thus, the assessors' meeting probably needs a straightforward measure like the 16PF or OPQ, which can be logically related and probably can be statistically related to the competency dimensions. On the other hand, participants might well feel more informed by, for example, Myers-Briggs®, FIRO-B, and Schein's measure of Career Anchors.

If an inventory is used for counselling, the feedback must be very sensitive and avoid giving the impression that the person is at the mercy of unchangeable dispositional forces. Unless feedback is given with great care, this is the message he or she will receive. Rightly or wrongly, the personality measure has the image of showing something enduring and not open to change, and so it seems to give a rather pessimistic message. Whoever carries out the feedback will need to have a good model of the relation between the competencies and the test/inventory dimensions and be able to feed back to participants their performance on the exercises with information about their dispositions and abilities. It is a job for someone properly qualified in the use of the test or inventory.

Although I would urge caution in adopting tests and inventories, it is clear that they are popular with many organisations. Holbeche and Glynn (1999) report that 85 per cent of their respondents used either personality questionnaires (92 per cent of the users) or ability tests (81 per cent) in their assessment centres. The use was less in development centres, with 68 per cent of people using either personality measures (95 per cent of the users) or ability tests (57 per cent).

In-depth psychological assessment

Instead of using a simple self-completion inventory on its own, a great deal more added value might come from an in-depth assessment to find out about the enduring themes of a person. It is these themes that lie behind the behaviour at the assessment centre. For example, a person's lack of self-confidence might be part of a deep-seated problem. This type of information will only come from an expert assessment which will yield insights into the person that are valuable to understanding their competencies, and to revealing the fundamental ways in which the person will need to grow and develop. Indeed, it is only by understanding them that fundamental change is possible. To carry out the assessment, a psychologist would need to be included among the assessment centre personnel. At a development centre, the psychologist's assessment would be used in counselling the individual. At an assessment centre, the psychologist would provide information over and above that provided by the exercises. In such cases, careful consideration is needed on how the psychologist's information will be combined with that from the exercises.

The danger with the psychologist's report at an assessment centre is that it might be seen by others at the centre as unarguable and particularly powerful information. However, it carries no guarantee of accuracy. This is less of a problem in counselling, where tentative ideas can always be amended, but it is a very real problem in assessors' meetings that are taking decisions. The problems with individual assessments are illustrated by Ryan and Sackett (1989) who showed that there was a low level of agreement between psychologists in their assessments of the same people based on the same material.

Projective techniques

One controversial way of getting in-depth information is through the use of projective techniques, (eg Thematic Apperception Test; Rorschach; Incomplete Sentences Blank). For example, Bray (1985) describes their inclusion on the AT&T mid-career assessment centre in the Management Progress Study. He recommends considering developing projective exercises that are targeted on the organisation's own dimensions rather than using the ready-made originals. Developing such material and interpreting the results is a job that requires great expertise.

11 GETTING READY FOR THE CENTRE: PRE-SELECTION, BRIEFING DOCUMENTS, AND TIMETABLES

Pre-selection

The decision over whether to have pre-selection will depend upon the use of the centre. The arguments in favour of a valid and acceptable pre-screen are that it will reduce the overall cost of the centre, and – if the centre is for internal selection – it will also reduce the number of people coming away from the centre feeling they have failed. In addition, the pre-screen might have an incremental validity over the assessment centre, so raising the validity of the overall process.

External selection

There will almost certainly be a system of pre-selection if the centre is for external selection. Depending upon the numbers coming through the centre, even a small reduction via a valid pre-screen will yield a saving in the overall costs of selection. However, a pre-selection that excludes a lot of candidates carries the penalty of the number of people mistakenly rejected. If there are many applicants for each vacancy then it might be justifiable to exclude a large number, including a lot of people who would have been good, because the vacancies will still be filled with the good people that remain.

On the other hand if there are few applicants per vacancy, the assessment centre becomes a placement centre, and a harsh pre-screen will not be appropriate.

The pre-selection is likely to be a combination of the application form and the preliminary interview. Both of these pre-selection devices should be targeted upon the same job-relevant dimensions that the assessment centre is examining. The application form should be designed to elicit as much information as possible on the competency dimensions, and a system should be devised for scoring the information from the form. This does not necessarily mean going for the expensive, and often unsatisfactory, alternative of biodata. What it does mean is designing the application form around the target competencies, and then scoring it against those same dimensions.

The pre-selection interview should be used to sift out people who would be obvious non-starters at the assessment centre, rather than to make fine distinctions between applicants. The interview is not a fine-grade measure, and it is illogical to invite to the sophisticated assessment centre only those people who have survived the far less sophisticated interview. The interview should be given a clear focus and it should be structured so that there is not a great deal of leeway for idiosyncratic interviewers.

A cognitive test is a third possible component of the pre-selection system. It would have to bear a strong theoretical relationship to one or more of the competency dimensions. Its use would be validated if there was confirmation of a strong relationship between the test and the overall assessment centre decision, or at least between the test and the assessment ratings for some competencies. Of course, this confirmation can only come after the assessment centres have been in operation. For example, in one organisation's assessment centre, I found that a test of critical thinking was related strongly to the overall assessment rating. It would have made sense to exclude from the centre people who were clearly poor performers on the test.

Internal centres

With internal centres, the question of pre-selection is much trickier. The main issue is whether any people in the eligible category should be prevented from attending the centre. For that matter, should all eligible people be required to attend? The answers depend upon the use of the centre. Boehm (1985) found that early identification programmes are often highly selective, whereas diagnostic and remedial programmes are usually open to all interested participants and are almost always voluntary. Development centres clearly fall into this voluntary and open category.

Pre-screening was reviewed by Warmke (1985), and he specifies the following possibilities:

Management nomination or recommendation. Spychalski *et al* (1997) found that more than 50 per cent of organisations responding to their survey used supervisor recommendations to select people for a centre. The problem with this is the motivation of the nominator, especially if the nomination is by just one person acting alone and is not accompanied by any real documentation. Good people might not be nominated in case they are lost to the manager; poor people might be recommended to teach them a lesson or move them on. These problems can be overcome by requiring that nominations are ratified, and that they are accompanied by adequate documentation.

Self-nomination. The problem is that it might do little to reduce the overall numbers, but it is likely to be viewed favourably by participants.

Setting minimum requirements, such as tenure or performance. This is easy to administer, is objective, and is likely to be acceptable.

Pre-screening interviews. Warmke recommends these to be used more as a counselling session, in which the potential participant learns more about the job and – it is hoped – selects out him or herself if it clearly is not appropriate to attend the centre.

Aptitude tests. For internal candidates, I believe the problems of acceptability must be weighed very carefully against the test's validity. If tests are used, then those who 'fail' must be counselled very carefully and sensitively.

Biodata. Biodata gained some popularity during the mid-1980s as a method of pre-selection. In essence it uses the person's past (or biographical) data to predict the future. It might be aspects of the past over which the person had no control (eg rural or urban upbringing) or past behaviour, and attitudes. Warmke says that biodata has a favourable to neutral participant reaction. My experience is the opposite. As a client of mine once said 'It's a pretty difficult job, telling someone they've failed the biodata'. I agree and I do not think this lack of acceptability is outweighed by the biodata's validity. People will see biodata as an unfair method of deciding eligibility for advancement. They will be right, as well. While biodata might have a statistical relation with success, there will always be anomalies, and nobody wants to be the anomaly.

Peer nominations. Again, Warmke seems impressed by the potential use of peer nominations. In contrast, I would be fearful of the tensions it might generate if someone is not nominated.

Job knowledge tests. These have a quite good validity – maybe because they provide an estimate of genuine motivation. However, Warmke reports their acceptability to be low. They are, anyway, more applicable for supervisory than managerial jobs.

In addition to these options considered by Warmke, some organisations use a loose quota system to allocate the scarce and expensive places on development centres. Each part of the organisation for which the centre is designed gets the opportunity to send a certain number of staff to the centre each year.

Lowry (1994) examined the validity of judgements based upon reviewing the personnel records of promotion candidates. Judges from the same profession as the candidates were given the records alongside candidates' statements about their major accomplishments. They evaluated the management potential of candidates from this information. Lowry found that these evaluations were related to supervisor ratings and to assessment centre scores. He concludes that the evaluation adds to the predictive power of the centre. If the records are systematic, they would seem to be a reasonable basis for selecting people for the centre.

There is no need to be confined to one pre-screen. Instead, they can be used in a battery. For example, the process might start with self-nomination to exclude people who are insufficiently motivated. Self-nominations could then be submitted to a management group to evaluate the nomination in the light of performance and experience. Then there might be a pre-screen interview and tests to decide on the priorities for attendance at the assessment centre rather than as a means of excluding people. In deciding how to prescreen, I think acceptability should be the major consideration. Of course, what is unacceptable in one company – eg administering psychological tests – might be routine for others. However, I believe it is preferable in general to define the eligible category and then leave it to self-selection, perhaps after a counselling interview. Excluding people from the centre on the basis of a personality inventory, cognitive test or biodata form is too demotivating to be acceptable. The grounds for exclusion should be criteria that people feel they can do something about, such as a minimum length of service, or a minimum performance record.

With a development centre, the organisation needs to be quite clear on the target audience. It might just be people who have already been selected for the fast track. Alternatively, it might be confined to people who can demonstrate their willingness and ability to learn. A pre-screen is needed to implement the decision. In deciding how to confine the target audience a consideration will be whether the pre-screen can be devised successfully and implemented without acrimony. Goodge (1991) advocates pre-screening to ensure that low-potential people do not attend the centre. However, the centre might be aimed at a mass market, with one objective being for people to reach their own understanding of their potential. Indeed, there is something of a paradox in limiting a development centre to people with the least need to develop.

Once the target audience has been defined, there is little justification in excluding anyone in the eligible category from attending, apart from cost. If this is such a problem that few in the eligible group can attend, it would be better to think imaginatively for a cheaper design (eg, a peer- and self-assessment centre) than to sacrifice the developmental opportunity for most people.

Briefing material

The general communication of the centre was dealt with in Chapter 7. There is also a need to give a detailed briefing to interested parties before a centre is held. Briefing materials are required for the participants and for others in the organisation. For external candidates, at a minimum, the briefing document needs to set the tone of the centre, and nowadays the emphasis will be upon the candidate finding out about the potential employer as much as the employer finding out about the candidate. The objective is that both can reach a rational and well-informed decision. The briefing should give details of how the assessment centre is made up in terms of exercises and interviews, etc, and there should be a note about the roles of the various people at the centre. It should also be clear how the decision on employment will be reached and conveyed to candidates. Finally, the document will make clear domestic details such as the time of arrival and likely time of departure.

Although some organisations give quite limited briefing to candidates, the weight of evidence is in favour of giving as thorough a briefing as possible. This might extend to providing practice material to put all candidates on the same footing. This is not being kind to candidates. It is ensuring that the organisation does not reject people who just do not know the 'knack' of tackling an in-tray or a role-play. If the knack can be taught quite readily, this would be a most stupid way of losing otherwise talented people.

A further reason to make the assessment centre as transparent as possible is that candidates will make up their own hypotheses about what is required in an exercise. They might be right. They might be wrong. Kleinmann (1993) showed that assessment centres tend not to be transparent. He says 'it is surprising how much assessment center dimensions actually lack transparency' (p992). He also found that 'participants received better ratings on dimensions that they recognised' (p991). For the organisation, the problem is that you risk losing a person who could have produced the desired behaviours if only they had guessed right what was required. However, critics might think this is an invitation to play-act. Kleinmann *et al* (1996) consider this objection. They counter it by saying that transparency ensures that candidates show their maximum ability. It can be added that if the candidate shows in the assessment centre that they are capable of performing in the desired way, then it is an issue of performance management if they fail to behave in that way when employed. Some people revert to driving badly after the driving test. One would hardly use this as an argument for some kind of 'secret' driving test.

There is also an equal opportunities implication to briefing that is inadequate. If there is the case that minorities will have had less exposure to the centre's settings than other candidates, a lack of adequate briefing and not providing the opportunity for practice is adding to their disadvantage.

For internal centres, the briefing should always aim to be comprehensive. It needs to explain the centre and how it fits into the career system in the organisation. Participants should be reminded of the purpose of the centre, especially if it is development. Steps (eg manager's appraisal or application sift) that take place before attendance at the centre should be described, along with what to expect after the centre. Particular emphasis should be given to the centre's role in the training and development process if it is an internal centre. It is useful with internal centres to summarise the briefing in the form of a flow chart that shows who does what and when.

In briefing for an internal centre, I believe that participants should be told as much as possible about the centre itself, especially the competencies. Transparency should be the aim. It seems wholly illogical to know the competency dimensions of success in an organisation, and then to keep them a secret. It seems far better to be open and specify exactly what dimensions will be examined in the centre. In any case, the competency dimensions cannot be kept a secret for long because they will be central to the management development workshops or modules. However, there seems often to be the worry that somehow the assessment will be contaminated if people know what they are being assessed against. This has some truth only if the measurement of the competency dimensions in the exercises is particularly gross. For example participants at a centre with achievement motivation as a dimension must not gain points merely by parroting the words 'We must do this excellently.'

I also think it is desirable to give the participants some foreknowledge of the exercises, at least in outline terms. They will come to learn of them anyway through their peers. Clearly it would not be sensible to go into detail, but an outline will put everyone on equal terms, and will not invalidate the centre. If there are parallel exercises, just the common denominator of the different versions could be given. For example, the briefing might say that one of the exercises requires participants to tackle an in-tray that might typically be found on the desk of someone at the target level.

The broad argument of giving more information rather than less is the same for internal centres as for external.

Aside from the briefing for participants, there needs to be a briefing document for each participant's manager. This should stress the primary purpose of the centre, especially if that purpose is developmental. It will give a very mixed message if people come back from a developmental centre and are asked by their managers whether they passed. The document must stress that it is not a pass/fail system and that participants are attending it to help their development. The briefing will need to pay particular care not to appear critical of managers' abilities to rate current performance. The emphasis can often be that the centre focuses upon participants' performance in a different job from the present one.

A contract

The expectations about the assessment or development centre can be summarised in the form of a learning contract between candidates/participants and the organisation. Shuttleworth and Prescott (1991) describe how they drafted such a contract in a development centre at Pilkingtons. It made clear the participant's right to withhold information from the reports and development plan and the company's right to make use of the information contained in the 'approved' report and plan.

The *Guidelines and Ethical Considerations for Assessment Center Operations* (Task Force on Assessment Center Standards, 1989 and reproduced in Appendix A) recommend having an Organisational Policy Statement for an assessment centre. It should cover the following areas:

1. the objective of the centre
2. who will go to the centre as participants/candidates
3. who the assessors/observers will be
4. what use will be made of the data from the centre
5. who the internal and external consultants responsible for designing the centre were, together with their professional qualifications and related training
6. what model to validate the centre is being used.

Timetables

The final material needed before the centre can get under way is the timetable. The timetable for an assessment centre should give assessors sufficient time to complete their ratings after each interactive exercise. They must not get behind in the work to be assessed. The utility of the centre will be destroyed if the assessments cannot be carried out conscientiously and if assessors cannot be given pause for thought. A rule of thumb will be to allow assessors 15 minutes to mark each candidate after an interactive exercise (ie they will need 30 minutes after a group exercise and quarter of an hour after each one-to-one exercise). A certain amount of leeway can be gained by leaving the marking of written exercises until the evening if the centre is lasting more than a day.

While assessors need gaps, participants at assessment centres, by contrast, should be involved without lengthy waiting between exercises. Normally these requirements can only be reconciled by dividing the participant group and running the written exercises and tests in parallel with the one-to-one exercises and interviews. By contrast, at a development centre, some slack time is an advantage. People need time to reflect upon the feedback they are receiving.

Obviously the timetable should have a starting time that allows people to travel without being rushed; alternatively, arrangements should be made for them to stay the night before the centre. The centre's chairperson should welcome participants and brief them, as described in the next chapter. The participants can then fill out any pre-centre self-assessment. Some centres also include a warm-up exercise before

Table 11
EXAMPLE OF AN ASSESSMENT CENTRE TIMETABLE

Day 1	
10.30	assemble and coffee
11.00–11.15	welcome and introduction
11.15–12.15	complete pre-assessment centre questionnaire
12.15–13.00	warm-up exercise
13.00–14.00	lunch
14.00–14.15	managers' meeting – preparing
14.15–15.15	managers' meeting – discussion
15.15–15.30	managers' meeting – write-up
15.30–15.50	tea
15.50–17.20	analytical written exercise (participants 1, 2 & 3)
15.50–17.00	subordinate 1:1 (participants 4, 5 & 6)
15.50–16.10	prepare
16.10–16.40	role-play
16.40–17.00	write-up
17.30–19.00	analytical written exercise (participants 4, 5 & 6)
17.50–19.00	subordinate 1:1 (participants 1, 2 & 3)
17.50–18.10	prepare
18.10–18.40	role-play
18.40–19.00	write-up
Day 2	
08.30–08.45	group negotiation – prepare
08.45–09.45	group negotiation – discussion
09.45–10.15	coffee
10.15–11.45	in-tray
11.55–12.25	interview (participants 1, 2 & 3)
12.35–13.05	interview (participants 4, 5 & 6)
13.05–13.30	debrief on assessment centre with administrator
13.30	lunch and participants depart
15.00–17.00	assessors' meeting

the assessors become involved. It gives people a chance to settle and get used to the sound of their own voices.

The centre itself might well start with a group exercise. Putting it first can help settle people down further. Then it should move on to the written exercises and one-to-one exercises. Preferably, each participant should be allocated a number to identify their written answers. These numbers will only be known to the collator of marks so that assessors mark these exercises blind of the impressions they have reached from the interactive exercises. An example of a timetable that gives assessors some leeway, but which keeps candidates/participants occupied, is given in Table 11 (opposite).

Each assessor and participant should be given a personal customised timetable derived from the master timetable. The timetable should show the room the person is in, and the activity. An example of an assessor's and a participant's time-table derived from the above master timetable are shown in Tables 12 and 13.

Table 12
EXAMPLES OF ASSESSOR 1'S TIMETABLE

Day 1		Room	Participant
14.15–15.15	observe managers' meeting group discussion exercise	D	1 and 4
15.15–16.10	mark discussion exercise		1 and 4
16.10–16.40	observe subordinate 1:1	B	5
17.00–18.10	mark subordinate 1:1		5
18.10–18.40	observe subordinate 1:1	B	2
Evening	mark subordinate 1:1		2
Evening	mark analytical exercises		3 and 6
Day 2			
08.45–09.45	observe group negotiation	D	2 and 5
09.45–11.55	mark group negotiation		2 and 5
11.55–12.55	interview	B	1
12.35–13.05	interview	B	4
13.00–13.30	mark interviews		
13.30–14.30	mark in-trays		
15.00–17.00	assessors' meeting	D	

Table 13

EXAMPLE OF PARTICIPANT 1'S TIMETABLE

Day 1		Room	Assessor
10.30	assemble	D	
11.00–11.15	welcome and introduction	D	
11.15–12.15	complete pre-assessment centre		
	questionnaire	D	
12.15–13.00	warm-up exercise	D	
13.00–14.10	lunch		
14.00–15.30	managers' meeting group exercise	D	I
14.00–14.15	managers' meeting – preparation		
14.15–15.15	managers' meeting – discussion		
15.15–15.30	managers' meeting – write-up		
15.30–15.50	tea		
15.50–17.20	analytical exercise	D	II
17.50–19.00	subordinate 1:1	A	III
17.50–18.10	preparation		
18.10–18.40	role-play		
18.40–19.00	write-up		
Day 2			
8.30–09.45	group negotiation meeting	D	II
08.30–08.45	prepare		
08.45–09.45	group meeting		
09.45–10.15	coffee		
10.15–11.45	in-tray	D	III
11.55–12.25	interview	B	I
13.05–13.30	debrief on assessment centre		
13.30	lunch and depart		

12 THE PEOPLE AT THE CENTRE

A question of language

Generally assessment centres have assessors assessing candidates; development centres have observers observing participants. The comments in the next three chapters generally apply equally to assessors/observers and candidates/participants. Referring continually to 'assessors/observers' and 'candidates/participants' makes reading irksome. I generally use the word 'assessor' if it is obviously covering both assessors and observers. Similarly, I use 'participant' if it is obviously covering candidates and participants. It's obvious to me, anyway!

Assessors

The group of assessment centre assessors or development centre observers will include people who have helped with the design of the exercise. They will have gained understanding and commitment to the process. If there are six exercises, and teams of two designers, then there are already twelve potential assessors. However, the group might need to be broadened to make sure there are enough people in it to cope with the number of participants or to include all the departments and interest groups in the organisation. Often, for political reasons, organisations have more trained assessors than are strictly required by the number of participants. A convenient time for including more people is when parallel exercises are developed. Another six people can be brought into the panel, each working alongside one of the experienced assessors.

The number of people who must be trained in the first assessor training courses depends upon the number of participants who will go through the initial centres, and the ratio of assessors to participants at each centre. Group exercises should always be observed in the ratio of one assessor for no more than two participants. An assessor cannot be expected to follow more than two participants. The advice that each assessor should observe only two candidates is echoed by Boyle *et al* (1995). However, they found in a survey of practice that one-third of organisations expect assessors to observe more than this number.

Even with the restriction of one person observing only two candidates in the group exercise(s), it is still possible to timetable a batch of 12 participants with three assessors. Participants are divided into two sub-groups of six for the group exercise. The groups would run sequentially with the same three people acting as assessors for both sub-groups.

If batches of six are used initially and if there will be 60 participants in the first year, 15 assessors will be needed, on the assumption that each of them assesses twice a year, which is about the minimum necessary to keep in practice.

Generally, it is better for line managers to be in the majority as assessors. Using line managers ensures that they own the process and do not see it as the property of the HR department. However, the extent to which this is an issue depends upon the organisation, and certainly there might be a disproportionate number of assessors from HR without the rest of the organisation feeling that it has lost ownership. For development centres, the presence of line managers as observers is a clear sign of the commitment of the business to people's development, and can be very motivating. As an example, Hardingham (1996) describes a development centre for middle managers at the accountancy firm KPMG. The observers included some of the firm's most senior managers.

In choosing potential assessors, Glynn (1996) advises picking people with a good track record in staff assessment and development. It is also important to take note of the consistent research that shows that job-applicants like to be dealt with by people who are personable, informed and informative (Connerley and Rynes, 1997). Although the research is based upon interviewers, it seems reasonable to suppose that it extends to assessors. Certainly, it is wise to choose assessors who can be friendly and warm and to encourage them to be so at the centre.

Generally, it is best for assessors not to know the participants and certainly not to have had a reporting relationship with them. This is particularly true for development centres. Jackson and Yeates (1993) found that knowing each other was off-putting both for participants and observers. They say 'the most significant difficulty came in delivering feedback' (p16).

There should be no problem in getting line managers to serve as assessors or observers if the groundwork has been laid correctly. First, the process will hopefully have top-level endorsement. If it is driven from the top, line managers will be more willing than if it appears they are doing a favour for an HR department scheme. Second, the system should have been sold to the line by involving them from the outset. Likely assessors should have been included in the job analysis interviews; then involved in one of the exercises. Most likely, they will then want to see the process through and act as assessors. After all, by this stage they will be convinced of the utility of the centre.

The level of the assessors in the organisation is important. If the process is to be seen as credible they must be senior to the participants. If the centre is looking at long-term potential, assessors should be from the level upon which the centre is targeted. There is going to be a distinct credibility problem if future senior managers are chosen by middle managers, just as there would be a problem if people on the shop floor assessed people's supervisory skills. Equally, it is possible to err in the direction of having assessors who are too senior. I know one large organisation whose managing director acts as an assessor for their fast track centre. This is excellent from the point of top-level endorsement and commitment. My reservations are whether he will bow to other assessors' opinions, or at least whether they will feel able to argue their points of view; whether he will have the time to be trained properly and whether his presence will make the process unnecessarily daunting for candidates.

Some organisations make considerable use of a small number of people as assessors. These people might even be seconded to the centre for a while to act full-time in the role. The benefit is in terms of these people developing an expertise. However, the risk, as Thornton (1992) notes, is that they will start to make their own modifications to the process, for example taking inadequate notes.

Aside from line managers and people from the HR department, it is also possible to have expert assessors of the exercises. Gaugler et al (1987) found that assessment centres were more predictive of performance when the assessors were psychologists than when they were managers. This might be used as a reason to replace line managers, but I think that the loss in terms of involvement and commitment will be unacceptable. As Greatrex and Phillips (1989) observe, for BP 'the lack of expert assessors is traded off against the high ownership of senior management for the programme and its high face validity with participants' (p39).

An assessment centre might still include an external expert, but to do a different job from the exercise assessors. The expert might be a psychologist whose role is to find out about the enduring themes that underlie a person's life, as described in Chapter 10. For example, the Civil Service Selection Boards include a psychologist and they find this person's insights and independent view to be of considerable value. Nevertheless, use of a consultant will add considerably to the costs of the centre, and his or her presence must not take undue emphasis from the simulation exercises. It could also be demotivating for the line assessors, who might feel they must bow to the expert.

The chairperson

An assessment centre normally has a chairperson to be in charge of the centre. For a development centre, the person in charge can quite readily be one of the facilitators from HR. The chairing role at an assessment centre is normally taken by a person of appropriate seniority from the management development function. Often it will be the management development manager who acts as the chairperson. However, a graduate selection centre or a team leader centre might be chaired by someone of lesser status. If there are a lot of centres each year, the chairing role might be delegated during the running of the centre, with the manager arriving for the assessors' meeting. Indeed, in some large organisations assessment is a year-round activity, and so the management development manager cannot be present even at the assessors' meetings. In such cases an equally credible chairperson must be found. Maybe it will be someone who is carrying out the role full-time on secondment. The full-time nature of their role gives them a credibility and authority they otherwise might not have.

The function of the chairperson during the centre is to ensure its smooth and fair running. It is essentially a job of quality control, and involves overseeing the participants, the assessors, and the role-players. The function at the assessors' meeting is both to chair the meeting and to hear – at first hand – the assessors' comments upon candidates.

Overseeing the participants

At an assessment centre, candidates should be well briefed, not suffer unnecessarily from stress, and approach each exercise with a fresh mind. To help achieve this, the chairperson should brief them on their arrival. The briefing needs to remind them of a number of points that will also have been mentioned in the pre-centre written briefing, and should deal particularly with what they can expect during the centre. They should be made familiar with the timetable, and reminded that each person is responsible for being in the right place at the right time. The exercises should be described to ensure everyone has an understanding of the different types of exercise.

The ground rules for the assessment centre should also be laid down. These will include a request that once the day is under way candidates should not talk to each other about the exercises. The timetables are individual to each candidate, and some people may not yet have done an exercise that others have finished. Finally, the chairperson must stress that people are not in competition with each other, but rather are being assessed against general standards. During the centre, the chairperson is a point of reference if they have any problems. In particular, the chairperson will need to deal with anyone who is suffering from stress, getting unduly despondent, or who is reacting very negatively to the centre. Finally, at the end of the centre it is a good idea to spend at least some time with candidates in a debriefing session. They can give their views on the centre, and clear up any doubts or anxieties.

At a development centre, the role of the chairperson is to set and maintain the developmental tone, make sure that the centre is running to its plan and sort out any problems that arise.

Overseeing the assessors

A second key role for the chairperson during the assessment centre relates to the assessors. The validity and reliability of the assessment centre process rests on the assessors' abilities in the three key areas of observing and recording candidates' behaviour, categorising behaviour and rating behaviour. To ensure that standards are met, the chairperson should be satisfied that assessors are taking full observation notes. The chair should also be alert to whether assessors are using the behavioural criteria to categorise their responses, and whether they are rating each competency dimension using the scale properly and independently of the other competency dimensions.

In practice, problems with categorising and rating are more likely to become evident at the assessors' meeting than during the centre. The chairperson should also make sure that assessors do not talk to each other about the candidates they have been observing until the assessors' meeting at the end of the centre. Such talk may well influence the assessors of subsequent exercises. Assessors should also not share information with candidates before the feedback meeting.

At a development centre, the chairperson will also want to be alert to the quality of the observation and feedback that the observers are delivering. The chairperson will be available to help observers with any problems or doubts they might have in their role.

Overseeing the role-players

Finally, the chairperson must monitor the role-players, as far as possible. Feedback on the role-plays will come from assessors and participants, and any obvious problems in the role-plays must be discussed.

Role-players

As Rodger and Mabey (1987) remark, the key contra-indicator for a role-player is an interest in amateur dramatics. People are needed who will play the parts in an undramatic way. One possible source of people for role-playing is the training department, but it can also be a useful way of bringing new people into the assessment centre system who will go on to become assessors. I try to keep down the number of people involved in the role-plays at any time. If there is a choice between using a small number of role-players frequently for a short period and then phasing in a new group versus using a large number infrequently then I would go for the small number. They can then become 'experts' at their roles.

While amateur dramatics is a contra-indicator, the same is not true for professional dramatics. There are now several companies of professional actors who offer their services to organisations for assessment and development centres. If your budget can stand it, this is a very satisfactory solution to ensuring that the role-plays are carried out professionally.

Role-players will need to be thoroughly familiar with the briefs, and it is important to have a meeting with the group of role-players to resolve any doubts and ambiguities in the parts they are to play. This is best done after the trial and videotaping of the one-to-one exercises. The role-players should then practise the role among themselves, and keep a record of any points that arise.

The starting-point for the role-playing is the brief that the exercise designers have written. The role-player meetings will then put extra detail on this brief. By the time of the centre, all the role-players should approach the role in the same way as far as possible. What role-players must establish is their general approach to the exercise and their answers to key questions that might be asked by participants.

At the centre itself each role-player should act in a similar manner with each participant, for example by giving the same information in response to the same question. The aim is to provide a standardised backdrop against which each person's competencies can be demonstrated. However, the role can never be scripted as it is most important that the interaction is natural. Role-players should not be obstructive by keeping information hidden when it is asked for directly. However, neither should they volunteer information to the participants too readily. Participants are required to elicit information and to identify a logical approach to a problem. Information should be volunteered only if the candidate is unable to direct the discussion. In such cases, volunteering is helpful as it will avoid participants feeling that they have failed the exercise. Detailed guidelines on when to volunteer information should be agreed and included in the role-players' brief. For example, it might say 'If, after ten minutes, the person appears to be getting nowhere, start to volunteer information. Do not, however, do this too soon.'

Role-players should feed back any points that arise during the playing of the role with participants. It is also a good idea to have occasional meetings – say every six months – among role-players to update, collate and implement any enhancements to playing the role.

A criticism that some people voice about role-plays is that they are unfair. It is argued that because of their interactive nature no two participants face the same stimulus. Of course, this is true at a micro-level, but the role-player training is aimed at ensuring that participants receive a similar stimulus at a broader level. The theme for the role-player is standardised, even if the precise words are not. The argument about standardisation can be applied to any assessment other than a written exercise. The practical answer is to go for a level of standardisation that does not destroy the basis of the exercise.

Facilitators

As well as the observers, development centres need facilitators who will work with the participants during the centre. The facilitator can brief participants before each exercise. The facilitator should also help the participant make best use of the feedback received from observers. In particular, facilitators can help to integrate the feedback from different observers with the participant's self-view and the view from 360-degree feedback, etc. The facilitators can also run the pure development sessions such as those on the competencies, career anchors, and how to write a development plan.

Normally, the same person will act as facilitator to a participant throughout the centre. The facilitator can also follow-up the participant's progress after the centre. In general, two facilitators will be needed for a development centre and one of them will take on the chairing responsibilities. They will generally be from the training and development function.

The administrator

A capable administrator is the key to the successful running of the centre. It is vital to have someone bright and energetic who can get on top of the co-ordinating activities of the centre. He or she must also, of course, be able to handle confidential information. The administrator should be in charge of all the preparation for the centre, including getting the materials ready, corresponding with assessors, role-players and participants and arranging accommodation. All this work is done before each centre. It will not be necessary for the administrator to be in full-time attendance at the centre itself once it has run a couple of times and any problems have been ironed out. Once the centre is running smoothly there will be long gaps during the exercises with the administrator having nothing to do. Instead of the administrator, the chairperson can start and stop the exercises, etc. It may sound uneconomic to have the expensive chairperson doing the administration at the centre, but he or she must be there anyway.

Checklists for running the centre

Working through the running of the centre chronologically, the following are the major checklists. Many of these matters will fall to the administrator.

Well before the centre

❏ Assessors and role-players must be informed in plenty of time that they are being asked to take part in the centre.

❏ Invitations must be sent to the candidates/participants, together with briefing documents.

❏ Briefing documents must also be sent to participants' managers, if the centre is internal.

❏ If there are managers' rating forms or 360-degree feedback material, they must be sent out. Accommodation for the centre must be booked.

Shortly before the centre

Having got everyone and everything booked, there is the checklist of materials for the centre itself. The centre's administrator needs to ensure that sufficient numbers of the following (obvious and less obvious items) are all ready for the start of the centre:

❏ exercises

❏ marking-guides

❏ role-players' briefs

❏ answer paper/booklets

❏ observation sheets

❏ rating sheets

❏ marking-grids

❏ clip-boards for assessors when observing

❏ individual timetables for assessors and participants

❏ psychometric test material

❏ self-assessment sheets

❏ end of assessment centre evaluation sheets

❏ pens, pencils, pencil sharpeners and erasers

❏ paper clips, staplers

- name badges/table place-labels
- labels for room doors
- calculators
- flipchart paper and pens.

Of course, some of these will not be relevant to a particular centre, and there will be other specific things that must be included. The overall message is to make an inventory and make sure that all the materials are despatched to the centre.

On the day

During the centre, there should be no need for a checklist if all the preparation has been carried out. The most important thing is to make sure that timetables are adhered to. Otherwise the centre will get out of synchronisation. The chairperson will also have to sort out any unlikely emergency, such as someone suffering from the stress of the occasion.

Accommodation for the centre

The minimum space for an assessment centre with six candidates is:

- assessors'/administrator's office
- candidates' relaxing room
- one large room for group exercises and written exercises
- three small rooms for one-to-one exercises, and interviews, if applicable

For a development centre, it is a definite advantage if participants can have their own rooms. They will do all the exercises in their own rooms, apart from the group exercises. The development centre therefore needs:

- observers'/facilitators' office
- one large room for group exercises and group development sessions
- six small participant rooms for one-to-one and written exercises, receiving feedback and development planning.

Hotels are often used for centres, but this amount of space will clearly add to quite a large bill. On top of the cost of the assessment rooms, meals and extras comes the cost of overnight accommodation for assessors, participants and the chairperson. Furthermore, there is a need to be careful of the sort of rooms the hotel is offering for the centre. A set of converted bedrooms at an airport hotel can be a dismal prospect. It is far preferable to get a private annexe or wing. However, such space is in short supply and will need to be booked well in advance. The hotel should also be flexible about mealtimes to allow assessors to get on with their marking in the evening and to eat when they want.

Despite its expense, I think it is preferable to hold centres for internal people away from the organisation's normal premises. This avoids interruptions and helps the psychological immersion in the centre's activities. Certainly, if it is to be held within the organisation, a space that is private is required, such as a training centre.

In contrast, it is preferable to hold graduate selection centres at the organisation's premises. An Incomes Data Services study (1998) found several companies that believed that 'visiting the working environment gave candidates a better feeling for the company culture' (p3). This must surely be true. It seems far better to be 'at home' to external candidates than to have the assessment centre at a hotel.

13 HOLDING THE CENTRE

Observing and recording the exercises

In the group exercises, the assessors observe two participants in a room laid out approximately as shown in Figure 9. Assessors must take a reasonably detailed record of what their participants do and say. An assessor may also note down significant events by other participants which could account for their own participants' behaviour. For example, another participant might be extremely rude to one of the participants being assessed. The assessors should record these contextual events in the column marked 'comments' on the observation sheet (please see Figure 7, p140).

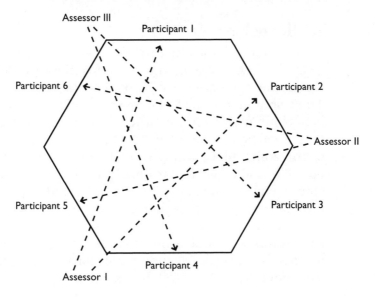

Figure 9
LAYOUT OF ROOM FOR GROUP EXERCISE

In the one-to-one exercises, the assessor is alone in the room with the participant and role-player. The assessor should record the participant's behaviour, but again might make the occasional note of what the role-player did and said. In the written exercises, the observing and recording is, of course, done by the participant. However, if there is a debriefing session after a written exercise, the assessor will again need to record the participant's comments.

Working in pairs

Some organisations prefer assessors to work in pairs, at least in the early runs of a centre. Each assessor marks the candidate in an exercise and then they compare marks. Clearly, this adds to the overall number of assessors needed for a group exercise. For a one-to-one exercise, it is possible for the second opinion to come from the role-player. However, this person will have been less focused on remembering, let alone recording, the candidate's behaviour and it would be wrong for their impressions at the end of the role-play to carry equal weight to the assessor's views. In the written exercises it is, of course, entirely possible for two assessors to provide a mark. It does, however, add to the overall time required for the assessment.

Classifying the behaviour

In the group and one-to-one exercises (the interactive exercises) the assessors must classify the recorded behaviour under the competency dimensions that are being assessed. They should not feel the need to classify every piece of behaviour under one or other dimension. It might well be that a particular piece of behaviour is an instance of none of the competency dimensions being assessed. Equally, it is possible that a particular observation covers more than one competency dimension. For example, 'puts forward an accurate summary of the other person's views' will be positive evidence of incisiveness and sensitivity. However, even in this example it is possible, strictly, to separate the evidence on incisiveness (the accurate summary) from the sensitivity (the other person's views). It is good discipline if assessors try not to double-classify their observations, but make a decision under which dimension the behaviour is to be classified.

Once assessors have gained experience and confidence, classifications can be made while the exercise is in progress, with a margin note, such as 'in+' for a positive example of incisiveness. This is better than waiting until the end of the exercise because the assessor has the richness of the behaviour itself available to classify rather than the note of the behaviour. However, inexperienced assessors must not miss a chunk of an exercise while they ponder on the classification of an item of behaviour.

Classification is easier in the written exercises. Assessors have a guide to the dimensions that different parts of the exercise are addressing, and they have time to reflect upon and consider their classification.

Rating the behaviour

At the end of the exercise, and only at the end, assessors at an assessment centre should bring together a summary of their classified observations for each competency dimension on the rating sheets. They should separate their positive and negative evidence for each of the dimensions. They must then summarise the balance of evidence by assigning a rating to the dimension. For making a selection decision, there seems little practical benefit in having a scale with more than five points. These equate approximately to:

❑ outstanding
❑ good
❑ acceptable
❑ requires development to be acceptable
❑ definite weakness.

It adds nothing to know that someone was extremely outstanding or very weak.

The problem with five points is that people will drift towards the middle. On the other hand, four points might seem too restricting to some organisations, which will introduce an informal mid-point by rating people 'b/c'. The choice is finely balanced.

The precise wording of the scale will depend upon the organisation. An example of a five-point scale is given below.

Showed multiple clear evidence of a high level of competence on the dimension and no substantial negative evidence	5
Showed clear evidence of competence on the dimension and little negative evidence	4
Showed more positive evidence of competence on the dimension than negative evidence	3
Showed sufficient negative evidence to be judged lacking in competence on the dimension	2
Showed multiple clear evidence of lack of competence on the dimension and no substantial positive evidence	1

The scale does not ask for a simple count of the instances of positive and negative evidence. It asks assessors to weigh both the quality and quantity of evidence, and to make a judgement. The judgemental nature of the assessment is inevitable, and is one reason for having highly paid assessors do the task.

At a development centre, a rating will normally be given as a way of summarising the feedback. However, the emphasis should be on the feedback itself and not the rating. We have used three-point rating scales at development centres because that is all that is needed for the summary. In effect, the scale is:

❑ strong

❑ competent

❑ development needed.

It is important that all assessors abide by the rating scale that is defined, so that two assessors mean the same thing by a given rating. Assessors must also be encouraged to use the whole of the rating scale. The wording of the high and low points should deliberately not be at the absolute extremes of competence. If they are so worded, they will be used extremely rarely and will effectively be redundant.

No evidence and negative evidence

In making their ratings, assessors need to know how to interpret a lack of evidence for a competency. A clear example of the problem is in an interactive exercise when participants give no evidence that can be noted down for, say, breadth of awareness even though it should be measured in the exercise. No evidence is different from demonstrating a muddled ignorance of the world. What happens when assessors fill out the rating sheet? Do they put 'said nothing to show breadth' as negative evidence, in just the same way that they would note the confused ignorance? The same issue arises with the written exercises if an item is left out. For example, if a report is not written in an in-tray exercise, does that count as negative evidence for the dimensions that the omitted item was meant to measure?

The ambiguity can lead to assessors feeling that they have insufficient evidence to make a rating for a dimension. There is nothing positive under the competency dimension, but no negative observations either. In practice, if assessors cannot have faith in their rating, it is better to give a 'not rate' than a '3', which will be misleading at the assessors' meeting.

If assessors are unable to make ratings, this is most likely because they cannot take as negative evidence the failure to display the competency dimension. The exercises should be designed and administered so that these ambiguities do not arise. The design and administration of the exercises should allow 'no evidence' to be counted as negative evidence. The design of the exercise must demand the demonstration of the target competency dimensions, rather than allowing it to be optional; and the administration of the exercise must give the participant every opportunity to display the dimension. This is where the 'light-touch' chairing of group exercises is important. For example, if each participant is gently drawn into the group discussion and given the opportunity to show breadth, then someone who still shows no breadth can be assumed to be lacking on this competency dimension rather than being, for example, shy. With written exercises, the instructions must be clear and, as a final measure, there can be a quick interview at the end of the in-tray exercise to cover any omitted items.

Rating by exercise

I have concentrated upon rating each competency dimension separately. Another possibility is to rate each exercise as a whole with an overall mark, or to rate each of the outputs or roles in an exercise. However, if there is to be feedback, the competency dimension ratings should not be substituted by the overall exercise rating or ratings in terms of outputs or roles. People need to be told what they should do to perform better, and this feedback must be in terms of the competencies. For example, if someone does badly in the business development role on the customer one-to-one exercise, the poor performance must be fed back in terms of the need to develop listening skills, etc. The overall mark or the marks for the roles must be mediated by the competencies.

Assessors cannot mark successfully by exercise and by competency dimension at the same time. Marking by exercise will serve only to encourage the halo effect across dimensions. If an overall mark for the exercise is wanted for some reason, I think it should be calculated simply as the mean of the dimension ratings, rather than something upon which assessors focus their attention.

The assessors' meeting

At an assessment centre, once the exercises are completed, the assessors must finish off their assessments. These should be handed to the chairperson/administrator, who will be collating marks by filling in a grid. The end result will be a completed grid, such as that in Table 14. Each grid should be photocopied for each assessor and for the chairperson, and the assessors' meeting can then be held.

Until the assessors' meeting, assessors have observed and rated behaviour independently of each other across the various exercises. At the meeting, assessors share these ratings and the behavioural examples in order to come to a

Table 14
EXAMPLE OF A COMPLETED GRID FOR RATINGS

Assessment Centre Grid **Name** Ruth Naylor **Number** 03

Measure / Dimension	Group negotiation	Group problem-solving	In-tray	Analytical	Subordinate one-to-one	Interview	RESULT
Breadth of awareness		5	3	4		5	1 2 3 4 5
Incisiveness	4	3	4	3			1 2 3 4 5
Imagination	2		3	3	4		1 2 3 4 5
Organisation		3	1	2	2		1 2 3 4 5
Drive		4	3		5	4	1 2 3 4 5
Self-confidence	5	4	3		4		1 2 3 4 5
Sensitivity	2		3	3	2		1 2 3 4 5
Co-operativeness		1	3		2	1	1 2 3 4 5
Patience	4		4	3		3	1 2 3 4 5
ASSESSOR	NM	JLV	CMC	JLV	CMC	NM	
FINAL RESULT							

common view of candidates on each competency, particularly a view on each candidate's strengths and development needs. The focus of the meeting is the observed behaviour on the exercises at the centre. Anecdotal information collected outside the assessment day must not be introduced. For example, an assessor may have met one of the candidates and have private views on that person. These views must be kept private.

The procedure for the meeting is to take one candidate at a time and to go through each of the competencies in turn. For each competency, the chairperson reads out the ratings. If there is a discrepancy among the ratings, the chairperson asks for behavioural examples from the different exercises. Once information on all the exercises measuring the competency has been shared it is considered by assessors, who must produce an overall rating on the competency. Minor discrepancies of just one point are usually resolved easily. Larger discrepancies might take quite a few minutes if the centre is for promotion, and assessors have to be satisfied about the accuracy of the resolved rating.

Boyle *et al* (1995) advocate two other ways of pooling information to arrive at a final rating. One is for an assessor to report the evidence without the rating. The group then discusses the evidence and agrees a rating. This seems to be for each cell in the grid, ie the grid would not be filled out before the meeting. A second variant on this approach is for the assessor to present the evidence, and then the other assessors give ratings individually based on the evidence. Finally, they agree the rating. These approaches seem very laboured. Boyle *et al* advocate them because they feel assessors are unlikely to dispute each other's ratings. However, there is no need for dispute if the ratings for a competency are in agreement across exercises. If the ratings are not in agreement, the assessors are forced to resolve the differences. In other words, dispute is built into the process.

Boyle *et al*'s approach is akin to that adopted by AT&T in their pioneering work on assessment centres. Their approach was not to rate until the end of all the exercises. Dobson and Williams (1989) reported that the same approach is used by the British Army's Regular Commissions Board. It also seems the same as the approach put forward by Drakeley and White (1999). They suggest pooling the evidence from different exercises to arrive at an overall rating across exercises. They see this as better than considering individual ratings each based on a subset of evidence. The argument does not seem particularly weighty. Giving ratings for each exercise simply points up where there are disagreements that need to be discussed. If there is disagreement, it is, of course, the evidence that is discussed to arrive at an agreed rating. The only real argument is whether it is more practical to summarise the evidence in terms of ratings after each exercise has been assessed. Not giving ratings means that all evidence must be presented and discussed at the final meeting, and that seems a waste of time. Furthermore, and notwithstanding the fact that there is written evidence, it also seems better to give the rating when the exercise is still vividly in the mind of the assessor than perhaps two days later. The delay seems at odds with what we know about information decay.

Whatever precise method is chosen to combine the information, the objective is the same. The assessors aim to arrive at a profile in terms of the competencies, such as that in Table 15. If it is a promotion centre, they must then arrive at a recommendation on the person's promotion and career development. This comes from reviewing the overall profile, together with the person's apparent strengths and limitations. It will need to have been agreed whether there is any weighting to be applied to the competency dimensions, or whether all are to be regarded as equal. Assessors will also need some advice upon the ease of overcoming limitations on the different dimensions. A weakness on a less improvable dimension is a bigger problem than on a readily improvable dimension. They will also be able to make use of any available information upon potential as shown by tests and inventories or by an in-depth psychological report.

The meeting for a centre that involves internal people who are being assessed for promotion or for a fast rack can be difficult and lengthy. The centre places a heavy responsibility upon assessors, and they could need an hour for some participants. (Indeed, Deloitte Haskins and Sells are reported to spend 1.5 hours per individual (Stevens, 1985).) They will

Table 15

EXAMPLE OF A COMPLETED GRID FOR RATINGS AND RESOLVED PROFILE

Assessment Centre Grid Name **Ruth Naylor** Number **03**

Measure / Dimension	Group negotiation	Group problem-solving	In-tray	Analytical	Subordinate one-to-one	Interview	RESULT
Breadth of awareness		5	3	4		5	1 2 3 (4) 5
Incisiveness	4	3	4	3			1 2 (3) 4 5
Imagination	2		3	3	4		1 2 (3) 4 5
Organisation		3	1	2	2		1 (2) 3 4 5
Drive	5	4	3		5	4	1 2 3 4 (5)
Self-confidence		4	3		4		1 2 3 (4) 5
Sensitivity	2		3	3	2		1 (2) 3 4 5
Co-operativeness		1	3		2	1	1 (2) 3 4 5
Patience	4		4	3	2	3	1 2 3 (4) 5
ASSESSOR	NM	JLV	CMC	JLV	CMC	NM	
FINAL RESULT							

need this if only to feel satisfied that they have done justice to each participant. They will need time to compare evidence in arriving at an overall rating for each competency dimension, and in weighing the profile to make a decision. I would not advise trying to shorten this process. It is important that the assessors feel they have done a thorough job and that they are comfortable with their decision.

The length of the meeting will be increased if it is intended to compile a report on each person at the meeting. I do not see the need for this. It seems more sensible to nominate before the meeting the assessors who will give the feedback to each participant. These people will be responsible for writing reports after the meeting, for which they will be given the rating sheets of their fellow assessors at the end of the meeting. It is better to do this, and give the participant the fullest possible feedback rather than to write brief reports at the centre, which consist of only a few rushed lines for each competency dimension.

Selection centre meetings for external candidates are much shorter than those for internal promotion. There is less feeling of onerous responsibility, and assessors might well scan the marks for a dimension and, if there is an obvious resolution, agree it speedily and move to the next dimension. Assessors will give their comments for individual exercises only in the case of discrepancies that are harder to resolve. Usually the meeting can consider each person in 15 minutes. There is no real need to write an integrated report on each person. Once the profile has been agreed in external selection centres, it will probably be sufficient to collect assessors' rating sheets and attach these to the marking grid and profile.

In the case of development centres, there is often no particular need for an observers' meeting. Participants can be given feedback after each exercise and compile their own overall report and development plan. This seems a much better option than the observers taking a lofty position and writing their reports on the participants.

If the assessment centre is for selection, research suggests that it is technically better to use a mathematical formula to combine scores on the individual dimensions for making decisions instead of having a discussion by assessors. The scores for the dimensions are put into a formula (which might be a simple or weighted average) to arrive at the decision. For example, Feltham (1988c) demonstrated the superiority of the mathematical composite score over assessors' decisions for predicting five performance criteria.

One reason for the superiority of the mathematical method might be that the process of arriving at a group consensus involves group dynamics. Sackett and Ryan (1985) point out that the mechanical approach avoids any pulling of rank by a more powerful assessor over the others. An example of group dynamics at the assessors' meeting is provided by Herriot *et al* (1985). They got groups of four assessors to make a pre-discussion rating of candidates; have their discussion; and then give a final rating individually. They found the more powerful assessors were less likely to shift their ratings after the group discussion, and that an assessor whose rating is an exception is more likely to shift downwards than upwards.

Despite the evidence, I prefer to have assessors make the decision. If the centre is for external selection, assessors can usually decide quite quickly by examining the profile, and it is more acceptable for them to do so than to arrive at a result by a formula. Building a computer algorithm to make the decision appears a state-of-the-art solution. However, it is a step that might well detract from assessors feeling they have power in the decision. Certainly, there are problems of acceptability if the futures of internal people are decided by a computer, however superior that might be over assessors sitting in committee. From the assessors' point of view, the use of the computer ignores their need to feel they have done the right thing by each person and considered each case on its merits. A compromise is the suggestion by Goodge (1987) for the use of computers to produce averages and to highlight those individuals whom assessors need not spend time discussing. But is a computer really needed for this?

Assessors' reports

In internal assessment centres, a report will usually be compiled out of the rating sheets. Normally this report will be under the sub-headings of the competency dimensions.

Throughout the assessment centre the focus has been on behaviour rather than on judgements. This is particularly important in the final write-up. To be useful for the participant, the descriptions of strengths and development needs should maintain the focus on behaviour. When the assessor group has identified a strength or a development need, it is important to write about actual behaviour, giving as many examples as possible. For example, the following description is behavioural and useful.

Strengths
Sensitivity: Throughout the group session and individual exercise she demonstrated a high level of sensitivity. For example, in the managers' meeting she was attentive to others and demonstrated that she listened to their needs and requirements. In the feedback exercise the team member felt he had a fair chance to say what he wanted. She showed empathy, yet remained committed to increasing performance.

This description is useful because it focuses on actual behaviour, with examples across a range of exercises. On the other hand, the following description would not be helpful.

Weaknesses
Self-confidence: A bad performance throughout, obviously a weakness. He is not confident with others, and it shows.

The example is evaluative. He is described as 'bad' but it gives no example of what he actually did. Words like 'good' and 'bad' are judgemental rather than descriptive. They do not describe what happened, but simply judge. Such comments will be difficult to feed back to participants and will fail to give them any clues about why they were good or bad or what they could do to modify their behaviour.

The report might also comment upon the participant's overall performance in each exercise. If the exercises are designed around the different settings in which people work within the target job, it might well be that people perform better in some settings than in others.

The usefulness of the assessment centre for development stands or falls by the quality of assessors' reports and of the feedback meeting. Unfortunately, there are all too many examples of centres that spend a lot of time and money on the centre itself, but then rush the report, I have seen assessors' reports that contain just a few cliches against each competency dimension, and read more like an end-of-term school report than something that can be useful for someone's development. The problem can be tackled by giving assessors adequate time to write the report and by ensuring they are properly briefed on what is expected of them. The next chapter deals with the issue of assessor training.

Privacy

Discussion of the writing of assessors' reports introduces the issue of appropriate control of the circulation and retention of these reports. As Finkle (1976) notes, 'when personal information is requested and disseminated with little or no evidence of need or of professional control, concerns for invasion of privacy may well arise' (p883). He recommends basing a control policy upon the clear 'identification of the principal type of decision to be made from the information' (p883). For example, if the system is to identify long-term potential, it is not strictly necessary for the current supervisor to see the report. However, Finkle's advice needs to be tempered with the goal of involving supervisors in the assessment centre process, so that they buy into the development phase. As Rodger and Mabey (1987) observe, if line managers are alienated from the process they can be highly destructive. Ideally, line managers will be involved at the stage of development planning with their subordinate. They must not have been alienated so that at best they say development is nothing to do with them or, at worst, they rule that there is certainly no time for such activities.

An approach that could resolve this dilemma is to decide whose property the information is seen as being. If it is the participant's then he/she would be advised but not obliged to share it with the line manager. For truly developmental centres, the information might well be entirely the property of the participants. Indeed, Herriot (1989) argues that even the information given by applicants should be seen as essentially their property. On the other hand, if it is viewed as the joint property of the participant and the management development function, both parties should agree to its being shared with others.

A second and related issue is for how long the information remains on file. Rothwell (1985a) reports that BP removes reports after three years. For more enduring competency dimensions, the reports might be seen as having a longer validity than BP allows, whereas for dimensions that should have been developed after the centre, the validity will be only until the development has been undertaken.

Using information technology (IT) with assessment centres

IT can clearly be a help in assessment centres. For example, ratings can be entered on to spreadsheets, allowing an instant check on whether assessors are discriminating between competencies. However, IT can also be a mixed blessing. As long ago as 1989, *Personnel Management* (August 1989, p14) carried a report of how British Nuclear Fuels managers had taken part in an assessment process that examined 50 skills, characteristics and aspects of behaviour. The managers went through workshops with 15 to 17 events. The marks were fed into the computer, which pointed up where differences between assessors lay. These were discussed and reconciled, and the computer then averaged scores over events for the 50 skills. Their pattern of strengths and weaknesses was considered against the profiles required for 23 different managerial jobs. This is very seductive, if only because it is under the control of the computer. Of course, some might ask whether the differences between jobs and between people were sufficient for the allocation process really to be statistically sensible. It is also important to be sure that there really are 50 dimensions and a need for 15 to 17 assessment events. The risk is that expert systems will over-engineer the assessment centre and give a spurious validity to quite arbitrary decisions.

Virtual centres

Thornton (1992) describes ways in which assessment centres might depart from one or more of the *Guidelines and Ethical*

Considerations for Assessment Center Operations (Task Force on Assessment Center Standards, 1989 and reproduced in Appendix A) in the interests of efficiency or flexibility.

A particular innovation that Thornton mentions is to make the centre 'virtual'. Written exercises are completed at remote locations and videotapes are made of one-to-one exercises and presentations. Even the group exercise would be possible by video-link. The virtual centre has a clear appeal in the USA where people might normally have to travel great distances to attend a 'normal' centre.

The virtual assessment centre seems fine in theory. However, like all things virtual, it lacks the vital ingredient of human contact that is part of the success of centres. It is hard to imagine potential new recruits being impressed by attending a virtual centre and it clearly does not suit the development centre atmosphere.

Modular centres

Thornton (1992) also describes the trend of assessment centre exercises being administered on separate occasions rather than at a single centre. Clearly, this makes the time demands less for assessors and participants. With a development 'centre', it also enables participants to work on a development need before returning to another exercise.

14 TRAINING FOR ASSESSORS/OBSERVERS

The very best centre exercise will be rendered useless by inadequately trained assessors or observers. Holbeche and Glynn (1999) found in their survey that organisations recognised the challenge of training assessors to be objective and consistent. The key requirement at the centre is that they observe, record, classify, and rate the behaviour of participants with accuracy. In addition, with assessment centres for internal participants and development centres, it is vital that feedback is given properly to participants. Assessors will need training in all these skills.

Training timetable

Choosing to make the training residential avoids interruptions during the day and allows a continuation of discussions into the evening. It might even be cheaper than a non-residential course because it requires managers to give up fewer working days to be trained. It also helps build an esprit de corps among the assessors.

Not unreasonably, any request to take people away from their jobs for training is questioned and there is a pressure to keep training to a minimum. However, it cannot be cut and cut as if the courses of the past were needlessly lengthy. The *Guidelines and Ethical Considerations for Assessment Center Operations* (Task Force on Assessment Center Standards, 1989) suggests that two days of training are needed for each day of the assessment centre exercises.

A full two days, preferably three, will therefore be required for training new assessors to assess the exercises. The time for training will need to be increased if it has to cover any complicated tests and inventories. To me, it seems a false economy to jeopardise the assessment for the sake of a few hours of training. The training in feedback and counselling will require at least another day – preferably two. An example of a timetable for assessor training that embodies these preferred times is contained in Table 16.

So there is a minimum requirement of three days to include feedback skills, but five days might well be needed for the training to be thorough. This is a considerable amount of time for busy people. However, in my view, it should be reduced only if it is a very brief centre, or if the assessors have had prior training. Certainly I cannot see how the training of four hours reported by Walsh *et al* (1987) for an assessment centre that they studied could possibly be adequate. By way of comparison, Cascio (1982) notes that training can last 'several weeks' (p245), and Russell (1985) quotes the example of a centre for which the training was three weeks. Hakstian and Harlos (1993) describe training of five to six days simply for scoring an in-basket. Of course, this might be going from the sublime to the ridiculous. Dugan (1988) found no detrimental effect upon assessors of having two weeks instead of three weeks of training. She suggests that this might be due to a ceiling effect whereby further training yields no improvement in assessors' skills.

The first assessor training course will definitely take longer than subsequent courses because there will be issues that remain to be resolved and clarified at the training. In addition, having not seen the centre in action it will be harder for the course leader to be definitive in replies to all the many questions that will be asked.

Training areas

The *Guidelines and Ethical Considerations for Assessment Center Operations* (Task Force on Assessment Center Standards, 1989) recommends that assessors have a thorough understanding of the assessment dimensions as well as skill in the observation, integration, and evaluation of behaviour.

Table 16

EXAMPLE OF TIMETABLE FOR ASSESSOR TRAINING

Day 1

09.00–09.30	introduction to the course
09.30–12.00	the assessment centre approach
	the job analysis and competencies
	the assessment centre
12.00–13.00	introduction to observing, recording, classifying, and rating behaviour
14.00–15.30	video of subordinate 1:1 exercise: observe; record and classify
16.00–18.00	rating the subordinate 1:1 exercise
18.00–18.30	review of exercise
18.30–19.30	the in-tray exercise I
Evening	mark in-tray answers

Day 2

09.00–12.00	the in-tray exercise II
12.00–13.00	the managers' meeting exercise I
14.00–16.30	the managers' meeting exercise II
17.00–19.30	the analytical exercise I
Evening	mark analytical exercise answers

Day 3

09.00–11.00	the analytical exercise II
11.00–13.00	subordinate 1:1 exercise, video 2
14.00–16.30	group negotiation exercise
17.00–19.30	the assessors' meeting and recommendations
Evening	complete Myers-Briggs Type Indicator™* and FIRO-B

Day 4

09.00–09.30	the Egan model of counselling
09.30–11.30	introduction to feedback and phase I counselling skills
11.30–13.00	score and debrief on Myers-Briggs Type Indicator®* and FIRO-B
14.00–19.30	counselling a problem area

Day 5

09.00–10.00	phase II counselling skills
10.15–12.15	feedback of poor performance
12.30–13.00	phase III counselling skills
14.00–14.30	the career development system
14.30–16.30	career counselling
17.00–18.00	final issues
18.00	close

*Copyright Oxford Psychologists Press

The timetable in Table 16 includes these major areas of assessor training.

Going through the sections of the timetable, I would make the following comments on what should be covered:

Introduction

The centre should be placed within the context of the organisation's HR system, and the fundamental purpose of the centre, whether it is selection or development, should be discussed.

The job analysis

Assessors should be made familiar with how the job analysis was carried out and become completely familiar with the competency dimensions: They are the key to the system. It might well also be appropriate to have training exercises that reinforce the dimensions in the assessors' minds. One such exercise is a behavioural classification exercise. This consists of a set of behaviours, each of which must be classified under one of the competency dimensions, as a positive or negative example of the dimension. A second exercise is a behaviour-generating exercise in which assessors produce examples of positive and negative behaviour for each competency. Apart from these exercises, the most important learning will come from discussing the competency dimensions and the distinctions between them.

The assessment centre approach

Having gone through the competency dimensions required for the job or job level, the assessment centre approach should be introduced as the means of measuring the dimensions. It is important to stress that assessment centres combine a number of other approaches (interviews, tests, self-assessment), but that they emphasise getting people to perform in actual simulations of the target-level job. Assessment centres give the best of all worlds, and that is what gives them their power of prediction. Some of the evidence in favour of assessment centres can be summarised. You should also cover what can go wrong, perhaps ending on the motivating thought that these pitfalls can be countered by good assessor training.

Skills of assessment

The main part of the assessor training is in the observation, recording, categorising and rating of behaviour. It is combined with assessors gaining a good working knowledge of the exercises.

Observing and recording behaviour

The key point to get across is that assessors need to have an accurate and complete record of what the participants did and said in the interactive exercises. (In the written exercises participants themselves provide the record.)

Having this record means that assessors can back up their ratings with evidence at the assessors' meeting and at feed-back meetings. Of course, they should not aim for a verbatim transcript, but they must have an adequate record. One approach to getting the message across to assessors is to ask them to imagine they had to justify their ratings to an enquiry. For development centre observers, the need for notes is obvious: They have to give feedback.

Apart from being necessary for the meeting and for feed-back, the process of recording helps the assessor concentrate on observing the participants. It also helps counter people's natural tendency to judge and rate participants rather than just observing them. This will help overcome the pitfalls to accurate observation and recording, such as:

- the halo effect – a favourable or unfavourable impression on one dimension (eg neatness of appearance) clouds across to the other dimensions
- the primacy effect – early observations count for far more than later ones
- stereotyping – the participant's membership of a particular category leads to characteristics being imputed to him/her that are supposed to be typical of that category (eg the participant is a woman; women are sensitive; therefore the participant is probably good on sensitivity)

❑ implicit personality theory – we carry around ideas of how dimensions go together; we believe information on one dimension allows us to make inferences to other dimensions; while the dimensions might go together more often than not, assessors must judge each dimension on its merits in case the person being assessed is one of the many exceptions to the rule.

This is all standard material for assessor and for interviewer training. The points to emphasise are the need to concentrate and the need to leave rating/judgement/evaluation to the end. Taking good notes helps both of these needs to be met. It will also deliver the raw material for feedback and for the assessors' meeting.

Assessors should practise observation and recording by looking at the first of the videotapes. If the centre includes one-to-one exercises, it is better to play one of these than a video of a group exercise, simply because assessors have only one person upon whom to concentrate. It is best to start with about a quarter of an hour of the tape, which should be played through with assessors taking observation notes. The tape can then be played again to allow assessors to flesh out their notes. During this exercise, the trainer should check out that assessors are taking adequate notes. An eye should be kept on the volume of notes everyone is taking, and the trainer should make sure that the notes are not judgemental and evaluative. Once assessors have been through the tape in full, there needs to be a discussion of key learning-points.

Classifying and rating

After the observation and recording phase, assessors must classify their observations against the competency dimensions being measured in that exercise. They should concentrate upon the dimensions that the exercise is targeting. However, particularly good evidence of any additional dimensions should also be classified.

I try to get assessors to move as quickly as possible to making margin notes of the competency classification while they are observing. It is far easier to classify at the time what was revealed by the observation than to leave it until later. However, right at the beginning of training they will have to postpone classifying until after they have completed their observing. Otherwise their decisions on classifying will interfere with the observation process.

The first time around, about one hour will be needed to classify and to collate the evidence of the individual competencies on the rating sheet. The tape might be played once more to let them add to their observation notes, and to help them classify. Once the classification is complete and any points discussed, assessors should make ratings from their evidence. It is crucial to impress the need for everyone to use the same rating scale so that like is being compared with like when the scores given by different assessors are compared. Assessors should rate their evidence – and now comes the moment of truth, when the ratings by different assessors are compared.

It is better not to dwell upon minor disagreements at this stage, but major discrepancies must be discussed. For example, if one person has the competency rated as a definite strength (a '4') and another has it as a definite weakness (a '1') these two assessors should compare their evidence. The person who gave '1' should outline the negative evidence and the person giving a '4' should outline the positive. Disagreements over ratings can often be tracked back to misclassifying evidence. In such cases, assessors should be reminded of the indicators for the competency dimensions. Disagreement can also come about by assessors having differences in standards. A way of overcoming this is frame-of-reference (FOR) training (Stamoulis and Hauenstein, 1993). Trainees focus on particular examples of performance on particular competencies and agree on the 'correct' rating for each example. FOR training is used particularly in appraisal training, but it seems as applicable to assessor training. Woehr (1994) found that apart from increasing the accuracy of ratings, FOR training serves to 'enhance the feedback and development process' (p532). Hopefully, there will be an encouraging level of agreement in the ratings, and certainly this will hearten the assessors (as well as the trainer!).

I normally move on to one of the written exercises and get the assessors to mark one of the answers done on the trial day. Marking will probably take at least 45 minutes the first time, after which assessors can compare their marks. Two hours should be allowed for the whole process for the first answer. After a break, they should mark another answer to the same exercise, with the aim of doing it faster.

The last type of exercise for them to practise is the group exercise. Assessors need to observe and rate the two people upon whom the video-recording concentrated. Again, ratings should be compared and differences discussed. By this stage assessors will have covered the three different types of exercise, and should be developing some confidence in their abilities to assess people. They will be able to get further practice in the skills of assessment by going through and familiarising themselves with any further written exercises included in the centre, together with other one-to-one exercises and group exercises.

Interviews and tests

The training will also need to cover the interview, and to make assessors familiar with any tests/inventories that are being used. The assessors do not need a detailed knowledge of the tests, but they certainly need to know enough to make use of the scores at the assessors' meeting.

Assessors should undergo the special training prescribed by test publishers if they are to give the feedback on the test and to help the participant integrate information from the test with exercise performance. Generally, it will be better to leave making use of the test results to a person who already has the expertise. Assessors cannot be turned into experts on psychological measures in a few days. If a complicated personality measure is included in the centre, it will be necessary for someone with expertise to interpret its meaning to the assessors' conference, and for that person to carry out the feedback with the participant after the assessor has fed back the results of the behavioural exercises.

Assessors' conference

The assessor training should also cover the assessors' meeting, including the collation of marks from the different exercises, and how the chairman will lead the discussion through each candidate. The main point that the assessors' training is likely to raise is how decisions are taken after the marks for each competency dimension have been resolved. This will need to be discussed and agreed.

A particular issue that needs to be covered at the training is the equal opportunities aspect of setting relevant standards. As Ballantyne (1999) points out, it is possible for an organisation to operate in a discriminatory way if it sets unnecessarily high standards and these standards disadvantage particular groups in society. Assessors need to be given a clear understanding at the training as to the standard of a 'pass'. This should be a standard that is justified by the work the candidates will be doing. If there is a surplus of candidates who pass, the assessment centre manager must check that taking the best people is not indirectly discriminatory.

Feedback and counselling

Apart from the training in the skills of assessment, assessors will also need training in the skills of feedback/counselling if it is to be one of their responsibilities. Certainly, it is a key part of the training for development centre observers.

The intention is not that assessors/observers become expert counsellors. Rather, they must build upon the skills they need anyway if they are to be good managers. In particular, they must learn to listen and to empathise. They must also learn to give feedback that will be useful to the participant. As Boehm (1985) says, to be useful, feedback must be detailed, behaviourally specific, and related to job demands. It must concentrate upon particular instances of good and bad performance on the competency dimension. It must also be given in a provisional and tentative way, rather than dogmatically. It should concern areas about which the person can do something, rather than matters that are unalterable. In essence, the content of good feedback is the same as the content of the good report.

The training on feedback and counselling requires plenty of practical work. It is important that assessors learn to give participants feedback with sensitivity. The training in feedback and counselling will need to include the nature of good feedback, and what is an effective counselling relationship. It will also need to cover basic communication skills, particularly the skills of active listening. A useful model for counselling is that provided by Egan (1986), and the stages of counselling in his model should be covered. A simplified treatment of Egan's approach, with particular reference to counselling at work is provided by Reddy (1987).

Generally, the line assessors are asked to give only straightforward feedback on what they observed at the centre. It is the role of the management development professional to discuss the career implications of the feedback from an assessment centre. At a development centre, it will be dealt with by the facilitators. They can help the participants integrate the feedback with any psychological and self-insight instruments that have been used, and to look at career path plans and options.

The assessor and feedback training might be split rather than requiring assessors to be away from their jobs for a lengthy period of time. Aside from this convenience, splitting the training also allows assessors to consider any points arising from the first part of the training for discussion at the second part. However, there should not be a big gap between the two blocks of training.

Assessors should use their skills of assessment as soon as possible after their training. Training should be scheduled so that at least some of the newly trained assessors are able to be at a centre within a month, and the remainder as soon as possible after that.

15   AFTER THE EXERCISES

The usual follow-up after all the exercises at an internal assessment centre is the feedback of assessors' views, drafting a development plan, and carrying out development. Much the same is true for a development centre, though the feedback will often be given after each exercise and development planning can be part of the centre itself.

It is vital that the mechanisms for the follow-through are in place before the centre is run. It is equally important that the follow-through takes place. Jackson and Yeates (1993) suggest that the eventual acceptance of the programme will be decided by how the first few centres are perceived by participants and what happens to them afterwards. Thornton (1992) describes the failure to follow through as a major reason why assessment centres fail. He describes a case where people went on a centre to identify talented people and development needs, but then nothing was done with the results. Jackson (1994) claims that problems in implementing the development process to follow a centre happen 'all too often' (p17). The follow-through has various strands, starting with feedback.

Feedback on exercise performance

The need to give feedback to participants extends to all centres. Feedback might well be offered even to external people who have attended a selection centre, but who are not to be offered employment. Indeed, Jackson (1994) declares this to be an ethical necessity. The feedback need not be lengthy and certainly must not turn into a dispute or negotiation. It is probably best handled centrally, by the HR function. Such feedback is a courtesy. It might well enhance the organisation's reputation among applicants. Word spreads quickly among tight-knit groups, such as graduates.

People who are selected and join the organisation via an assessment centre should be given a fuller feedback of their performance once they have joined the organisation. Obviously this should be a reasonably up-beat feedback and it will normally be carried out by someone from the HR function. It can include one or two areas that the new recruits should consider for development, and it can also be used as a way of discussing their initial posting (which might capitalise on their strengths).

In the case of promotion centres, the feedback should be as soon as possible after the centre, preferably the next day and certainly within a week. The feedback on the exercises at internal centres might well be given by the assessors. They were the people who observed and rated the participants, and they should give the feedback. The feedback is direct, in contrast to it being delivered by, say, the management development manager, who would have to report second-hand upon what the assessors saw. Having the assessors take responsibility also makes the assessment quite clearly a line event, rather than one belonging to management development. Assessors might also make a start upon discussing the career implications of the assessment centre with the participant. However, the major part of this will probably fall to the management development function.

The most important consideration with centres used for promotion is to retain the motivation of people who are, after all, among the organisation's most able employees at their level. The danger lies in giving a lot of these people the impression they have 'failed'. It is most important that the feedback is carried out in a way that avoids this outcome. As Holbeche and Glynn (1999) observe from their survey, feedback is a special challenge if it is to someone who has not done well but who has an unrealistic self-perception.

The inherent tensions in promotion centres are the very reason that many organisations have moved to full development centres. The centre is no longer the decisive event for promotion and the labelling of potential. However, it is pointless trying to fudge the issue if the performance at the centre is going to make a major contribution to promotion decisions in the near future. Everyone will know this anyway.

Feedback at a development centre is best carried out after each exercise in a collaborative meeting between observers and participants. It makes sense to let participants write their own report. The ideas of immediate feedback and of participants writing their own reports were advocated by Goodge (1991). They were employed with success by Woodruffe and Wylie (1994) in the NatWest centres they designed.

It is vital that feedback at development centres is perceived to be accurate. Goodge (1995) showed that accuracy is perceived to be greater if the feedback is clearly explained and backed up by 'strong supporting evidence and examples' (p55). The perceived accuracy of feedback was shown by Goodge to affect the quality of people's plans for both self-managed learning and training courses. Mahoney-Philips (1991) recommends that the feedback is packaged so that people can focus on 'key learning points'. Otherwise, they might be overwhelmed with information. At the same time, the feedback needs to be thorough and detailed.

Career implications

The management development specialists are probably best placed to discuss the person's career ambitions and possibilities, as well as to go into detail on their development priorities. There should not be a paternalistic attempt to persuade people around to the organisation's view. The aim is for the organisation to be honest with participants. Participants must own the implications of the centre for their careers, not have the implications imposed on them.

There will also need to be an integration of the person's exercise performance with their responses to any tests and inventories that were used at the centre. Finally, the person's self-assessments should be discussed in the light of the exercises and other measures.

All this adds up to a quite complex agenda, and counselling skills are particularly important so that participants are helped to see their options for themselves rather than being told them. I am not suggesting the organisation turns into a deeply introspective collection of people undergoing analysis. However, some people going through a centre will find the feedback at odds with, or a challenge to, their expected career path. Indeed, as Gratton (1984) observes 'there may be occasions when people need to be referred to a skilled professional counsellor' (p9). Even if the centre is basically developmental (ie there are no direct implications for promotion or potential) there will still be the indirect implications. For example, some participants will be asking themselves 'If that is what I am like, am I really going to get as far as I had assumed?' People are very good at hiding any feelings of hurt and upset. However, beneath the façade there will be people who are demoralised as a result of their attendance at the centre. If only from an economic view, that is an undesirable state of affairs. They will underperform, and might leave. Macho organisations might say good riddance, but few can afford the luxury of this response nowadays. Evans (1993) describes how senior UK police officers were offered feedback by occupational psychologists. Among the objectives was the desire to 'maintain the contribution of those who could not be recommended' for promotion (p164).

Although some people will react badly to the implications of the centre, Goodge (1991) suggests that in many cases it will only amount to 'openly discussing what everyone knows' (p10). He says that people whose prospects are limited by their professional specialism will benefit from talking about what is available to them and how they might increase their options.

However, Fletcher (1991) conducted a study of the effects of a UK bank's assessment centre on participants that led him to conclude that there is 'cause for concern about the unsuccessful candidates' psychological well-being' (p125). They have stronger status needs and material needs but lower self-worth than the successful, and he suggests this to be a recipe for frustration. He argues that they need both 'particularly careful handling of feedback' as well as the availability of supportive counselling. Fletcher supports the belief that people who have many areas of development need identified are likely to require sensitive treatment. This is as true of a development centre as a promotion centre.

Development planning

Integrated with the feedback on performance and the consideration of career implications, should be consideration of the development opportunities open to the participants. This is the message of hope, and for development centres it is their main focus.

Assessors will need to be thoroughly familiar with the developmental options open to participants so that they can carry out initial discussions with the participant. For this to happen, of course, the developmental opportunities must be in place! The discussion with assessors will be followed up by the management development function. The overall goal must be that participants work out for themselves a plan over which they feel ownership and commitment. To do this, they must see for themselves the areas of development need, and work out ways of overcoming their needs that they see as useful and practicable.

The ownership of development needs will happen only if all the earlier stages of the process, from the definition of the competencies through to the assessor feedback are working correctly. For example, people will not take on board a need to develop a competency that is plainly unnecessary to successful performance.

Unfortunately, Jackson and Yeates (1993) found that many centres broke down at the point of development planning. They found it rare for participants to leave development centres with a plan. Instead, the assumption was that participants would return to work and draft a plan with their manager. There was, however, no formal mechanism for ensuring this happened. It seems highly desirable to set aside time at the development centre itself for development planning. Goodge (1991) suggests that half a day is needed and says that superficial and scanty reports are the signs of a poor centre.

To gain line managers' commitment, it is vital that they are informed properly of the nature of the centre and management development system. They will then be able to carry out their role, which is to agree with participants the development actions that the participant will be taking, and give active support to these actions. If this is to happen, line managers must feel involved in the management development process. Otherwise, there, is the danger of managers coming out with dreaded cliches like 'now you're back in the real world' to participants. Goodge (1995) found that the manager's direct involvement in development planning contributed to the centre leading to better job performance. One possibility is to invite managers to the centre when the development planning is being carried out. Another is to ensure that a meeting with the participant is in the manager's diary shortly after the centre. The meeting might also include the management development manager.

A problem noted by Jackson and Yeates (1993) is that a 'significant minority' (p21) of participants in their survey did not discuss their results with their managers. The reason is that they had not been working with their present manager for sufficient time to build the relationship necessary to discuss development needs. As Jackson and Yeates (1993) observe, frequent job changes are increasingly common and so it might be necessary to consider providing for the long-term relationship in other ways. Their specific suggestion is to use a mentoring scheme.

Development actions

There is a series of integrated management development activities that might follow the centre and make up the development plan. Unfortunately, with many centres, there is little systematic follow-up, and so many potential benefits of having the centre are lost. The development plan is never implemented. Goodge (1991) describes the failure to follow through as the most common symptom of a poor centre and Holbeche and Glynn's (1999) survey found that the primary challenge facing development centres is the follow-up. They say it is important to manage expectations about what follow-up is possible and then ensure that development plans are acted upon.

The follow-up system must be installed before the centre. Otherwise, participants are being asked to live on promises, and expectations might well be unrealistic. Aside from changes of job, and entry to special development schemes for a few people, one development system that can cope with the majority of participants will be a set of highly practical competency development workshops coupled with a system of action learning. The system is clearly focused upon the competencies, and is designed to assist people to understand and acquire higher performing behaviours for each competency. Clearly, it will not turn an extremely weak competency into a major strength, but it can certainly yield significant improvements.

Competency development should be an ongoing activity. It needs to be a process of continuous development (Wood, 1988). Once participants have improved one competency, they will hopefully be keen to select another and decide the activities to develop it.

Behavioural workshops

It is possible to have separate workshops to concentrate on each particular competency and give the participants intensive coaching at that competency. Alternatively, some of the competencies might be grouped together and dealt with at a joint workshop. Different labels might be employed for the competencies and the workshops, but the relationship between the competencies and the workshops must be clear. For example, 'sensitivity' might be dealt with at the 'listening skills' workshop. Participants should attend the workshop early in their development programme and then the action learning allows them to practise the new competence that they acquire. Each workshop should be behaviourally based. Both the workshops and action learning emphasise learning to be competent, rather than learning about the competency. The courses and workshops relate directly to the competencies of the organisation.

Having gone to all the trouble of finding the dimensions that mark out the high performer, it seems thoroughly worthwhile to invest in workshops tailored to their development. The danger is that organisations with an existing system of development will be reluctant to start afresh with the competency list, but it might well be needed to ensure proper coverage of the competencies. A suite of specially designed competency workshops has a number of advantages over trying to make do with existing courses, and over sending people away to take part in a generic course at an educational establishment. Each workshop need take participants away from their work for only one or two days, depending upon the competency. The workshops are highly practical, and involve the acquisition or development of the specific behavioural skills that make up the competency for the organisation. Participants will see that the workshop is a direct and specific answer to their competency development needs. Furthermore, the system emphasises to participants that development is a continuing process. Once one competency has been addressed and developed they move on to the next one.

The workshops can be at different levels and can be integrated with a series of assessment centres. For example, an organisation could have a set of workshops following an entry-level centre to present the core skills of the competencies, and then have another set following a middle-level centre to build upon the competency development. Apart from its overall coherence, this system means that people come to the middle centre having been able to make specific preparation on the competencies. This is a more logical order when the aim is for the organisation to get an indication of potential from the middle centre. It is not measuring competency deficits that could have been remedied easily.

Because they are so strongly oriented to practical work, the implementation of these workshops need not be onerous. The most direct way is to have a project team for the overall project and a small design team for each workshop who would do the bulk of the detailed work. Finally, delivery teams – which would include the design team – would deliver the workshops.

Work-based learning

Although courses and workshops can help people develop, many organisations put particular emphasis on people developing within their jobs, with the help of coaching. The emphasis is well founded. For example, Goodge (1995) found that self-managed learning activities made a greater contribution to people's performance than attending courses. For it to be successful, as Jackson (1994) points out, 'the organisation must believe in and understand self-development' (p12).

Self-managed learning can be seen as an adaptation of action learning. There are well-documented examples of action learning schemes that are essentially project-based. They might take participants away from their regular activities for months (eg Casey and Pearce, 1977 on action learning at GEC).

The more elaborate schemes will necessarily be limited in the numbers that can benefit from them. Self-managed learning adapts the system for larger numbers. One possibility is for learning to take the form of the participants doing an aspect of their existing jobs with a much greater consciousness of the competency they are trying to develop and exhibit. For example, if the job involves even minor project work, and they want to develop their competency at 'achieving results', then they might increase this competency by deliberately setting out to list the phases of a project, work out the resources that are needed, and the timing, etc. Alternatively, self-managed learning might involve participants taking on a new activity at work that helps to develop the targeted competency. For example, it might be that oral communication is the competency being focused upon. A person working in a branch office might volunteer to make presentations to staff in the branch on communications from head office.

Participants must think carefully about the competencies they wish to develop, and how this can best be achieved in their particular place of work. They can gain ideas if there is a session on self-managed learning during the centre. Such a session would start by getting participants to break down their jobs into the component tasks. These tasks can be written as the left-hand rows on a task × competency matrix. Along the top, and making up the columns, will be the list of competencies. Participants then match competencies against the tasks, which will enable them to see how they can develop particular competencies within their own jobs.

The matrix also allows participants to see at a glance which competencies they require most in their jobs, and this information will help them settle their development priorities. Participants can also consider taking on additional duties, which involve tasks that are particularly relevant to developing the competencies. The methodology for choosing self-managed learning can be repeated whenever the participant changes job.

The learning is primarily up to the participants to organise and monitor. If the participants are not really keen to develop, their learning is likely to be ineffective. Unfortunately, there is a paradox, identified by Carrick and Williams (1999), which is that people with a lot of development needs are likely to be less motivated to develop themselves than those who receive more positive – and motivating – feedback. Even if they are motivated, development is not something people can easily do single-handed. They need a coach. Goodge (1995) found that coaching from senior managers had a particular impact on performance after a centre. Aside from their coach, participants can gain feedback on how their development is progressing from a range of people. They should identify the person most able to observe the behaviour they are developing and ask for feedback. For example, if they are developing presentation skills, they might get a colleague to observe their presentations and rate them, and discuss the rating. More elaborately, a 360-degree feedback process will inform the participant of people's views on their development.

Participants might also get specific feedback if they have available a process of mentoring (Clutterbuck, 1985), whereby the mentor guides and offers feedback to the learner. Glynn (1996) advocates the appointment of a mentor for each participant. The same advice is given by Gammie (1994). She notes the mentor's or sponsor's role in setting up developmental activities as well as giving feedback. Gammie also describes the benefit this might give the mentor as well as the participants.

Job changes and challenges

Work-based development might be best achieved by a change of job or by introducing a challenging new feature to the job.

Job changes might be permanent or the person might have a secondment. Worts (1996) describes how the Skipton Building Society has a scheme called Trading Places. It is a job-swap programme that gives people exposure to different parts of the business.

The job change must, of course, be planned to meet a development need. McCauley *et al* (1994) describe a method called the Developmental Challenge Profile (DCP). It is used to assess the developmental components of managerial jobs. It is based on the premiss that development comes from facing novel or challenging situations. The DCP presents 15 scales grouped under three headings of job transition (eg 'unfamiliar responsibilities'), task-related challenges (eg 'creating change') and obstacles (eg 'lack of top management support'). While obstacles would not be deliberately created to help people develop, they might seek out situations that offer the other two types of challenge. McCauley *et al* found the amount of learning varied depending on the type of challenge. Learning also depended on the stress the challenge induced and the amount of support the person perceived to be available.

Fast-track development

The system of behavioural workshops and self-managed learning is designed to cater for everyone going through the internal assessment centre or development centre. It means that there is a system to address any weaknesses identified at the centre, and it is essentially a remedial system. A centre that aims to identify potential, by contrast, needs to be backed up by a system for building upon and capitalising on people's strengths. This might include sending high-potential people away to business schools and to short management courses, as well as ensuring they have developmental job changes. Again, the focus should be upon competency development, but for this system the competencies will be those required by the senior and general manager.

Reunions

It can be a spur to their motivation if development centre participants meet periodically after the centre. Goodge (1995) demonstrated the value of such regular meetings. If people cannot meet face-to-face, participants might, at least be encouraged to keep in contact with each other to discuss their progress with development.

Worts (1996) describes how the Skipton Building Society ran workshops on a quarterly basis for participants to exchange ideas and share experiences. The workshops 'encouraged those who have not made much progress with their own development to become more active' (p37).

Feedback to the resourcing function

The ultimate aim of the centre itself and of the management development system is to ensure that the organisation has the resources it needs when it needs them. This means checking that the organisation has available the pool of talented people it needs. The pool is made up of individuals and so the organisation needs to compile an overview of people's capabilities. The management development function will need to know people's performance at the centre and to keep track of their development following the centre. They also need to know people's career aspirations. There is no point in earmarking people as future general managers if they really want to follow a more technical career path.

The information from the centre can be used to pencil in people's likely potential. While some people will have more glorious careers than the centre predicted and others will do less well, the organisation will have a good idea of the overall resources available, and of significant gaps and gluts. This information can be used to set priorities for training and development programmes, as well as for recruitment. It can also be used to feed back to the organisation's strategic planning function. If the human resources simply cannot be envisaged to support a particular strategic plan then the plan is best adapted to come into line with reality. For example, the plan might be for all managers to carry out a particular amount of business development. If the present managers generally lack the business development competencies, the strategy will need to be altered, or specialist business developers will need to be recruited.

16 VALIDATING THE CENTRE

There needs to be a check that the centre is doing what it was meant to do. In deciding the way to validate the centre, it is therefore important to return to its original purpose. It might have been for selection, and in this case the most appropriate validation is whether the centre is measuring the competency dimensions efficiently, and whether these measurements are related to people's future performance. A quite different validation will be required if the centre was meant to provide an impetus to the management development programme. If this were the aim, it would seem to matter less that the assessments are perfectly accurate than that they provide a spur to individuals and to the organisational culture in the direction of development.

There are a number of strands to the validation work that might be undertaken. Broadly, these will fall under the headings of qualitative and quantitative validation. In addition, there is an audit against best practice, which determines whether the centre is at least set up in a way that makes it likely to work.

Qualitative validation

Qualitative research will concentrate on the reactions of participants and assessors to the assessment centre. The focus will be on how people experience the centre, and upon whether it is achieving its qualitative aims.

Validation with assessors

The questions for assessors will need to cover such issues as:

❑ Was the centre, for them, timetabled correctly or stressful and rushed?

❑ Did the exercises seem relevant and fair and easy to mark?
❑ Were the exercises getting at the dimensions they were meant to?
❑ Does the centre seem to be fulfilling its developmental purpose?

Validation with participants

Participants should be asked about their experience of the centre itself as well as about the helpfulness of pre-centre briefing, and of the post-centre feedback and development planning. The questions will also cover the accommodation, travel, etc. Precise topics will readily suggest themselves, and these can be tackled by questionnaire or interview.

The time to start asking these questions is at the debrief that takes place at the end of the centre. Participants can fill out – anonymously if they wish – a form to give their immediate reactions to the centre. They should also have a chance to discuss their views – maybe over a drink. The debrief should be with the most neutral person at the centre. At an assessment centre this is the chairperson. At a development centre, it will be the person's facilitator. It is also a good idea to follow-up the immediate feedback with a questionnaire, after perhaps a month, to find out participants' considered feelings about the centre.

The feedback from participants should be taken seriously. If the centre is switching off applicants or existing staff, there is a clear problem. If a series of adverse reactions is received, the format of the centre should probably be altered. The price of leaving it unaltered could be people being demotivated and performing poorly, and maybe seeking employment elsewhere. Alterations will usually entail changing the emphasis or presentation of the centre, rather than a radical rethink of the exercises.

The questioning of participants is a critical part of the validation of selection centres. It helps determine whether the centre combines acceptability alongside the quantitative validity that it might enjoy. Qualitative validation will probably outweigh the quantitative evidence for a development centre. The crucial question is whether the centre has succeeded as a catalyst to people deciding their areas of development need and getting on with developing those areas.

Validation with the organisation

The co-ordinator of the centre will want to know line managers' reactions to the centre, as well as the views of potential participants. For example, people might be put off coming to an internal centre because they have heard that it can be stressful and threatening. The co-ordinator should know about the centre's image generally in the organisation. Some assessment centres gain nicknames such as 'assassination centre'. Hopefully, this is not true for your centre.

Quantitative validation

Quantitative research might of course be carried out upon the above qualitative data, but the real technical validation deals with the analysis of the relationships among the assessment ratings, and between the assessment ratings and other quantified data. A number of statistics can be computed after the centres have run on, say, 60 people. These analyses should be re-run as the numbers build up, but the process should start early to give an early warning of any problems.

The individual ratings

First, the mean and standard deviation should be computed for each cell in the rating matrix, eg on the ratings for sensitivity in the subordinate one-to-one exercise, and the ratings for sensitivity in the group exercise, etc. Comparing the means for the same competency dimension measured in different exercises will show whether a particular dimension gains higher marks in one of the exercises in which it is marked than in another. The standard deviations will show if assessors/observers are differentiating between participants or giving everyone pretty well the same mark. It might be uniformly very low or very high, suggesting that the exercise is at the wrong level of difficulty for that competency dimension. On the other hand, if all the marks are around the middle of the range, this is usually a sign that assessors are not really able to measure the dimension in the exercise, and are seeking safety in the middling mark. Whatever the explanation, if there is little differentiation between people the measurement is in practice of no particular use. The way the competency dimension is brought out in the exercise will need to be changed, or assessors will need additional training. As a last resort, the dimension might have to be measured in one of the other exercises.

Another way to find out whether raters are using the full scale as intended is to examine the percentage of people being given each of the possible ratings for each cell in the rating's matrix. For example, for the five-point rating scale, as defined in Chapter 13, about 35 to 40 per cent of ratings would be expected to be '3'; 20 to 25 per cent would be expected to be '2' or '4', and about 10 per cent of ratings might be expected to be '1' or '5'. Anything markedly different might be due to the ease or difficulty of the exercise, or some particularly good or weak group of participants. It might also be due to the assessors not making proper use of the scale. If this seems the most likely cause, assessors must be alerted to the problem.

The statistics that are computed from the centre's ratings will have various rival explanations, and it will be a matter of judgement to decide which is the most plausible. However, they will enable the monitoring of the centre. For example, the mean for one competency dimension – say communication skill – might be '4', and only 1 per cent of ratings might be '1'. This could be because of an excellent course in communication, and so participants are generally very good on this dimension. Alternatively, it might be very easy to do well on that dimension in the exercises. The calculation of the statistics will prompt these questions, but it cannot answer them.

Exercises and dimensions

The mean and standard deviation should be computed for the ratings for each exercise averaged across dimensions, and for each dimension, averaged across exercises. The means for the exercises will show whether some exercises are performed at a higher standard than others – perhaps because they are easier. The standard deviations will show the amount of differentiation between participants. Likewise, the dimension means will show whether some dimensions gain higher ratings than others and the standard deviations will show the amount of discrimination between participants for each competency dimension.

Once the number of people who have been through the centre is sufficient, all these statistics can be computed separately for participants with different backgrounds in the organisation. For example, it might be found that people from the marketing function do better on the customer exercise than people from personnel. The data will show what is happening and then it is a matter of deciding whether it is reasonable or whether some amendments need to be made to the exercises.

Most importantly, the statistics can also reveal whether the centre seems to be affording people equal opportunities. If a group (for example, an ethnic minority) is achieving weaker ratings than most people, this will need to be investigated.

The exercise effect

If the grid of ratings is factor-analysed, the hope would be to find one factor for each of the assessment dimensions. The expectation is that the ratings for each dimension across exercises would 'go together' and be separate from the ratings for all the other dimensions. They would be like the simplified example in Table 17.

However, what is found quite typically are separate factors for each exercise rather than for each dimension. The ratings for the competency dimensions that are measured in each particular exercise are similar to each other, and form exercise factors. The ratings look rather like those in Table 18.

This phenomenon, labelled the exercise effect, will be considered in more detail in the next chapter. For the moment, the first thing to ask is whether the assessors' discrimination between dimensions within each exercise can be increased by further assessor training. Alternatively, the exercise effect might be due to a problem with the exercises. For example,

Table 17

EXAMPLE OF A GRID OF RATINGS WITHOUT AN EXERCISE EFFECT

Assessment Centre Grid   Name _____   Number _____

Measure / Dimension	Group negotiation	Group problem-solving	In-tray	Analytical	Subordinate one-to-one	Interview	RESULT
Breadth of awareness		4	5	4		4	1 2 3 4 5
Incisiveness	3	3	3	4			1 2 3 4 5
Imagination	2		3	2	2		1 2 3 4 5
Organisation		5	4	5	5		1 2 3 4 5
Drive		2	1		2	2	1 2 3 4 5
Self-confidence	5	5	4		5		1 2 3 4 5
Sensitivity	1		1	2	1		1 2 3 4 5
Co-operativeness		3	3		2	3	1 2 3 4 5
Patience	4		4	3		4	1 2 3 4 5
ASSESSOR							
FINAL RESULT							

Table 18
EXAMPLE OF A GRID OF RATINGS WITH AN EXERCISE EFFECT

Assessment Centre Grid   Name   Number

Measure / Dimension	Group negotiation	Group problem-solving	In-tray	Analytical	Subordinate one-to-one	Interview	RESULT
Breadth of awareness		3	2	1		4	1 2 3 4 5
Incisiveness	4	3	1	1			1 2 3 4 5
Imagination	4		1	2	5		1 2 3 4 5
Organisation		4	2	2	4		1 2 3 4 5
Drive		4	3		5	4	1 2 3 4 5
Self-confidence	5	3	2		4		1 2 3 4 5
Sensitivity	4		1	1	4		1 2 3 4 5
Co-operativeness		3	2		5	4	1 2 3 4 5
Patience	3		1	2		5	1 2 3 4 5
ASSESSOR							
FINAL RESULT							

if a group exercise is trying to get at various cognitive competencies, then the person who says little or nothing might well be marked down against a broad sweep of competency dimensions, thereby creating the exercise effect. A further approach to the exercise effect would be to check that the competency dimensions are worded clearly, and that they are definitely separate from each other in their definitions.

Dimension scores and their components

The assessors' resolved ratings for each dimension should be compared with the simple additive sum of the ratings for the dimension in the various exercises. The two sets of final ratings can be correlated with each other. The analysis will show the extent to which all the discussion that goes into resolving a score for a dimension could be dispensed with, simply by adding up the scores. It also shows the extent to which assessors are moving away from the individual scores in arriving at their resolved scores.

A model of the process leading to the assessors' resolved rating can be derived by regressing the individual ratings for the competency in the different exercises on to the assessors' resolved rating. This will show whether particular exercises contribute more than others to the assessors' resolved rating for the competency dimension.

In addition, the scores on each of the competency dimensions can be correlated with the overall assessment centre rating. One or two competency dimensions might be found to exhibit very low correlations with the total, which suggests that these dimensions contribute little in the minds of the assessors in forming their overall rating.

The results of these analyses should be discussed with assessors, and there should be a decision on whether the devaluing of some dimensions is desirable. If not, drawing the issue to the attention of assessors should contribute to its correction.

Redundancy of dimensions

A very high correlation between the overall ratings for two dimensions suggests either that they are closely related and one of them is redundant, or that a meaningful and important distinction is not being made by the assessors. If the latter is the case, there might be an argument for some additional assessor training.

Assessment ratings and tests/inventories

The assessment ratings should be examined in relation to scores on the cognitive tests and personality inventories that are being used. The tests and inventories will have been chosen because of their assumed relationship to the competencies, and these assumptions should now be checked. If no relation is found between the test's scores and the competencies, the value of the test to the assessors' decision appears very doubtful.

Criterion validation

The relation between the assessment ratings and subsequent performance is a major aspect of the centre's validation. The competency dimensions are meant to lie behind overall job performance. The centre's ratings should predict job performance. The exercise effect casts doubt upon whether the link to performance is as straightforward as this, but the pragmatic question might be 'does it work?', rather than 'why does it work?'

The speediest answer will be obtained by correlating the ratings for the competency dimensions that are given by the assessors with ratings of the same dimensions by the participants themselves or by their line managers. The difficulty in concluding much from these statistics, however, is that it is unknown which set of ratings is more accurate.

Some of the dimensions might be clearly visible only after the person has moved into the job or job level upon which the centre was targeted. It is therefore advisable to wait and correlate assessment centre scores with future performance. However, it may not be possible to reach firm conclusions even from these correlations, because of the practical constraints on having a neat design to assessment centre research. One problem is the amount that will have happened between the assessment centre and people taking up the target-level jobs. For example, they will have attended development workshops, etc. Furthermore, people who performed badly at the centre will not be included in the sample as they will not get through to the target-level. Conversely, the people who performed well go to the next-level job with their performance known by others. This can give rise to a self-fulfilling prophecy. People who perform highly become known as the rising stars. They get more developmental experience and go to the target-job with people expecting and looking for the good news and excusing the bad.

It can be seen that carrying out a validation study that will pass critical scrutiny is difficult. However, that should not lead to the effort being abandoned. At least the validation will prompt the right questions to be asked.

Developmental validation

If the centre is primarily for development, the key validation questions are whether development takes place at the centre, and whether attending the centre acts as an impetus for subsequent development. In turn, these subsequent development activities should also be validated. The validation must determine whether people who attend the development modules or take part in action learning really improve their performance as shown, for example, through the performance appraisal system or perhaps at a subsequent assessment centre.

Given their cost, it seems unfortunate that development centres are infrequently validated. This was the conclusion of Spychalski *et al* (1997) from a survey of practice in US organisations. An approach to evaluating development centres that is advocated by Lee and Beard (1993) is to estimate the costs of failures before and after the centre. The costs are determined by interviewing managers to uncover critical incidents that have occurred before and after the centres. As an example, they describe how a development centre for BT's sales force is estimated to have saved the company over £60 million in failures.

Validating existing centres

A centre that has been operating for some time should definitely be examined to make sure that it is working properly. At the very least, there should be an analysis of the ratings that have been produced at the centre. Blackham and Smith (1989) provided a very good example of how such an analysis can lead to subsequent modifications of a centre. As Blinkhorn (1986) observed, the problems brought to light when the enlightened company audits its practices are likely to compare favourably with the problems of companies who prefer to remain in ignorance. It might be found that assessors are not making much differentiation between people on some dimensions for some exercises. An example is the centre mentioned in Chapter 8, which included self-monitoring as a dimension. None of the assessors really understood what was meant by this dimension, let alone how to rate it. Typically people got a rating of '3' on it. Problems like this will show up when the statistics are computed on the assessors' ratings. An exercise effect might well be found when the ratings are factor-analysed. For example, Blinkhorn (1986) cites one company's centre, which had 12 dimensions but, when the ratings were analysed, just one global factor was shown to be used by assessors in making decisions. Somewhat similarly, Blackham and Smith (1989) found that ratings on ten dimensions yielded just three factors. They labelled these 'interpersonal skills and initiatives' (sic), 'ability to organise' and 'ability to relate to others'.

Existing centres should also be examined for how well they offer equal opportunities to all participants. Lapses are often due to a lack of forethought. For example, setting standards way above those required for the job might have an adverse impact on people who are perfectly suitable for the job but not judged to be the very best candidates.

Inferential evidence: conformity to best practice

The validation work that has been suggested gives direct evidence of whether a centre is working. A different approach is to examine the centre to determine whether it is being operated correctly and in a way that should make it work properly. It is examined or audited against best practice. A first aspect of best practice is the features of the centre that help or hinder it to be a reliable measure of people on the dimensions. In order to have validity, it is necessary that the assessment centre is reliable. This means that participants should make similar responses between one day and the next, and assessors should assess these responses in the same way. Making the same responses will depend upon being presented with the same stimuli. Problems of reliability will come if, for example, role-players differ among themselves in the part they are playing, or if the same role-player chooses to play the part differently from day to day. Difficulties can also occur if the exercises are constructed so that much of a participant's behaviour on the target competency dimensions depends upon what the other participants are like. For example, a leaderless group discussion exercise might be used to measure 'leadership'. However, the amount of leadership manifested by any one participant will depend upon the leadership of the other participants. The participant of average leadership might appear quite strong in an otherwise weak group, or weak in an otherwise strong group.

Steps can be taken to overcome these problems. One step is to give careful and comprehensive briefing and training to role-players. Another is to stop trying to measure competency dimensions in group exercises that clearly depend on the particular mix of people in the group. It is also possible to set up the group exercise in a way that minimises the group mix effect, for example, by including the light-touch chairperson.

Even if participants are presented with the same stimuli and respond the same way from day to day, it is also necessary for these responses to be assessed the same way by different assessors. If there is a lot of variation between assessors, the assessment will end up saying more about the assessor than the participant. The reliability of assessments is achieved by good assessor training, and by making exercises assessor-friendly. For example, I have discussed targeting items in an in-tray on specific dimensions so that assessors are in no doubt as to the dimension being marked.

Aside from reliability, validity will also depend upon accurately identifying the competency dimensions, and upon ensuring the fidelity of the exercises as a simulation of the target job. In the best practice audit, there will be a need to review the competency dimensions to check that they are the critical dimensions for high performance in the job. There is also a need to check the exercises for how well they correspond to the target job. There is, for example, no point in having quasi-military outdoor exercises as part of an accountants' assessment centre. Similarly, I was told of an assessment centre conducted in English for people whose mother tongue was not English. Although it was argued that a good knowledge of English was important for the people being assessed, there was really no logic in letting a language deficit prejudice the assessment of people's competencies.

It is also important to ensure that assessors are focusing upon the competency dimensions as they are defined, and not upon their interpretations of what makes a person suitable. Assessment centre decisions or recommendations must be based upon performance on the competency dimensions. They must not be diluted by assessors taking an overview of the person against the image of a 'good type'. The overview will be likely to take little account of performance on the expensively designed exercises.

All these aspects of best practice deal with the centre's usefulness as a means of assessment. Equally, there is the best practice for the developmental aspects of centres. This will focus largely upon the way participants are treated; indeed, whether they are called participants or candidates. It will also cover observers' feedback and the reports and plans that participants write. The audit should examine a sample of plans to determine whether they are feasible with measurable outcomes or just a set of wishful generalities. Best practice will also cover the implementation of development plans and the steps that are taken to follow up the centre to encourage people to implement their plans.

17   VEXED ISSUES

Assessment centres are very much a live topic in the journals, particularly, the *Journal of Applied Psychology*, *Personnel Psychology*, and the *Journal of Occupational and Organisational Psychology*. There are a number of issues and developments in these journals that have influenced the earlier chapters of this book, but which now merit discussion in their own right. I shall deliberately introduce some of the terminology from the journals, and I hope that I have translated it to make it more digestible.

The exercise effect

A problem for assessment centres, noted in the previous chapter, is the exercise effect. The effect is found when ratings of assessment centres are analysed. Assessment centres are designed with the explicit expectation that there will be more agreement about the same dimension across exercises (called monotrait-heteromethod correlations) than about different dimensions within the same exercise (heterotrait-monomethod correlations). However, typically, the analysis shows the opposite: there is more in common between ratings of different dimensions within each exercise than there is in common between ratings of the same dimension across exercises. Assessors seem to be paying more attention to an overall halo for each exercise than to making distinctions between dimensions.

The most famous study showing the effect was by Sackett and Dreher (1982). They took the ratings of three different assessment centres, and found for each centre that the heterotrait-monomethod correlations were larger than the monotrait-heteromethod correlations. The centres lacked convergent validity (viewings of the same dimension in different exercises did not converge on the same answer) and divergent validity (viewings of different dimensions within an exercise did not diverge from each other). When they factor-analysed the matrix of correlations between individual ratings, they obtained exercise factors for all three centres.

In a related study, Turnage and Muchinsky (1982) examined a centre that rated all dimensions in all exercises. They found that the correlation between different traits within an exercise was about the same as the correlation between the same trait across exercises. Finally, Bycio *et al* (1987) examined a centre that had five exercises, and again found that exercises were dominant even after they had combined clearly overlapping dimensions. The conclusion (also replicated by Robertson *et al* 1987 in the UK) suggests that there is a pervasive halo across ratings within an exercise.

Indeed, the pervasiveness of the effect was demonstrated by Silverman *et al* (1986) who appeared to do everything possible to destroy it. They got assessors to rate the candidates on the dimensions for each exercise only as an afterthought once the overall ratings for each dimension had been agreed among assessors. Even with this approach to rating, which is a modification of that used by AT&T, the correlations between exercises for individual dimensions were not much greater than the correlations between dimensions within exercises. Furthermore, when they factor-analysed the matrix of correlations, they still did not obtain factors clearly corresponding to the dimensions. Broadly the same result was obtained by Harris *et al* (1993).

There are various ways to react to the exercise effect. One is to try to improve the assessment process to get rid of it. A first step is to ensure that the dimensions can be revealed independently in each exercise. A lack of independence will be found, for example, in a group exercise in which one dimension (say, lack of self-confidence) clouds the other dimensions that are being measured. The exercise effect will also be found if a dimension is not properly understood or if the dimensions are badly defined. Assessors will tend to use the other dimensions as a rough guide to a poorly understood dimension. If the dimensions are not clearly separated from each other in terms of their definitions, then it is most unlikely that there will be a differentiation between them in terms of ratings.

The effect could also be attributed to participants differing in their familiarity with the different exercise settings. For example, if a person is familiar with the one-to-one setting perhaps performance will be better across a series of dimensions than for an exercise in which the setting is less familiar. This might be tackled by giving everyone the chance to practise and be developed before the centre. For example, if one of the exercises is a subordinate meeting, people without experience of this type of interview could be given some practice before the centre.

In a similar way, the exercise effect could be due to a lack of transparency in the assessment centre. If candidates do not know what qualities are sought, they will guess. Sometimes they will guess correctly; sometimes wrongly. As Kleinmann et al (1996) point out, this guessing is likely to reduce the consistency whereby competencies are displayed across exercises. They compared a non-transparent and a transparent assessment centre and found that in the former there was an exercise effect whereas in the latter the abilities were marked as independent factors. The exercise effect that remains in the transparency condition is put down by Kleinmann et al as due to the difficulty of gaining good evidence for some dimensions in some exercises. This leads assessors to be influenced in their marking of those dimensions by the candidates' general exercise performance.

So the exercise effect should be met in the first instance by refinements to the processes of defining dimensions, revealing the dimensions via the exercises, and marking performance in the exercises. These refinements were not all present in the studies showing the exercise effect. First, it is possible that there was not the opportunity for participants properly to demonstrate all the dimensions in the exercises that were measuring them. This is particularly relevant to the studies by Turnage and Muchinsky, and Bycio et al, in which all dimensions were rated in all exercises. Second, it is possible that the assessor training was inadequate. There are plenty of assessment centres for which assessors have received less than one day's training.

To help explore the exercise effect, Schneider and Schmitt (1992) proposed that there are two aspects of exercises that need to be considered. The first of these is exercise form, which refers to whether it is a written, one-to-one, or group exercise. The second is exercise content, for example whether it is co-operative or competitive. They manipulated both form and content and took all possible steps to remove the exercise effect by ensuring that assessors had the maximum possibility to view the dimensions, by giving assessors a high level of training, and by making sure they did not have to rate too many dimensions. After all these precautions, Schneider and Schmitt still found an exercise effect. They also found that the form of the exercise accounted for an important amount of the variance in ratings, whereas the content did not. In other words, people tended to perform similarly across exercises of the same form, but there was no consistency to their performance on exercises of the same content.

Schneider and Schmitt conclude from their study that it is vital to ensure that the centre's form reflects the kinds of interpersonal relations a person will encounter on the job. If the centre is made up of written exercises, but the job is mainly one-to-one, there is little guarantee that the person who has done well at the centre's written exercises would have done as well at one-to-one exercises in the centre. By extension, there is little reassurance that they will do well in one-to-one situations at work. Schneider and Schmitt also conclude that their results 'do not raise a great deal of hope that efforts aimed at improving the mechanics of assessment centers (such as rater training, dimension definitions, and scoring format) will significantly change the finding that exercise factors account for variance in assessment center ratings' (p40).

The exercise effect is as important to development centres as to assessment centres. People are given feedback in terms of the competencies. The exercise effect suggests this feedback is flawed. If the grid of observers' ratings is analysed, the likelihood is that they will be found to be rating more by global exercise performance than by the individual competencies.

The pervasiveness of the effect has led some people to advocate rating by exercise rather than continuing to try to get valid ratings for each dimension. For example, Herriot (1986) concludes that the rationale of rating by dimension is unsound, and that it is much better to ensure that the exercises give a valid sample of the job and to rate overall performance in each exercise. The centre becomes a series of work samples (Klimoski and Brickner, 1987) and task analysis is important as part of the job analysis, (Robertson *et al* 1987). Indeed, Payne *et al* (1992) go so far as to describe as 'second generation' those assessment centres that rate by the samples of exercises rather than the signs of dimensions.

Giving in to the exercise effect seems at odds with the presumption that assessors' impressions of performance in an exercise must be mediated by dimensions. They do not say someone did well in the in-tray, full stop. They say the person did well in the in-tray because he or she communicated clearly, planned and organised, etc. It therefore seems premature to give up upon dimensions. Furthermore, feedback has to be in terms of the dimensions. Giving up is not an option, if the centre is to be used for development (Bycio *et al*, 1987). For example, telling someone they need to improve in meetings with customers begs the question of what is wrong at the moment. The explanation must return to the dimensions of competence. He or she should be told that it is listening skills or presenting a point of view that needs to be improved.

As noted above, the original AT&T approach did not rate each dimension in each exercise. Instead, dimensions were rated after all exercises had been observed. A return to this AT&T method is an alternative response to the exercise effect rather than deciding simply to mark exercises. This approach was taken by Shore *et al* (1992) on the basis that measuring dimensions after all exercises had taken place will be based on more evidence and on a pooling of assessors' views. However, this does not seem to get away from the fact that the pooled views of dimensions across exercises are based upon the individual views of dimensions in each exercise. The AT&T approach seems only to conceal the process that takes place at the assessors' meeting when the ratings of each relevant dimension in each exercise are considered.

Cause for optimism might be adduced from a study by Sagie and Magnezy (1997). They obtained ratings both by psychologists and managers in an assessment centre. Ratings were for two interpersonal dimensions (human relations and sensitivity) and three performance dimensions (initiative, organisational acumen and analysing). They found that psychologists maintained distinctions between the five dimensions while managers produced ratings that merged the two interpersonal dimensions and the three performance dimensions. They did not, however, produce just one exercise-effect rating. The result reinforces the notion that the exercise effect might be countered by having expert assessors. It also underlines the importance of reducing the number of dimensions.

Reliability and validity

The basic findings on the validity of assessment centres were covered in Chapter 6. It was noted that the evidence tends to be summarised as showing the power of assessment centres. In fact, the position is more complex than that summary suggests, and relates back to the exercise effect. The evidence must be examined against the different types of validity that a centre might have.

Content and construct validity

The content validity of the centre is established if it can be shown to be a good and accurate simulation of the target-level job. Construct validity deals with the centre as a measure of the job dimensions presumed to underlie job performance. To build in both types of validity, Byham (1980) says that the centre must be based on a thorough job analysis. The aim is to ensure that the exercises represent at the correct level of complexity the most common and significant job activities and that the centre measures competency dimensions that are related to performance in important job activities. Furthermore, the dimensions must be observable in the exercises. Sackett (1987) adds the importance that assessors are properly trained, and that all candidates are put on an equal footing by good instructions and briefing.

Developing an assessment centre along the lines laid out in this book does everything possible to promote construct and content validity. By way of contrast, construct validity is not assisted if generic dimensions are used without a proper check of their applicability to the target job. Content validity is not promoted if the centre consists of the Lego or piranha-ditch exercises, which bear little relation to the job of a manager. The problem is that although the textbook approach should give construct validity, the evidence from the exercise effect suggests that the effort is in vain. This leads Klimoski and Brickner (1987) to say that 'the available research consistently demonstrates a lack of evidence for the construct validity of assessment center dimension ratings' (p246).

Criterion validity

Assessment centres might not work by measuring the dimensions as planned, but they do seem to achieve their ultimate goal, which is to predict the criterion they are meant to predict. The criterion might be immediate performance in the job, or immediate ratings of potential, or performance over time (indexed by final level or final salary in the organisation). Thus, they have a validity when judged against concurrent (concurrent validity) or future (predictive validity) criteria of performance. An immediate problem with criterion validity was summed up by Robertson and Makin (1986) who wrote 'for different reasons almost all of the current criteria with which we work are unsatisfactory' (p52). Performance measures generally concentrate upon the individual's own performance, and often this has to be rated by supervisors. Relying on such ratings as the criterion measure means that negative evidence can always be explained away as due to a problem with the supervisors' ratings rather than with the centre.

One alternative criterion to performance is salary progression and promotion, which Meyer (1987) calls performance-over-time measures. In their favour, promotion decisions are frequently based upon a collective judgement, rather than upon one supervisor's viewpoint. They are also cut-and-dried, carrying with them no errors of measurement. However, promotions and salary progress might not be linked closely to performance. In some organisations they are more a result of political acumen than ability. Overall, Turnage and Muchinsksy (1984) found only a weak relationship between performance and promotion.

The third commonly used criterion is ratings of potential. Studies of validity have tended to show a higher correlation between assessment centres and ratings of potential than between assessment centres and current performance. For example, Turnage and Muchinsky (1984) found potential ratings to be the criterion measures most highly correlated with assessment evaluations. Similarly Gaugler *et al* (1987) found higher validities for potential than performance in their meta-analysis.

Explanations of criterion validity

The paradox is that assessment centres appear to predict criteria, but the exercise effect suggests that they do not do so by measuring the dimensions. This has led people to speculate on how the centres work. One possibility is that assessors arrive at some kind of rating of overall 'goodness' in each exercise, and that these ratings relate to job performance because the exercises simulate the job. This is the obvious conclusion from the exercise effect, and in many ways is the most optimistic answer to how the centres work. At least it says that it is performance on the exercises that is the predictive variable.

Russell and Domm (1995) took this explanation and designed a centre in which assessors used the evidence from the exercises to make ratings of how well candidates perform various tasks that make up the target job. They also rated 27 dimensions. Russell and Domm found the sum of task ratings were more strongly related to subsequent performance than the sum of the dimension ratings. They take the result as further evidence for the explanation that assessment centres work by providing forecasts of task performance rather than by measuring the dimensions that lie behind performance.

This does not seem wholly logical. Some of the 27 dimensions were poorly related to subsequent performance, but one dimension was more strongly related than any of the task ratings. Summing across the 27 dimensions will have depressed the apparent predictiveness of dimensions. Russell and Domm do not seem to have shown conclusively that assessment centres should measure tasks rather than dimensions.

The issue of whether to concentrate on performance in terms of the competencies or exercises is an issue of which is the better predictor of subsequent job performance. There is no question that assessment centres work by previewing future performance. Other explanations of why they work are more complicated. They suggest that the relationship between assessment centre marks and the criteria is based on a statistical artefact. One such explanation is advanced by Klimoski and Strickland (1977) and Gaugler *et al* (1987) who suggest that assessors and the people providing the criterion information hold in common a prototype of a good manager that intrudes upon both the assessment centre ratings and ratings of potential and performance. Of course, there would be no problem if the prototype were in terms of the assessment centre dimensions. The worry however is that it is a much grosser stereotype of a 'good type'. For example, Dobson and Williams (1989) are clear in their own minds that the British army's assessment centre ratings correlate with performance because the board concentrates upon an overall rating of character, which will also be a major influence upon ratings of subsequent performance. Any centre that follows the AT&T model of rating dimensions globally across exercises rather than taking one exercise at a time seems particularly susceptible to the intrusion of the 'good type' halo.

The correlations between assessment centres and promotion might also be explained in terms of a self-fulfilling prophecy. People's assessment centre performance is well known. Those labelled as 'good' raise their performance in line with the label, get extra opportunities to develop, and benefit from people perceiving them in terms of their label. The assessment centre result therefore leads to performance and to promotion, and is not independent of the criteria it is meant to predict. Apparently going against this explanation are studies, notably the AT&T studies, which kept the assessment centre results secret but which still found a relationship with promotion.

A further artefactual explanation is that assessors might be evaluating what they know of the individuals already, and using this as the basis for their assessment centre judgement. As Klimoski and Brickner (1987) point out, assessors have a good deal of information from application forms, in the case of external applicants, or from organisational repute, in the case of internals. Past success might reasonably be expected to relate to future success.

Klimoski and Brickner (1987) also discuss the possibility that both assessment centre and job performance are determined by intelligence. This is not just the narrow psychologists' definition of intelligence but the broader conception of practical intelligence (Sternberg and Wagner, 1986; Wagner, 1987). This argument amounts to stating that the dimensions measured by the assessment centre are neither the dimensions that matter in the job nor those that matter as the centre. What matters in both cases is practical intelligence. If these writers are correct, it is easy to take account of their views. It is not an argument against assessment centres. It is simply an argument to analyse properly what causes superior job performance and to ensure the centre overtly measures the same qualities. It might well be that practical intelligence is as important as is claimed. In that case, it should be reflected in both the competencies and the centre.

A related argument is advanced by Kleinmann et al (1996). They note that assessment centres tend not to be transparent. They say that the ability to identify the requirements of non-transparent situations might not only contribute to success at the centre but also at work. This ability therefore links assessment centre and at-work performance. The link would, of course, be compromised by following Kleinmann et al's general advice to make centres transparent. A way forward would be to ensure that the ability to identify non-transparent requirements is deliberately measured at the centre, rather than operating artefactually.

There is no neat answer to the debate about why assessment centres work. Indeed, Turnage and Muchinsky (1982) suggest that drawing firm conclusions from assessment centre research might not be possible. Perhaps different centres work for different reasons. In some cases, undoubtedly both the centre and the performance criterion are saturated with whether or not the participant is a 'good type'. Other centres just might work by measuring the dimensions that underlie performance in the job. Certainly I believe that this should still be the goal of assessment and development centre designers, who should do everything possible to achieve it. Assessors should be well trained, the dimensions must be clearly specified and kept simple, and the exercises must be well designed. The design of the exercises should enable the dimensions to be seen with confidence by assessors. In addition, the exercises should be good simulations of the job so that at least content validity will be achieved.

Choosing the appropriate type of validity

It has been seen that assessment centres can be designed to achieve content validity by ensuring that they replicate the job. Furthermore, they are likely to have predictive validity, even if its basis is open to debate. However, Sackett (1987) points out that these different types of validity are not interchangeable. It is not enough just to establish any sort of validity and heave a sigh of relief. He says that content validity is particularly appropriate if the centre is being used to establish people's current level of competence to perform in the target-level job now or in the immediate future. Under these circumstances, the assessment centre is being used to sample the candidates' competence. On the other hand, the centre might be used to establish potential to perform at the target level in some years' time. Under these circumstances, Sackett says that the centre is being used as a sign, and criterion validity is more appropriate. There is no point in loading the centre with simulated activities that will be learned between the time of attending the centre and arrival in the target-level job. The centre should still simulate the job, but the learned components should be stripped out of the simulation, and a proper predictive validation is required to ensure the centre is achieving its purpose.

Implications for development centres

As development centres use the same broad approach to measuring competencies as assessment centres, it can be assumed that the ratings are subject to the same problems. The exercise effect leads to a questioning of whether people receive accurate feedback about individual competencies. Carrick and Williams (1999) describe the assumption of accuracy as the 'foundation on which the supposed worth of DCs is based. Unfortunately, the assumption is found wanting' (p83).

This might be an over-pessimistic conclusion. If people receive feedback after each exercise, and synthesise for themselves the feedback across exercises, then they would seem to have had a useful input to deciding their development priorities. The feedback is from well-trained observers and is therefore likely to be accurate. The exercise effect might just make the synthesis more complex. We need to take account of the interaction between the competencies and the situation and not expect to be uniformly competent across situations. The same is likely to be true in 'real life', for which the feedback we receive might well also vary between situations. We have to make sense of it and decide to identify particular competencies in particular situations (eg I must be more assertive with the boss) rather than necessarily expecting to identify strengths and weaknesses across situations.

Equal opportunities

The fidelity of exercises has importance under 'The American Uniform Guidelines on Employee Selection Procedures' (Equal Employment Opportunity Coordinating Council, 1978, and see Appendix B for weblink). These might serve as a guide to good practice in the UK even if the law is somewhat different. All that the guidelines ask is that the assessment centre appears likely to work to select the best people for the job. That must be in everyone's interest. The approach to designing and validating assessment centres that has been described in this book falls within the guidelines. The centre is based upon a careful analysis of the dimensions required for the job, and the exercises are based on job simulations. However, a centre might be held to be discriminatory if there had not been a job analysis preceding it or if the exercises did not simulate the target job.

As the second chapter made clear, the actual evidence on the equality of impact of centres tends to be favourable. However, people have residual doubts about the contamination of ratings. An aspect of equality was investigated by Robertson and Iles (1988). Their hypothesis, based upon an assumption of inequality, was that ratings of femininity in women would be negatively correlated with perceived appropriateness for 'male' jobs (including managerial jobs) while masculinity in men would be positively correlated with the same criterion. The hypothesis was investigated using 78 participants in a UK clearing bank's promotion centre, and was not upheld.

A worrying phenomenon for centres was reported by Bogan (1991). She described how managers tend to give middling ratings to people who are unfamiliar to them. People they know are given ratings that are more extreme – both high and low. Bogan defines familiarity in terms of whether the person behaves or looks differently from what managers are used to. She suggests that if managers are male the familiarity phenomenon will result in them giving women middling ratings, while men will enjoy more extreme ratings. In turn, the people hitting the upper extreme will be chosen for high-potential groups. The same argument would apply to ethnic minorities and the disabled. In turn, this phenomenon ties in with the risk of adverse impact from setting standards above those required for successful job performance. The familiar people get the highest marks and will be chosen in favour of those with slightly lower marks who could have performed the job competently.

International assessment centres

Multinational organisations might wish to use the same assessment or development centre in different countries. This is less easy than it might at first seem. Littlefield (1995) reports how Novotel's French assessment centre required an Anglo-Saxon slant for use in Britain and North America. He describes the need to take account of different business cultures and environments.

The converse of this problem was encountered by the international investment bank, J. P. Morgan. Their assessment centre was designed for Anglo-Saxons and Platt (1996) reports how their psychologist was aware of concerns about putting continental Europeans though it.

Cultural differences in the way people approach development centre exercises are dealt with by Schofield *et al* (1993). Exactly the same comments apply to assessment centres. Schofield *et al* discuss the emphasis on communal activity and conformity by some Asian cultures, particularly the Japanese. They contrast this with the emphasis in centres, which is upon the individual. They also summarise the differences between Western and Asian management styles. By their very nature, these summaries are generalisations that will not apply to each and every person from the different cultures and, indeed, there will be subcultures to the Western or Asian style. Nevertheless, the designer of a centre from any particular culture needs to be aware of such cultural differences. The differences extend to:

- *causation*. Westerners look for causes; Asians look for circumstances.
- *probability*. Westerners extrapolate from the present; Asians are more fatalistic.
- *time*. Westerners see time as linear; Asians place less importance on time.
- *self*. Westerners emphasise the individual; Asians emphasise society.
- *morality*. Westerners have an absolute moral code; Asians do not.

These differences give rise to different solutions to standard assessment or development centre exercises. Schofield *et al's* views on the different solutions to exercises by those from a Western and Asian culture are reproduced in Table 19.

There are also cultural differences in the norms of behaviour. These lead Ballantyne (1999) to expect that ethnic Asian men and women will do less well at group exercises than in written exercises or interviews. He also suggests that ethnic women will perform less well in the presence of Asian men than otherwise, because they will be less assertive.

Clearly, this is potentially a very vexed issue. Organisations that wish to extend the use of an assessment or development centre across cultures need to decide whether there is one best way to tackle the exercises or if the ways of different cultures are equally valid. If the latter is the case, it should be reflected in the competencies.

However, the discussion also returns us immediately to the issue of equal opportunities within a country. Organisations need to be clear that they are not being needlessly prescriptive in the way situations are dealt with by their staff, and hence in the centre's exercises.

There is a further problem for organisations that try to recruit globally and to use their staff across cultures. For example, airlines want to recruit cabin crew globally. They have to be very careful to allow different cultures to tackle the exercises at the assessment centre or development centre in their own ways, as long as those ways are acceptable to multicultural customers.

It becomes quite clear that assessors and observers need to be aware of these issues and make sure they do not place needless cultural restrictions on the way an exercise is approached.

Contrast effects

A potentially worrying finding for assessment centres is that the ratings an individual receives partly depend on the strength of other participants at the centre. This was demonstrated by Gaugler and Rudolph (1992). They made videotapes of three participants in three exercises. If one of the three was consistently poor across the exercises, judges gave this

Table 19

IMPACT OF CULTURAL DIFFERENCES ON DEVELOPMENT CENTRE DESIGN

Exercise type	Western approach to a solution	Asian approach to a solution
In-tray and analysis	Identify symptoms of a problem and deduce the causes. Establish basic principles on which to generate a solution, and plan action to prevent a recurrence.	Adopt a contingency approach to problem definition, seeing any problem as situation-specific, and not necessarily linked to other wider issues.
	Answer may emphasise cause – effect and be linked to underlying principle or theory.	Answer may emphasise conditions which created the specific problem, and provide action-oriented solution.
Planning	Identify required action and plan activity by various deadlines.	Identify the main issues to be resolved.
	Answer may emphasise short, medium and long term, and look at the strategic implications	Answer may concentrate on concrete action with detailed contingencies for each issue. Good solutions are more important than planning within artificial deadlines.
Group	Objectives are agreed, together with a process for achieving objectives. Within the exercise, some form of egalitarianism exists, even if roles are assigned. Informal roles emerge and are accepted. Individual identity is not determined by the group, and most people participate.	Group members take their identity from the group, and will be reluctant to contribute until the hierarchy of group members has become established. Pre-group discussion role assignment is important. There is little heated debate and group members defer to the 'chairman'.
One-to-one	Participants are often assertive in explaining their position, and will be able to disagree with the view of an adversary, while still accepting the validity of opposing views.	Participants maintain 'face' and harmony by avoiding the clear expression of opposing views, by not fully explaining their own position, and by seeking compromise.

Reprinted with the kind permission of McGraw-Hill Publishing Company from G. Lee and D. Beard, *Development Centres: Realising the potential of your employees through assessment and development*, 1993, London, McGraw-Hill.

person better (and less accurate) ratings if the other two were also poor than if they were high performers. Judges also gave better (and less accurate) ratings to a poor performance in the final exercise if it followed two other poor performances than if it followed two good performances.

The conclusion from Gaugler and Rudolph is that having a contrast increases accuracy. The finding might be less troublesome than it appears. Hopefully, homogeneously weak performers will not pass through the pre-selection for an assessment centre. However, the person running the centre certainly needs to be alert to the potential problem. The general supposition must be that the way any particular person is rated depends upon the performance of the others at the centre. The contrast effect could also decrease the accuracy of development centres if a fairly weak group of people attend together. The problem is, of course, not peculiar to assessment and development centres and it might be reduced by making assessors aware of the phenomenon.

Back to the real world

A major problem for development centres is that participants quickly get engulfed in their jobs and all the development resolutions get forgotten.

One way of countering this is to make sure there is a generally developmental culture in the workplace. It might be thought that having a development centre was a sure sign of a development culture. This is not really so. All line managers might not have 'bought into' the process, particularly those at the top. They might tolerate it rather than embrace it.

Maurer and Tarulli (1994) studied employees' development activity and found that the variable with the most consistent relationship was people's 'perception that policies, rules, guidelines, and regulations within the organisation facilitated participation in such activity' (p11). They also found a positive effect from a general emphasis by the company on employee learning and development. This suggests that development centres will work best in a learning culture. They will not work in isolation.

Conclusion

The issues for assessment centres and development centres should not be allowed to get out of proportion. A well-designed and carefully monitored assessment centre is a practical way of selecting people. It is the best way, as judged by the twin yardsticks of accuracy and acceptability. Likewise, a development centre is definitely seen by participants as an invaluable experience. It is a symbol of the organisation's commitment and it helps them focus on moving forward.

Assessment and development centres show no sign at present of losing their popularity. Their use is increasing. As a prediction, I would expect assessment centres to be the more enduring of the two. There does not seem to be any better way of selecting people. On the other hand, there are apparent alternatives to development centres such as 360-degree feedback. It could be helpful for the cause of development centres if some evidence were to be assembled on their effectiveness in comparison to these alternatives. Otherwise, organisations might be tempted to save time and money by moving away from development centres. This would be unfortunate, because the centres appear to offer an extremely powerful and positive experience to participants, observers and facilitators.

APPENDIX A: GUIDELINES AND ETHICAL CONSIDERATIONS FOR ASSESSMENT CENTER OPERATIONS

Task Force on Assessment Center Guidelines
Endorsed by the Seventeenth International Congress
on the Assessment Center Method
May 17 1989 – Pittsburgh, Pennsylvania

These guidelines replace the 1979 Standards and Ethical Considerations for Assessment Center Operations. The primary purpose of this document is to provide professional guidelines for users of the assessment center method. As such, these guidelines include explanations of the most important concepts common to all assessment centers and suggestions which if followed should maximize the benefits obtained from use of this method. These guidelines have been developed and endorsed by practitioners who specialize in the use of the assessment center method.

Table of Contents

A Task Force Members
B Background
C Purpose
D References

Assessment Center Defined
F Organizational Policy Statement
G Assessor Training
H Informed Participation
I Validation Issues
J Rights of the Participant

A Task Force Members and Organizations Who Have Contributed to These Guidelines

Task force for 1979 edition

Albert Alon – Miracle Food Mart (Canada)
Dale Baker – U.S. Civil Service Commission
Douglas W. Bray, Ph.D. – AT&T
William C. Byham, Ph.D. – Development Dimensions International
Steven L. Cohen, Ph.D. – Assessment Designs, Inc.
Lois A. Crooks – Educational Testing Service
Donald L. Grant, Ph.D. – University of Georgia
Milton D. Hakel, Ph.D. – Ohio State University
Lowell W. Hellervik, Ph.D. – University of Minnesota
James R. Huck, Ph.D. – Western Airlines
Cabot L. Jaffee, Ph.D. – Assessment Designs, Inc.
Frank M. McIntyre, Ph.D. – Consulting Associates
Joseph L. Moses, Ph.D. (Chairman) – AT&T
Nicky B. Schnarr – I.B.M.
Leonard W. Slivinski, Ph.D. – Public Service Commission (Canada)
Thomas E. Standing, Ph.D. – Standard Oil of Ohio
Edwin Yager – Consulting Associates

Task force for 1989 edition

Virginia Boehm – Assessment & Development Associates
Doug Bray (co-chair) – Development Dimensions International
William Byham – Development Dimensions International
Ann Marie Carlisi – Bell South
Jack Clancy – Clancy and Associates
Joep Esser – Mars B.V.
Reginald Ellis – Canadian National Railway
Fred Frank – Electronic Selection Systems Corp.
Ann Gowdey – Connecticut Mutual
Dennis Joiner – Joiner and Associates

Rhonda Miller – New York Power Authority
Marilyn Quaintance – Laventhol & Horwath, Office of Personnel
   Management
Robert Silzer – Personnel Decisions Inc.
George Thornton (co-chair) – Colorado State University

B Background

The rapid growth in the use of the Assessment Center method in recent years has resulted in a proliferation of applications in a variety of organizations. Assessment Centers currently are being used in industrial, educational, military, government, and other organizational settings. Practitioners have raised serious concerns that reflect a need for standards or guidelines for users of the method. The Third International Congress on the Assessment Method Meeting (May 1975) in Quebec endorsed the first set of guidelines. These were based on the observation and experience of a representative group of professionals representing many of the largest users of the method.

Developments in the following five years concerning Federal guidelines related to testing, as well as professional experience with the original guidelines, suggested that the guidelines should be evaluated and revised. Therefore, the 1979 guidelines included the essential items from the original guidelines and changes in the direction of: 1. Further definitions, 2. Clarification of impact on organizations and participants, 3. Expanded guidelines on training, 4. Additional information on validation.

Since 1979 the use of assessment centers has spread dramatically to many different organizations assessing individuals representing widely diverse types of jobs. During this period pressures to modify the assessment center method have come from three different sources. First, there have been attempts to streamline the procedures to make them less time consuming and expensive. Second, there have been put forth theoretical arguments and empirical research evidence which some people have interpreted to mean that the assessment center method does not work as its proponents originally believed and that the method should be modified. Third, many procedures purporting to be assessment centers have not complied with previous guidelines because they were too ambiguous. Revisions in this third edition are designed to incorporate needed changes and to respond to some of the concerns raised in the last 10 years.

The current revision of these guideline was begun at the Fifteenth International Congress on the Assessment Center Method (April 1987) in Boston when Dr. Douglas Bray conducted a discussion with many attendees. Subsequently, Bray and Dr. George Thornton solicited additional comments from a group of assessment center practitioners. The (1989) Task Force named above provided comments on drafts of a revision prepared by Bray and Thornton. A subsequent draft was circulated and discussed at the Sixteenth Congress in May, 1988 in Tampa.

The present guidelines were written in response to comments at the 1988 Congress and from members of the Task Force. These guidelines were endorsed by a majority of the Task Force and by participants at the Seventeenth Congress in May 1989 in Pittsburgh.

Changes from prior editions include: 1. Specification of the role of job analysis. 2. Clarification of the types of attributes to be assessed and whether or not attributes must be used. 3. Delineation of the processes of observing, evaluating, and aggregating information. 4. Further specification of assessor training.

C Purpose

This document is intended to establish professional guidelines and ethical considerations for users of the Assessment Center method. These guidelines are designed to cover both existing and future applications. The title 'assessment center' is restricted to those methods which follow these guidelines.

These guidelines will provide (a) guidance to human relations specialists, Industrial/Organizational Psychologists, and others designing assessment centers, (b) information to managers deciding whether or not to institute an assessment center, and (c) instruction to assessors serving on the staff of an assessment center.

D References

The guidelines have been developed to be compatible with the following documents:

American Educational Research Association, American Psychological Association and National Council on Measurements in Education. (1985). *Standards for Educational and Psychological Testing*. Washington, DC: American Psychological Association, 1985.

Society for Industrial and Organizational Psychology Inc., American Psychological Association. (1987). *Principles for the Validation and Use of Personnel Selection Procedures*. (Third Edition) College Park, MD: author.

E Assessment Center defined

An Assessment Center consists of a standardized evaluation of behavior based on multiple inputs. Multiple trained observers and techniques are used. Judgments about behavior are made, in major part, from specifically developed assessment simulations. These judgments are pooled in a meeting among the assessors or by a statistical integration process. In an integration discussion, comprehensive accounts of behavior, and often ratings of it, are pooled. The discussion results in evaluations of the performance of the assessees on the dimensions or other variables which the assessment center is designed to measure. Statistical combination methods should be validated in accord with professionally accepted guidelines.

There is a difference between an Assessment Center and assessment center methodology. Various features of the assessment center methodology are used in procedures which do not meet all of the guidelines set forth here. Such personnel assessment procedures are not covered by these standards; each should be judged on its own merits. Procedures which do not conform to all the guidelines here should not be represented as Assessment Centers or imply that they are assessment centers by using the term 'assessment center' as a part of the title.

The following are the essential elements necessary for a process to be considered an Assessment Center.

1 A job analysis of relevant behaviors must be conducted to determine the dimensions, attributes, characteristics, qualities, skills, abilities, motivation, knowledge, or tasks that are necessary for effective job performance and to identify what should be evaluated by the assessment center.

The type and extent of the job analysis depends on the purpose of assessment, complexity of the job, the adequacy and appropriateness of prior information about the job, and the similarity of the new job to jobs which have been studied previously.

If past job analyses and research are used to select dimensions and exercises for a new job, evidence of the comparability of the jobs must be provided.

When the job does not currently exist, analyses can be done of actual projected tasks which will compose the new job.

2 Behavioral observations by assessors must be classified into some meaningful and relevant categories, such as dimensions, attributes, characteristics, aptitudes, qualities, skills, abilities, knowledge, or tasks.

3 The techniques used in the assessment center must be designed to provide information for evaluating the dimensions, etc. previously determined by job analysis.

4 Multiple assessment techniques must be used. These can include tests, interviews, questionnaires, sociometric devices, and simulations. The assessment techniques are developed or selected to tap a variety of behavior and information relevant to the predetermined dimensions, etc. The assessment techniques will be pretested prior to use to ensure that the techniques provide reliable, objective, and relevant behavioral information for the organization in question. Pretesting might entail trial administration with participants similar to Assessment Center candidates, thorough review by subject matter experts as to accuracy and representativeness of behavior sampling, evidence from the use of these techniques for similar jobs in similar organizations, etc.

5 The assessment techniques must include sufficient job-related simulations to allow multiple opportunities to observe the candidate's behavior related to each dimension, etc. being assessed.

A simulation is an exercise or technique designed to elicit behaviors related to dimensions, etc. of performance on the job requiring the participants to respond behaviorally to situational stimuli. Examples of simulations include group exercises, in-basket exercises, interview simulations, fact-finding exercises, etc.

If a single comprehensive assessment technique is used, then it must include distinct job related segments. For simple jobs, one or two job related simulations may be used if the job analysis clearly indicates that only one or two simulations sufficiently simulate a substantial portion of the job being evaluated.

The stimuli contained in a simulation parallel or resemble stimuli in the work situation, although they may be in different settings. The desirable degree of fidelity is a function of the purpose of the assessment center: fidelity may be relatively low for early identification and selection programs for non-managerial personnel, and may be relatively high for programs designed to diagnose training needs for experienced managers. Assessment center designers should be careful that content of the exercises does not favor certain assessees (e.g. assessees in certain ethnic, age, or sex groups) for irrelevant reasons.

6   Multiple assessors must be used for each assessee.

When selecting a group of assessors the following characteristics should be considered: diversity of ethnicity, age, gender and functional work area.

Peer- and self-assessment may be gathered as assessment information.

The maximum ratio of assessees to assessors is a function of several variables, including the type of exercises used, the dimensions sought, the roles of the assessors, the type of integration carried out, the amount of assessor training, the experience of the assessors, and the purpose of the assessment center. A typical ratio of assessees to assessors is 2 to 1. A participant's supervisor should not assess him or her in an assessment center.

7   Assessors must receive thorough training and demonstrate performance guidelines as outlined in Section G prior to participating in an assessment center.

8   Some systematic procedure must be used by assessors to record accurately specific behavioral observations at the time of their occurrence; this might involve handwritten notes, behavioral observations scales, behavioral checklists, etc.

9   Assessors must prepare some report or record of the observations made in each exercise in preparation for the integration discussion.

10   The integration of behaviors must be based on a pooling of information from assessors and from techniques at a meeting among the assessors or through a statistical integration process validated in accord with professionally accepted standards.

During the integration discussion, assessors should report information from the assessment techniques, but not information irrelevant to the purpose of the assessment process.

The integration of information may be accomplished by consensus or some other method of arriving at a joint decision. Methods of combining assessors' evaluations of information heard in the assessor discussion must be supported by research evidence showing reliable and valid aggregations of the observations.

The following kinds of activities *do not* constitute an Assessment Center.

1   Panel interviews or a series of sequential interviews as the sole technique.

2   Reliance on a single technique (regardless of whether a simulation or not) as the sole basis for evaluation. A single comprehensive assessment technique which includes distinct job related segments, i.e. large complex simulations with several definable components and with multiple opportunities for observations in different situations, is not precluded by this restriction.

3   Using only a test battery composed of a number of pencil and paper measures, regardless of whether the judgments are made by a statistical or judgmental pooling of scores.

4   Single assessor assessment, i.e. measurement by one individual using a variety of techniques such as pencil and paper tests, interviews, personality measures or simulations.

5   The use of several simulations with more than one assessor where there is no pooling of data; i.e., each assessor prepares a report on performance in an exercise, and the individual reports (unintegrated) are used as the final product of the center.

6   A physical location labeled as an 'Assessment Center' which does not conform to the requirements noted above.

F Organizational policy statement

Assessment Centers need to operate as a part of a human resource system. Prior to the introduction of a center into an organization, a policy statement should be prepared and approved by the organization. This policy statement should address the following areas:

1   Objective – This may be selection, diagnosis for development, early identification, affirmative action, evaluation of potential, evaluation of competency, succession planning, or any combination of these.

2   Assessees – The population to be assessed, the method for selecting assessees from this population, procedures for notification, and policy related to assessing should be specified.

3   Assessors – The assessor population (including sex and ethnic mix), limitations on use of assessors, number of times assigned, evaluation of assessor performance and certification requirements, where applicable, should be specified.

4   Use of Data – The flow of assessment records, who receives reports, restrictions on access to information, procedures and controls for research and program evaluation purposes, feedback procedures to management and employee, and the length of time data will be maintained in files should be specified.

5   Qualifications of Consultant(s) or Assessment Center Developer(s) – The internal or external consultants responsible for the development of the center should be identified and their professional qualifications and related training listed.

6   Validation – There should be a statement specifying the validation model being used. If a content oriented validation strategy is used, documentation of the relationship of the job content to the dimensions and exercises should be presented along with evidence of reliability to in observation and rating of behavior. If evidence is being taken from prior validation research, which may have been summarized in meta-analyses, the organization must document that the current job and assessment center are comparable to the jobs and assessment centers studied elsewhere. If local validation has been carried out, full documentation of the study should be provided. If validation studies are underway, there

should be a time schedule indicating a validation report will be available.

G Assessor Training

Assessor training is an integral part of the Assessment Center program. Assessor training should have clearly stated training objectives and performance guidelines.

The following are some issues related to training:

1 Training content

Whatever the approach to assessor training, the objective is obtaining reliable and accurate assessor judgments. A variety of approaches may be used, as long as it can be demonstrated that reliable and accurate assessor judgments are obtained. The following minimum training goals are required.

a Thorough knowledge of the organization and job being assessed.

b Thorough knowledge and understanding of the assessment techniques, relevant dimensions etc., to be observed, expected or typical behaviors, examples or samples of actual behaviors, etc.

c Thorough knowledge and understanding of the assessment dimensions etc., definitions of dimension, relationship to job performance, examples of effective and ineffective performance.

d Demonstrated ability to record and classify behavior in dimensions, including knowledge of forms used by the center.

e Thorough knowledge and understanding of evaluation and rating procedures, including how data are integrated.

f Thorough knowledge and understanding of assessment policies and practices of the organization, including restrictions on how assessment data are to be used.

g Thorough knowledge and understanding of feedback procedures, where appropriate.

h Demonstrated ability to give accurate oral and written feedback, when feedback is given by the assessors.

i Demonstrated knowledge and ability to play objectively and consistently the role called for in interactive exercises, e.g.

one-on-one simulations or fact-finding exercises, when this is required of assessors.

2 The length of assessor training may vary due to a variety of considerations that can be categorized into three major areas:

a Trainer and instructional design considerations

❑ The instructional mode(s) utilized

❑ The qualifications and expertise of the trainer

❑ The training and instructional sequence

b Assessor considerations

❑ Previous knowledge and experience with similar assessment techniques

❑ The use of professional psychologists

❑ Experience and familiarity with the organization and the target position(s) or target level

❑ The frequency of assessor participation

c Assessment program considerations

❑ The difficulty level of the target position

❑ The number of dimensions, etc. to be rated

❑ The anticipated use of the assessment information (immediate selection, broad placement considerations, development, etc.)

❑ The number and complexity of the exercises

❑ The division of roles and responsibilities between assessors and others on the assessment staff

❑ The degree of support provided assessors in the form of observation guides.

It should be noted that *length* and *quality* of training are not synonymous. Precise guidelines for the exact minimum number of hours or days required for assessor training are difficult to specify. However, extensive experience has shown that for the initial training of assessors who have no experience in an assessment center which conforms to the guidelines in this document, it is desirable to have at least two days of assessor training for each day of the administration of assessment center exercises. Assessors who have experience with similar assessment techniques in other programs may require less training so long as they meet the performance guidelines below. More complex assessment centers with varied formats of simulation exercises may require additional training.

In any event, assessor training is an important aspect of an assessment program. The true test of training quality should be provided by the performance guidelines and certification outlined below.

3 Performance guidelines and certification – each Assessment Center should have clearly stated minimal-performance guidelines for assessors

These performance guidelines should, as a minimum, include the following areas:

a The ability to administer an exercise, if the assessor serves as exercise administrator.

b The ability to recognize, observe, and report the behaviors measured in the center.

c The ability to classify behaviors into the appropriate dimensions, etc.

d The ability to rate behavior in a standardized fashion.

Some measurement is needed to indicate that the individual being trained is capable of functioning as an assessor. The measurement of assessor performance may vary and could include data in terms of (1) rating performance, (2) critiques of assessor reports, (3) observation as an evaluator, etc. It is important that, prior to their actual duties, assessor performance is evaluated to ensure that individuals are sufficiently trained to function as assessors and that such performance is periodically monitored to ensure that skills learned in training are applied.

Each organization must be able to demonstrate its assessors can meet minimal performance guidelines. This may require the development of additional training or other action for assessors not meeting these performance guidelines.

The trainer of assessors should be competent to develop the assessor skills stated above and to evaluate the acquisition of these skills.

4 Currency of training and experience

The time between assessor training and initial service as an assessor must not exceed 6 months. If a longer period has elapsed, a refresher course should be attended.

Assessors who do not have recent experience as an assessor (i.e.

fewer than 2 assessment centers over two consecutive years) should attend a refresher course before they serve again.

H Informed participation

The organization is obligated to make an announcement *prior* to assessment so that participants will be fully informed about the program. While the information provided will vary across organizations, the following basic information should be given to all prospective participants.

Ideally, this information should be made available in writing prior to the center. A second option is to use the material in the opening statement of the center.

1 Objective – The objectives of the program and the purpose of the Assessment Center.

2 Selection – How individuals are selected to participate in the center.

3 Choice – Any options the individual has regarding the choice of participating in the Assessment Center as a condition of employment, advancement, development, etc.

4 Staff – General information on the assessor staff to include composition and assessor training.

5 Materials – What Assessment Center materials are collected and maintained by the organization.

6 Results – How the Assessment Center results will be used. The length of time the assessment results will be maintained on file.

7 Feedback – When and what kind of feedback will be given the participants.

8 Reassessment – The procedure for reassessment (if given).

9 Access – Who will have access to the Assessment Center reports and under what conditions.

10 Contact – Who will be the contact person responsible for the records. Where will the results be stored.

I Validation issues

A major factor in the widespread acceptance and use of Assessment Centers is directly related to an emphasis on sound validation research. Numerous studies demonstrating the predictive validity of individual assessment center programs have been conducted and reported in the professional literature in a variety of organizational settings.

The historical record of the validity of this process cannot be taken as a guarantee that a given assessment program will or will not be valid in a new setting.

Ascertaining the validity of an Assessment Center program is a complicated technical process, and it is important that validation research meet both professional and legal guidelines. Research should be conducted by individuals knowledgeable in the technical and legal issues pertinent to validation procedures.

In evaluating the validity of Assessment Center programs, it is particularly important to document the selection of the dimensions, etc. assessed in the center. In addition, the relationship of assessment exercises to the dimensions, attributes or qualities assessed should be documented as well.

Validity generalization studies of assessment center research suggest that overall assessment ratings derived in a manner conforming to these guidelines show considerable predictive validity. Such findings support the use of a new assessment center in a different setting if the job, exercises, assessors, and assessees in the new situation are similar to those in the validation research and similar procedures are used to observe, report, and integrate the information. The validity generalization studies of the predictive validity of the overall assessment rating do not necessarily establish the validity of the procedure for other purposes, e.g. diagnosis of training needs, accurate assessment of level of skill in separate dimensions, the developmental influence of participation in an assessment center, etc.

The technical standards and principles for validation appear in *Principles for the Validation and Use of Personnel Selection Procedures* (Society for Industrial and Organizational Psychology, Inc. 1987) and *Guidelines for Educational and Psychological Testing* (APA, 1985).

J Rights of the participant

In the United States the Federal Government enacted the Freedom of Information Act and Privacy Act of 1974 to ensure that certain safeguards are provided for an individual against an invasion of personal privacy. Some broad interpretations of these acts are applicable to the general use of Assessment Center data.

Assessment Center activities typically generate a volume of data on an individual who has gone through an Assessment Center. These assessment data come in many different forms, ranging from observer notes, reports on performance in the exercises, assessor ratings, peer ratings, paper and pencil tests, and final Assessment Center reports. This list, while not exhaustive, does indicate the extent of collection of information about an individual.

The following guidelines for use of these data are suggested:

1   Assessees should receive feedback on their performance at the Center and be informed of any recommendations made. Assessees who are members of the organization have a right to read any formal summary written reports concerning their own performance and recommendations which are prepared and made available to management. Applicants to an organization should be provided at a minimum what the final recommendation is, and if possible, the reasons for the recommendation, if requested by the applicant.

2   For reasons of test security, Assessment Center exercises are exempted from disclosure, but the rationale and validity data concerning ratings of dimensions, etc., and recommendations should be made available upon request of the individual.

3   If the organization decides to use assessment results for purposes that can impact the assessees other than those originally announced, the assessees involved must be informed.

4   The organization should inform the assessee what records and data are being collected, maintained, used, and disseminated.

APPENDIX B: WEBLINKS

The following websites are worth checking out for information on development and assessment centres. I start with our own because there you will find an updated and expanded page of weblinks that you can access at a click of your mouse. The address is:

www.humanassets.co.uk

Other links

MCI Standards: www.meto.org.uk/Standards/a.cfm

US Uniform Guidelines on Employee Selection Procedures: www.doi.gov/pmanager/st13d.html

International Congress on Assessment Center Methods: www.assessmentcenters.org/pages/intlconference.html

UK Institute of Personnel and Development: www.ipd.co.uk

US International Personnel Management Association (Public Service body): www.ipma-hr.org

REFERENCES

ADAMS D. (1987) 'Assessment centre exercises – bespoke or ready to wear?' *Guidance and Assessment Review*. Vol. 3, No. 1. February. pp6–7.

ADAMS K. (1998) 'A pragmatic approach to recruiting and developing people'. *Competency*. Vol. 5, No. 4. Summer. pp11–14.

ADLER Z. (1990) 'Hill Street clues: The US police record on promoting women'. *Personnel Management*. Vol. 22, No. 8. August.

AITCHISON D. *and* WIGFIELD D. (1999) 'Invalid assessment centre? All is not lost'. *Selection and Development Review*. Vol. 15, No. 6. December. pp13–16.

ANDERSON N. *and* SHACKLETON V. (1993) *Successful Selection Interviewing*. Oxford, Blackwell.

ANSTEY E. (1989) 'Reminiscences of a wartime army psychologist'. *The Psychologist*. November. pp475–8.

ARKIN A. (1991) 'Turning managers into assessors'. *Personnel Management*. Vol. 23, No 11. November. pp49–51.

ASSOCIATION OF GRADUATE RECRUITERS. (1993) 'Assessment centres'. AGR Briefing. 4 October.

AUSTIN R. (1986) 'Why assessment centres are often necessary'. *Guidance and Assessment Review*. Vol. 2, No. 1. February. pp5–7.

BALLANTYNE I. (1999) 'Cultural diversity in graduate assessment centres'. *Competency*. Vol. 7, No. 1. pp12–15.

BALLANTYNE I. *and* POVAH N. (1995) *Assessment and Development Centres*. Aldershot, Gower.

BARTLETT C. A. *and* GHOSHAL, S. (1995) *Beyond the M-form:*

Toward a managerial theory of the firm. http://www.gsia.cmu.edu/bosch/bart.html.

BEARD D. and LEE G. (1990) 'Improved connections at BT's development centres'. *Personnel Management*. April. pp61–3.

BEARD D., COALEY K. *and* LEE G. (1991) 'Enhancing development for sales staff'. *The Occupational Psychologist*. No. 14. August. pp25–6.

BEDFORD T. (1987) 'New developments in assessment centre design'. *Guidance and Assessment Review*. Vol. 3, No. 3. June. pp2–3.

BLACKHAM R. B. *and* SMITH D. (1989) 'Decision-making in a management assessment centre'. *Journal of Operational Research Society*. Vol. 40, No. 11. pp953–60.

BLANKSBY M. *and* ILES P. (1990) 'Recent developments in assessment centre theory, practice and operation'. *Personnel Review*. Vol. 19, No. 6. pp33–44.

BLINKHORN S. (1986) 'Assessing management potential – retrospect and prospect'. *Guidance and Assessment Review*. Vol. 2, No. 6. December. pp1–3.

BOEHM V. R. (1985) 'Using assessment centres for management development – five applications'. *Journal of Management Development*. Vol. 4, No. 4. pp40–53.

BOGAN M. (1991) 'Fast tracks and the risk of running into sidings'. *Financial Times*. 7 August. p8.

BOUDREAU J. W. (1983a) 'Economic considerations in estimating the utility of human resource productivity improvement programs'. *Personnel Psychology*. Vol. 36. pp551–76.

BOUDREAU J. W. (1983b) 'Effects of employee flows on utility analysis of human resource productivity programs'. *Journal of Applied Psychology*. Vol. 68, No. 3. pp396–406.

BOYATZIS R. (1982) *The Competent Manager*. New York, Wiley.

BOYLE S., FULLERTON J. *and* WOOD R. (1995) 'Do assessment/development centres use optimum evaluation procedures? A survey of practice in UK organizations'. *International Journal of Selection and Assessment*. Vol. 3, No. 2. April. pp132–40.

BRAY D. W. (1964) 'The assessment center method of

appraising management potential', in D. W. Blood (ed.), *The Personnel Job in a Changing World*, New York, American Management Association.

BRAY D. W. (1985) 'Fifty years of assessment centres: a retrospective and prospective view'. *Journal of Management Development*. Vol. 4, No. 4. pp4–11.

BRITTAIN S. *and* RYDER P. (1999) 'Get complex'. *People Management*. Vol. 5, No. 23. 25 November. pp48–51.

BROGDEN H. E. (1949) 'When testing pays off'. *Personnel Psychology*. Vol. 2. pp171–83.

BUCKINGHAM, M. (1999) 'Clone-free zone'. *People Management*. Vol. 5, No. 19. 30 September. pp42–5.

BURKE K. (1997) 'Staff given formula to protect careers'. *Personnel Today*. Part 2. 3 July.

BYCIO P., ALVARES K. M. *and* HAHN J. (1987) 'Situational specificity in assessment center ratings: a confirmatory factor analysis'. *Journal of Applied Psychology*. Vol. 72, No. 3. pp463–74.

BYHAM W. C. (1980) 'Starting an assessment center the right way'. *Personnel Administrator*. February. pp27–32.

CARRICK P. and WILLIAMS R. (1999) 'Development centres – a review of assumptions'. *Human Resource Management Journal*. Vol. 9, No. 2. pp77–92.

CASCIO W. F. (1982) *Applied Psychology in Personnel Management*. 2nd edn. Reston, VA, Reston Publications.

CASEY D. and PEARCE D. (1977) *More than Management Development: Action learning at GEC*. Farnborough, Gower Press.

CHAN D. (1996) 'Criterion and construct validation of an assessment centre'. *Journal of Occupational and Organizational Psychology*. Vol. 69, Part 2. June. pp167–81.

CLAPHAM M. M. (1998) 'A comparison of assessor and self dimension ratings in an advanced management assessment centre'. *Journal of Occupational and Organizational Psychology*. Vol. 71, No. 3. September. pp193–203.

CLEMENTS A. (1994) 'Developing women leaders'. *Directions – The Ashridge Journal*. July. pp18–22.

CLUTTERBUCK D. (1985) *Everyone Needs a Mentor: How to foster talent within the organization.* London, Institute of Personnel Management.

COLLOFF S. and GOODGE P. (1990) 'The open track to élite status'. *Personnel Management.* Vol. 22, No. 11. November. pp50–53.

COMPETENCY A 'Competencies affect climate, style, results: IBM'. *Competency.* Vol. 6 No. 4. p2.

COMPETENCY B 'Competencies are the "glue" in a decentralised business'. *Competency.* Vol. 6 No. 4. p6.

COMPETENCY C 'Linking competencies to company values: KPMG'. *Competency.* Vol. 6 No.4. p8.

CONNERLEY M. L. *and* RYNES S. L. (1997) 'The influence of recruiter characteristics and organizational recruitment support on perceived recruiter effectiveness: views from applicants and recruiters'. *Human Relations.* Vol. 50, No. 12. pp1,563–86.

CRABB S. (1989) 'Man of the moment: David Duffield'. *Personnel Management.* Vol. 21, No. 12. December. pp36–7.

CRONBACH L. J. and GLESSER G. C. (1965) *Psychological Tests and Personnel Decisions.* 2nd edn. Urbana, IL, University of Illinois Press.

CRONSHAW S. F *and* ALEXANDER R. A. (1985) 'One answer to the demand for accountability: selection utility as an investment decision'. *Organizational Behavior and Human Decision Processes.* Vol. 35. pp102–18.

DAVIES M., STANKOV L., and ROBERTS R. D. (1998) 'Emotional intelligence: in search of an elusive contract'. *Journal of Personality and Social Psychology.* Vol. 75, No. 4. October. pp989–1015.

DOBSON P. *and* WILLIAMS A. (1989) 'The validation of the selection of male British Army officers'. *Journal of Occupational Psychology.* Vol. 62, Part 4. December. pp313–25.

DRAKELEY R. J. *and* WHITE A. (1999) 'Competencies: foundation garments or emperor's clothes?' *Selection and Development Review.* Vol. 15, No. 3. 3 June. pp7–13.

DUGAN B. (1988) 'Effects of assessor training on information use'. *Journal of Applied Psychology*. Vol. 73, No. 4. November. pp743–8.

DUKES J. (1996) 'Meta-analysis and the validity of assessment centres'. *Selection and Development Review*. Vol. 12, No. 2. April. pp1–2.

DULEWICZ V. (1989) 'Assessment centres as the route to competence'. *Personnel Management*. Vol. 21, No. 11. November. pp56–9.

DUNNETTE M. D. (1966) *Personnel Selection and Placement*. Belmont, CA, Wadsworth Publishing Co.

EGAN G. (1986) *The Skilled Helper: A systematic approach to effective helping*. 3rd edn. Monterey, Brooks/Cole.

EMERY F. E *and* TRIST E. L. (1965) 'The causal texture of organizational environments'. *Human Relations*. Vol. 18. pp21–32.

EMPLOYEE DEVELOPMENT BULLETIN No. 42 (1993) 'Development centres at Yorkshire Water'. *Review and Report No. 538*. Industrial Relations Services. June. pp11–14.

ENGELBRECHT A. S. *and* FISCHER A. H. (1995) 'The managerial performance implications of a developmental assessment center process' *Human Relations*. Vol. 48, No. 4. pp387–404.

EQUAL EMPLOYMENT OPPORTUNITY COORDINATING COUNCIL (1978) 'Uniform guidelines on employee selection procedures'. *Federal Register*. pp38, 290–315.

EVANS R. (1993) 'Assessment centre feedback and career counselling for senior police officers in the UK'. *International Journal of Selection and Assessment*. Vol. 1, No. 3. July. pp163–4.

FELTHAM R. (1988a) 'Validity of a police assessment centre: a 1–19-year follow-up'. *Journal of Occupational Psychology*. Vol. 61, Part 2. June. pp129–44.

FELTHAM R. (1988b) 'Justifying investment'. *Personnel Management*. Vol. 20, No. 8. August. pp17–18.

FELTHAM R. (1988c) 'Assessment centre decision making: judgmental vs. mechanical'. *Journal of Occupational Psychology*. Vol. 61, Part 3. September. pp237–41.

FERGUSON J. (1991) 'When is an assessment centre a development centre?' *Guidance and Assessment Review*. Vol. 7, No. 6. December. pp1–3.

FINKLE R. B. (1976) 'Managerial assessment centers', in M. D. Dunnette (ed.), *Handbook of Industrial and Organizational Psychology*, Chicago, IL, Rand-McNally, pp861–88.

FLETCHER C. (1989) 'The impact of demographic changes on selection'. *The Occupational Psychologist*. Vol. 8. August. pp3–4.

FLETCHER C. (1991) 'Candidates' reactions to assessment centres and their outcomes: a longitudinal study'. *Journal of Occupational Psychology*. Vol. 64, No. 2. June. pp117–27.

FOX S., BEN-NAHUM Z. *and* YINON Y. (1989) 'Perceived similarity and accuracy of peer ratings'. *Journal of Applied Psychology*. Vol. 74, No. 5. October. pp781–6.

FRANCIS-SMYTHE J. *and* SMITH P. M. (1997) 'The psychological impact of assessment in a development center'. *Human Relations*. Vol. 50, No. 2. pp149–67.

FREDERIKSEN N. (1986) 'Toward a broader conception of human intelligence'. *American Psychologist*. Vol. 41, No. 4. April. pp445–52.

GAMMIE A. (1994) 'Likely to succeed'. *Human Resources*. Summer. pp37–42.

GARAVAN T. N. *and* MORLEY M. (1998) 'Graduate assessment centres: an empirical investigation of effectiveness'. *Education and Training*. Vol. 40, No. 5. pp206–19.

GAUGLER B. B. *and* RUDOLPH A. S. (1992) 'The influence of assessee performance variation on assessors' judgements'. *Personnel Psychology*. Vol. 45. pp77–98.

GAUGLER B. B. *and* THORNTON G. C. (1989) 'Number of assessment center dimensions as a determinant of assessor accuracy'. *Journal of Applied Psychology*. Vol. 74, No. 4. August. pp611–18.

GAUGLER B. B., ROSENTHAL D. B., THORNTON G. C. *and* BENTSON C. (1987) 'Meta-analysis of assessment center validity'. *Journal of Applied Psychology*. Vol. 72, No. 3. pp493–511.

GERSTEIN M. *and* REISMAN H. (1983) 'Strategic selection:

matching executives to business conditions'. *Sloan Management Review*. Winter. pp33–49.

GHOSHAL S. *and* BARTLETT C. A. (1998) 'Play the right card to get the aces in the pack'. *Financial Times*. 28 July.

GLAZE T. (1989) 'Cadbury's dictionary of competence'. *Personnel Management*. Vol. 21, No. 7. July. pp44–8.

GLYNN C. (1996) *The Development of Assessment Centres*. Roffey Park, Roffey Park Management Institute, April.

GOLEMAN D. (1998) *Working with Emotional Intelligence*. London, Bloomsbury Publishing

GOODGE P. (1987) 'Assessment centres: Time for deregulation?' *Management Education and Development*. Vol. 18, Part 2. pp89–94.

GOODGE P. (1991) 'Development centres: guidelines for decision makers'. *Journal of Management Development*. Vol. 10, No. 3. pp4–12.

GOODGE P. (1994a) 'Development centres: design generation and effectiveness'. *Journal of Management and Development*. Vol. 13, No. 4. pp16–22.

GOODGE P. (1994b) 'Development centres for the 90s – third-generation design'. *Organisations and People*. Vol. 1, Part 3. pp18–20.

GOODGE P. (1995) 'Design options and outcomes: progress in development centre research'. *Journal of Management Development*. Vol. 14, No. 8. pp55–9.

GOODGE P. (1997) 'Assessment and development centres: practical design principles'. *Selection and Development Review*. Vol. 13, No. 3. June. pp11–14.

GRATTON L. (1984) 'Assessment centres: the promises and the pitfalls'. Paper presented to the *CRAC Annual Conference*. July.

GRATTON L. *and* SYRETT M. (1990) 'Heirs apparent: succession strategies for the future'. *Personnel Management*. Vol. 22, No. 1. January. pp34–8.

GREATREX J. *and* PHILLIPS P. (1989) 'Oiling the wheels of competence'. *Personnel Management*. Vol. 21, No. 8. August. pp36–9.

GRIFFITHS P. *and* ALLEN B. (1987) 'Assessment centres: breaking with tradition'. *Journal of Management Development*. Vol. 6, No. 1. pp18–29.

GRIFFITHS P. *and* GOODGE P. (1994) 'Development centres: the third generation'. *Personnel Management*. Vol. 26, No. 6. June. pp40–43.

HAGEDORN J. (1989) 'When the best fail the tests'. *The Guardian*. 11 April.

HAKSTIAN, A. R. *and* HARLOS K. P. (1993) 'Assessment of in-basket performance by quickly scored methods: Development and psychometric evaluation'. *International Journal of Selection and Assessment*, Vol. 1, No. 3. July. pp135–43.

HAKSTIAN A. R. *and* SCRATCHLEY L. S. (1997) 'In-basket assessment by fully objective methods: development and evaluation of a self-report system'. *Educational and Psychological Measurement*. Vol. 57, No. 4. August. pp607–30.

HALL P. *and* NORRIS P. (1992) 'Development centres: making the learning organisation happen'. *Human Resources*. Autumn. pp126–8.

HAMEL G. *and* PRAHALAD C. K. (1994) *Competing for the Future*. Boston, MA, Harvard Business School Press.

HARDINGHAM A. (1996) 'Why the top job is the beginning, not the end'. *People Management*. 12 September. p49.

HARRIS M. M., BECKER A. S. *and* SMITH D .E. (1993) 'Does the assessment center scoring method affect the cross situational consistency of ratings?' *Journal of Applied Psychology*. Vol. 78 No. 4. pp675–8.

HERRIOT P. (1986) 'Assessment centres revisited'. *Guidance and Assessment Review*. Vol. 2, No. 3. June. pp7–8.

HERRIOT P. (1988) 'Assessment centres: fashionable fad or flexible friend'. Paper delivered to Sectional Meeting 40, Institute of Personnel Management Conference, Harrogate, 28 October.

HERRIOT P. (1989) *Recruitment in the 90s*. London, Institute of Personnel Management.

HERRIOT P. *and* PEMBERTON C. (1995) *New Deals: The revolution in managerial careers*. Chichester, John Wiley.

HERRIOT P., WINGROVE J. *and* CHALMERS C. (1985) 'Group

decision making in an assessment centre'. *Journal of Occupational Psychology*. Vol. 58. pp309–12.

HIGGS M. (1996) 'The value of assessment centres'. *Selection and Development Review*. Vol. 12, No.5. October. pp2–6.

HOLBECHE L. (1999) 'Bonding training to strategy'. *Training Journal*. December. pp18–21

HOLBECHE L. *and* GLYNN C. (1999) *The Roffey Park Management Agenda*. Roffey Park, Roffey Park Management Institute. January.

HORNBY D. *and* THOMAS R. (1989) 'Towards a better standard of management'. *Personnel Management*. Vol. 21, No. 1. January. pp52–5.

HUCK J. R *and* BRAY D. W. (1976) 'Management assessment center evaluations and subsequent job performance of white and black females'. *Personnel Psychology*. Vol. 29, No. 1. Spring. pp13–30.

HUNTER J. E *and* SCHMIDT F. L. (1983) 'Quantifying the effects of psychological interventions on employee job performance and work-force productivity'. *American Psychologist*. Vol. 38, No. 4. April. pp473–8.

HUNTER J. E., SCHMIDT F. L. *and* JACKSON G. B. (1982) *Meta-Analysis: Cumulating research findings across studies*. Beverly Hills, CA, Sage.

HUTCHINSON S., VALENTINO K. E. *and* KIRKNER S. L. (1998) 'What works for the gander does not work as well for the goose: the effects of leader behaviour'. *Journal of Applied Social Psychology*. Vol. 28, No. 2. pp171–82.

ILES P. A. *and* FORSTER A. (1994) 'Professional forum: collaborative development centres: the social process model of assessment in action?' *International Journal of Selection and Assessment*. Vol. 2, No. 1. January. pp59–64.

ILES P. A. *and* ROBERTSON I. T. (1989) 'Unintended consequences and undesired outcomes in managerial selection and assessment'. *Guidance and Assessment Review*. Vol. 5, No. 3. June. pp4–5.

ILES P. A. *and* ROBERTSON I. T. (1997) 'The impact of personnel selection procedures on candidates', Chapter 27 in N. Anderson and P. Herriot (eds), *International Handbook of Selection and Assessment*, Chichester, John Wiley.

IMADA A. S., VAN SLYKE M. D. *and* HENDRICK W. W. (1985) 'Applications of assessment centres multinationally: the state of the art, obstacles and cross-cultural implications'. *Journal of Management Development*. Vol. 4, No. 4. pp54–67.

INCOMES DATA SERVICES (1998) *Assessment centres*. IDS Study 646. London: Incomes Data Services Limited (e-mail: ids@incomesdata.co.uk). April.

INDUSTRIAL SOCIETY (1996) 'Assessment and development centres'. *Managing Best Practice Series*, Number 29. November.

JACKSON C. *and* YEATES J. (1993) *Development Centres: Assessing or developing people?* IMS Report No. 261. Falmer, Sussex, Institute of Manpower Studies.

JACKSON L. (1989) 'Turning airport managers into high-fliers'. *Personnel Management*. Vol. 21, No. 10.October. pp80–85.

JACKSON R. P. (1994) 'Development through assessment centres'. *Organisations and People*. Vol. 1, Part 3. pp12–17.

JACOBS R. (1989) 'Getting the measure of managerial competence'. *Personnel Management*. Vol. 21, No. 6. June. pp32–7.

JANSEN P. G. W. (1997) 'Assessment in a technological world', Chapter 6 in N. Anderson and P. Herriot (eds), *International Handbook of Selection and Assessment*, Chichester, John Wiley.

JONES R. G. *and* WHITMORE M. D. (1995) 'Evaluating developmental assessment centers as interventions'. *Personnel Psychology*. Vol. 48. pp377–88.

KEENAN T. (1997) 'Selection for potential: the case of graduate recruitment', Chapter 25 in N. Anderson and P. Herriot (eds), *International Handbook of Selection and Assessment*, Chichester, John Wiley.

KLEINMANN M. (1993) 'Are rating dimensions in assessment centers transparent for participants? Consequences for criterion and construct validity'. *Journal of Applied Psychology*. Vol. 78, No. 6. December. pp988–93.

KLEINMANN M., KUPTSCH C. *and* KOLLER O. (1996) 'Transparency: A necessary requirement for the construct validity of assessment centres'. *Applied Psychology: An International Review*. Vol. 45, No. 1. pp67–84.

KLIMOSKI R. *and* BRICKNER M. (1987) 'Why do assessment centers work? The puzzle of assessment center validity'. *Personnel Psychology*. Vol. 40. pp243–60.

KLIMOSKI R. *and* STRICKLAND W. J. (1977) 'Assessment centres – valid or merely prescient?' *Personnel Psychology*. Vol. 30. pp353–61.

LEE G. *and* BEARD D. (1993) *Development Centres: Realising the potential of your employees through assessment and development*. London, McGraw-Hill.

LITTLEFIELD D. (1995) 'Menu for change at Novotel'. *People Management*. 26 January. pp34–6.

LOWRY P. E. (1994a) 'Selection methods: comparison of assessment centers with personnel records evaluations'. *Public Personnel Management*, Vol. 23, No. 3. Fall. pp383–95.

LOWRY P. E. (1994b) 'The structured interview: an alternative to the assessment centre?' *Public Personnel Management*. Vol. 23, No. 2. Summer. pp201–15.

LOWRY P. E. (1996) 'A survey of the assessment centre process in the public sector'. *Public Personnel Management*. Vol. 25, No. 3. Fall. pp307–21.

MABEY B. *and* ILES P. (1991) 'Human resource management from the other side of the fence'. *Personnel Management*. Vol. 23, No. 2. February. pp50–53.

MACAN T., AVEDON M. J., PAESE M. *and* SMITH D. E. (1994) 'The effects of applicants' reactions to cognitive ability tests and an assessment center'. *Personnel Psychology*. Vol. 47. pp715–38.

MACKINNON D. W. (1977) 'From selecting spies to selecting managers: the OSS assessment program', in J. L. Moses and W. C. Byham (eds), *Applying the Assessment Center Method*, New York, Pergamon.

MACLACHLAN R. (1998) 'Regeneration X'. *People Management*. 2 April. pp34–41.

MAHONEY-PHILIPS J. (1991) 'Development centres: a perspective on influencing factors'. *European Work and Organizational Psychologist*. Vol. 1, Issue 4. pp286–91.

MANAGEMENT CHARTER INITIATIVE (1990) *Occupational Standards for Managers*. London, MCI.

MANAGEMENT CHARTER INITIATIVE. (1999) *Standards*. http://www.meto.org.uk/Standards/a.cfm.

MANGHAM I. (1990) 'Managing as a performing art'. *British Journal of Management*. Vol. 1. pp105–15.

MANPOWER SERVICES COMMISSION (1987) *Standards of Performance for Administrative Business and Commercial Staff*. Sheffield, MSC.

MAURER T. J. *and* TARULLI B. A. (1994) 'Investigation of perceived environment, perceived outcome, and person variables in relationship to voluntary development activity by employees'. *Journal of Applied Psychology*. Vol. 79, No. 1. February. pp3–14.

MCCAULEY C. D., RUDERMAN M. N., OHLOTT P. J. *and* MORROW J. E. (1994) 'Assessing the developmental components of managerial jobs'. *Journal of Applied Psychology*. Vol. 79, No. 4. August. pp544–60.

MCDANIEL M. A., WHETZEL D. L., SCHMIDT F. L. *and* MAURER S. D. (1994) 'The validity of employment interviews: a comprehensive review and meta-analysis'. *Journal of Applied Psychology*. Vol. 79, No. 4. August. pp599–616.

MEGLINO B. M., DE NISI A. S., YOUNGBLOOD S. A. *and* WILLIAMS K. J. (1988) 'Effects of realistic job previews: a comparison using an enhancement and a reduction preview'. *Journal of Applied Psychology*. Vol. 73, No. 2. pp259–66.

MEYER H. H. (1987) 'Predicting supervisory ratings versus promotional progress in test validation studies'. *Journal of Applied Psychology*. Vol. 72, No. 4. pp696–7.

MEYER J. P. *and* ALLEN N. J. (1997) *Commitment in the Workplace: Theory, research, and application*. Thousand Oaks, CA, Sage.

MISCHEL W. (1968) *Personality and Assessment*. New York, Wiley.

MISCHEL W. (1973) 'Toward a cognitive social learning reconceptualization of personality'. *Psychological Review*. Vol. 80, No. 4. pp252–83.

MISCHEL, W. *and* SHODA Y. (1995) 'A cognitive-affective system theory of personality: reconceptualizing situations, dispositions, dynamics, and invariance in personality structure'. *Psychological Review*, Vol. 102, No. 2. pp 246–68.

NEILL A. (1989) 'Personal potential'. *Personnel Today*. 30 May. pp29–33.

PAYNE T., ANDERSON N. *and* SMITH T. (1992) 'Decision making and financial considerations in a second generation assessment centre'. Paper presented at The British Psychological Society Occupational Psychology Conference, Liverpool.

PERSONNEL MANAGEMENT (1989) 'Computer assessment identifies skills'. *Personnel Management*. August. p14.

PERSONNEL MANAGEMENT (1990) 'Strengthening the top team'. *Personnel Management*. Vol. 22, No. 8. August.

PFEFFER J. (1994) *Competitive Advantage through People: Unleashing the power of the work force*. Boston, MA, Harvard Business School Press.

PLATT S. (1996) 'Foreign accent'. *Personnel Today*. 1 October. pp42–4.

PYNES J. E. *and* BERNARDIN H. J. (1989) 'Predictive validity of an entry-level police officer assessment center'. *Journal of Applied Psychology*. Vol. 74, No. 5. October. pp831–3.

RANDELL G. (1989) 'A rejoinder to Handy: Is it what you are or what you do?' *The Occupational Psychologist*. Issue 9. December. pp8–9.

REDDY M. (1987) *The Manager's Guide to Counselling at Work*. Leicester, The British Psychological Society.

REILLY R. R. *and* CHAO G. T. (1982) 'Validity and fairness of some alternative employee selection procedures'. *Personnel Psychology*. Vol. 35. pp1–62.

RITCHIE R. J. *and* MOSES J. L. (1983) 'Assessment center correlates of women's advancement into middle management: a 7-year longitudinal analysis'. *Journal of Applied Psychology*. Vol. 68. pp227–31.

ROBERTSON I. T. *and* ILES P. A. (1988) 'Social representations in assessment centres: candidates' appearance and assessors' judgements'. Paper given to Occupational Psychology Conference of The British Psychological Society, Manchester. January.

ROBERTSON I. T. *and* MAKIN P. J. (1986) 'Management selection in Britain: A survey and critique'. *Journal of Occupational Psychology.* Vol. 59. pp45–57.

ROBERTSON I. T., GRATTON L. *and* SHARPLEY D. (1987) 'The psychometric properties and design of managerial assessment centres: dimensions into exercises won't go'. *Journal of Occupational Psychology.* Vol. 60, No. 3. September. pp187–195.

ROBERTSON I., ILES, P. A., GRATTON L. *and* SHARPLEY D. (1991) 'The impact of personnel selection and assessment methods on candidates'. *Human Relations.* Vol. 44, No. 9. pp963–82.

ROBERTSON S. (1990) 'The development of a company's vision and values to meet its business and people's goals'. Paper presented to the Institute of Personnel Management National Conference, Harrogate, 25 October.

RODGER D. *and* MABEY. C. (1987) 'BT's leap forward from assessment centres'. *Personnel Management.* Vol. 19, No. 7. July. pp32–5.

ROTHWELL S. (1985a) 'Manpower matters: the use of assessment centres'. *Journal of General Management.* Vol. 10, No. 3. Spring. pp79–84.

ROTHWELL S. (1985b) 'Manpower matters: assessment centre techniques'. *Journal of General Management.* Vol. 10, No. 4. Summer. pp91–6.

RUSSELL C. J. (1985) 'Individual decision processes in an assessment center'. *Journal of Applied Psychology.* Vol. 70, No. 4. pp737–46.

RUSSELL C. J. *and* DOMM D. R. (1995) 'Two field tests of an explanation of assessment centre validity'. *Journal of Occupational and Organizational Psychology.* Vol. 68, No. 1, March. pp25–47.

RYAN A. *and* SACKETT P. R. (1989) 'Exploratory study of individual assessment practices: inter-rater reliability and judgements of assessor effectiveness'. *Journal of Applied Psychology*. Vol. 74, No. 4. August. pp568–79.

SACKETT P. R. (1987) 'Assessment centers and content validity: some neglected issues'. *Personnel Psychology*. Vol. 40. pp13–25.

SACKETT P. R. *and* DREHER G. F. (1982) 'Constructs and assessment center dimensions: some troubling empirical findings'. *Journal of Applied Psychology*. Vol. 67, No. 4. pp401–10.

SACKETT P. R. *and* RYAN A. M. (1985) 'A review of recent assessment centre research'. *Journal of Management Development*. Vol. 4, No. 4. pp13–27.

SAGIE A. *and* MAGNEZY R. (1997) 'Assessor type, number of distinguishable dimension categories, and assessment centre construct validity'. *Journal of Occupational and Organizational Psychology*. Vol. 70, No.1. March. pp103–08.

SCHEIN E. H. (1978) *Career Dynamics: Matching individual and organizational needs*. Reading, MA, Addison-Wesley.

SCHMIDT F. L. *and* HUNTER J. E. (1981) 'Employment testing: old theories and new research findings'. *American Psychologist*. Vol. 36, No. 10. October. pp1,128–37.

SCHMIDT F. L. *and* HUNTER J. E. (1983) 'Individual differences in productivity: an empirical test of estimates derived from studies of selection procedure utility'. *Journal of Applied Psychology*. Vol. 68, No. 3. pp407–14.

SCHMIDT F. L. *and* HUNTER J. E. (1998) 'The validity and utility of selection methods in personnel psychology: practical and theoretical implications of 85 years of research findings'. *Psychological Bulletin*. Vol. 124, No. 2. pp262–74.

SCHMIDT F. L., HUNTER J. E., McKENZIE R. C. *and* MULDROW T. W. (1979) 'Impact of valid selection procedures on workforce productivity'. *Journal of Applied Psychology*. Vol. 64, No. 6. pp609–26.

SCHMIDT F. L., HUNTER J. E., OUTTERBRIDGE A. N. *and* TRATTNER M. H. (1986) 'The economic impact of job selection methods on size, productivity, and payroll costs of the federal workforce: an empirically based demonstration'. *Personnel Psychology*. Vol. 39. pp1–29.

SCHMITT N., GOODING R. Z., NOE R. A. *and* KIRSCH M. (1984)

'Meta-analyses of validity studies published between 1964 and 1982 and the investigation of study characteristics'. *Personnel Psychology*. Vol. 37. pp407–22.

SCHMITT N., FORD J. K. *and* STULTS D. M. (1986) 'Changes in self-perceived ability as a function of performance in an assessment centre'. *Journal of Occupational Psychology*. Vol. 59, No. 4. pp327–35.

SCHNEIDER J. R. *and* SCHMITT N. (1992) 'An exercise design approach to understanding assessment center dimension and exercise constructs'. *Journal of Applied Psychology*. Vol. 77, No. 1. pp32–41.

SCHOFIELD P. (1998) 'Give the transferable skill your vote if you want to get selected'. *Daily Telegraph*. 2 April.

SCHOFIELD S., HOGG B. *and* BEARD D. (1993) 'Cultural issues and development centres', Chapter 9 in G. Lee and D. Beard, *Development Centres: Realizing the potential of your employees through assessment and development*, London, McGraw-Hill.

SHORE T. H., SHORE L. M. *and* THORNTON G. C. III (1992) 'Construct validity of self- and peer evaluations of performance dimensions in an assessment center'. *Journal of Applied Psychology*. Vol. 77, No. 1. pp42–54.

SHUTTLEWORTH T. *and* PRESCOTT R. (1991) 'The hard graft way to develop managers'. *Personnel Management*. Vol. 23, No. 11. November. pp40–43.

SILVERMAN W. H., DALESSIO A. *and* WOODS S. B. (1986) 'Influence of assessment center methods on assessors' ratings'. *Personnel Psychology*. Vol. 39, No. 3. Autumn. pp565–78.

SKAPINKER M. (1989a) 'Playing the game is almost for real'. *Financial Times*. 15 February.

SKAPINKER M. (1989b) 'Fast track from the shop floor'. *Financial Times*. 3 July.

SMITH D. *and* TARPEY T. (1987) 'In-tray exercises and assessment centres: the issue of reliability'. *Personnel Review*. Vol. 16, No. 3. pp24–8.

SMITHER J. W., REILLY R. R., MILLSAP R. E., PEARLMAN K. *and* STOFFEY R. W. (1993) 'Applicant reactions to selection procedures'. *Personnel Psychology*. Vol. 46. pp49–76.

SPENCER L. M. *and* SPENCER S. M. (1993) *Competence at Work.* New York, John Wiley.

SPYCHALSKI A. C., QUINONES M. A., GAUGLER B. B. *and* POHLEY K. (1997) 'A survey of assessment center practices in organizations in the United States'. *Personnel Psychology,* Vol. 50, No. 1. Spring. pp71–90.

STAMOULIS D. T. *and* HAUENSTEIN N. M. A. (1993) 'Rater training and rater accuracy: training for dimensional accuracy versus training for ratee differentiation'. *Journal of Applied Psychology.* Vol. 78, No. 6. December. pp994–1003.

STAMP G. (1989) 'The individual, the organization, and the path to mutual appreciation'. *Personnel Management.* Vol. 21, No. 7. July. pp28-31.

STERNBERG R. J. *and* WAGNER R. K. (eds) (1986) *Practical Intelligence: Nature and origins of competence in the everyday world.* Cambridge, Cambridge University Press.

STEVENS C. (1985) 'Assessment centres: the British experience'. *Personnel Management.* Vol. 17, No. 7. July. pp28–31.

STRUBE M. J. ET AL (1986) 'Self-evaluation of abilities: accurate self-assessment versus biased self-enhancement'. *Journal of Personality and Social Psychology.* Vol. 51, No. 1. pp16–25.

TASK FORCE ON ASSESSMENT CENTER GUILDELINES (1989) 'Guidelines and ethical considerations for assessment center operations'. *Public Personnel Management.* Vol. 18. pp457–70. See Appendix A.

THERRIEN M. *and* FISCHER J. (1978) 'Written indicators of empathy: a validation study'. *Counsellor Education and Supervision.* Vol. 17. pp273–7.

THORNTON G. C. (1992) *Assessment Centers in Human Resource Management.* Reading, MA, Addison-Wesley Publishing Company.

TREADWELL D. (1989) 'How Courtaulds find graduates a material factor'. *Personnel Management.* Vol. 21, No. 11. November. pp54–5.

TURNAGE J. J. *and* MUCHINSKY P. M. (1982) 'Transsituational variability in human performance within assessment centers'. *Organizational Behavior and Human Performance.* Vol. 30. pp174–200.

TURNAGE J. J. *and* MUCHINSKY P. M. (1984) 'A comparison of the predictive validity of assessment center evaluations versus traditional measures in forecasting supervisory job performance: interpretive implications of criterion distortion for the assessment paradigm'. *Journal of Applied Psychology*. Vol. 69, No. 4. pp595–602.

WAGNER R. K. (1987) 'Tacit knowledge in everyday intelligent behavior'. *Journal of Personality and Social Psychology*. Vol. 52, No. 6. pp1236–47.

WALKLEY J. (1988) 'The use of assessment centres in management succession'. *Banking and Financial Training*. Vol. 4, No. 3. September. pp17–18.

WALSH J. (1998) 'Competency frameworks give companies the edge'. *People Management*. 17 September. p15.

WALSH J. P., WEINBERG R. M. *and* FAIRFIELD M. L. (1987) 'The effects of gender on assessment centre evaluations'. *Journal of Occupational Psychology*. Vol. 60. pp305–09.

WARMKE D. L. (1985) 'Preselection for assessment centres: some choices and issues to consider'. *Journal of Management Development*. Vol. 4, No. 4. pp28–39.

WEEKLEY J. A. *and* JONES C. (1997) 'Video-based situational testing'. *Personnel Psychology*. Vol. 50, No. 1. Spring. pp25–49.

WEEKLEY J. A. *and* JONES C. (1999) 'Further studies of situational tests'. *Personnel Psychology*. Vol. 52, No. 3. Autumn. pp679–700.

WHIDDETT S. *and* HOLLYFORDE S. (1999) *The Competencies Handbook*. London, Institute of Personnel and Development.

WOEHR D. J. (1994) 'Understanding frame-of-reference training: the impact of training on the recall of performance information'. *Journal of Applied Psychology*. Vol. 79, No. 4. August. pp535-43.

WOOD R. (1994) 'Work samples should be used more (and will be)'. *International Journal of Selection and Assessment*. Vol. 2, No. 3. July. pp166–71.

WOOD S. (ed.) (1988) *Continuous Development: The path to improved performance*. London, Institute of Personnel Management.

WOODRUFFE C. (1991) 'Competent by any other name'. *Personnel Management*. Vol. 23, No. 9. September. pp30–33.

WOODRUFFE C. (1997) 'Going back a generation'. *People Management*. Vol. 3, No. 4. 20 February. pp32–4.

WOODRUFFE C. (1999) *Winning the Talent War: A strategic approach to attracting, developing and retaining the best people*. Chichester, John Wiley.

WOODRUFFE, C. (2000) 'Employability: A strategic role for training'. *Training Journal*. February. pp22–5.

WOODRUFFE C. *and* WYLIE R. (1994) 'Going the whole hog: the design of development centres at NatWest'. *Competency*. Vol. 2, No. 1. Autumn. pp23–7.

WORTS C. (1996) 'Building a society with special skills'. *People Management*. Vol. 2, No. 2. 25 January. pp36–9.

WRIGHT P. M., LICHTENFELS P. A. *and* PURSELL E. D. (1989) 'The structured interview: additional studies and a meta-analysis'. *Journal of Occupational Psychology*. Vol. 62, Part 3. September. pp191–9.

WYLIE R. *and* WOODRUFFE C. (1994) 'Taking stock: some lessons from consulting in a large divisionalised company'. *Competency*. Vol. 2, No. 2. Winter. pp18–23.

INDEX

absenteeism, impact of organisational
  commitment on 17
acceptability by participants of a centre
  6, 102, 119, 125
action learning and action learning
  schemes 215, 229
administrative back-up for a centre 11,
  177–9
analysis
  as a problem-solving cognitive skill 5,
    12, 68, 119
  see also job analysis
analytical exercise(s) 3, 119–20, 147
appraisal interview(s) 17
  as a means of assessment by line
    manager 71
appraisal process, an integrated
  organisational 71
  as an alternative to development
    centres 72
  centres as contributory to 16–17
aptitude and ability tests, as sometimes
  better than a centre 64
  in comparison with a centre 68,
    159–60
assessing, methods and duties of see
  assessment techniques
assessment centre(s) 11–21, 232–50
  accommodation for 179–80
  acknowledged accuracy of
    assessments by 11, 57
  administration of 177–9
  and recruitment 17–19
  as a basis for personal development
    plans 27, 59
  as a collaborative process between
    participants and assessors 18
  as a means of anticipating the
    organisation's future staffing needs
    27, 96–7

as a means of choosing, developing
  and retaining talent 14, 22, 25, 218
as a means of making the best use of
  available talent 14, 25
as a means of selling the organisation
  17, 54, 59
as Extended Interviews 7
as handing power to line managers/
  assessors 74–5
as part of an HR strategy 22–36, 200
beneficial side-effects of 15–21
chairperson of 172–5
checklist for the running of 178–9
costs of 61–4, 65, 73–4
creating positive perceptions of the
  organisation/work 17–18, 42
debrief(ing) after 221
definition of 1–4
duration of 4, 11
economic justification for 54–9, 61–4
financial benefits of 61–4
forms and documentation for 139–44
graduate 37, 131, 145
greater perceived predictiveness of 17,
  55–8, 59, 63, 200
history of 6–9
international 246–7
meta-analysis to measure 'validity' of
  56–8
modular 196
perceived justice/validity in
  procedure/outcomes of 17, 18–19,
  38, 42, 54–9, 71, 220–32
potential demotivation nonetheless
  by 45
potential use of for redundancy
  selection 21
potential use of to alter business
  strategy 25–6

promotion board, comparison with 34, 55
promotion of people as an objective of 71
purpose of 1–2, 31–2
selection of people as an objective of 2, 11, 12, 13, 19, 20–1, 32, 35, 59, 78, 200; *see also* selection centre(s)
studies on the 'validity' of 54–9
supervisor rating(s) as an alternative to 55–6, 71
timetable/schedule for 165–8
to create 'talent pools' 30
to select teams/team leaders 19, 27, 34, 72
US court cases focusing on 19–20
US guidelines and ethical considerations for 252–65
widespread use of 9–10, 14
assessment centre exercises, nature of 4, 115–16, 197–8
assessment centre project *see* project management in introducing a centre
assessment techniques 2, 181–96, 197
classifying behaviour(s) 182–3, 197, 201, 202–4
combination of as essential to a centre 4, 197
filing a report after a centre 192–5, 197
grid of collated assessments 186–7, 190
halo effect as a pitfall 201, 233–8; *see also* exercise effect, the
marking overall exercise performance rather than individual dimensions 116, 125, 146, 186, 233–8
observing and recording exercises 181–2, 197, 201–2
primacy effect as a pitfall 201
rating 97–9, 139–44, 183–6, 197, 201, 202–4
stereotyping as a pitfall 201
use of information technology (IT) 195–6
with no evidence and/or negative evidence 185–6
working in pairs 182
assessors 169–72, 178, 181–96, 198, 200–6
a team of 4, 7, 12, 81
benefits of belonging to a team of 15–16
deciding who should be 79, 169–72
duties of 181–2; *see also* assessment techniques; assessor training
friendly and warm 171
HR function personnel as 49
judgemental nature of 184
level in the organisation of 171
line managers as 17, 49, 75, 78, 81, 123, 170–1, 194, 206
management personnel involved as 11
meeting of following a centre 166, 167, 174, 185, 186–92, 204–5
need (or no need) for 9, 77
need to involve in all components of a centre 149, 169
privacy of information from 194–5
rating documentation/systems for 97–9, 139–44
role of in development centre(s) 49, 81, 146
senior personnel as 20, 170
skills required by 4, 12, 49, 137; *see also* assessment techniques; assessor training
training of *see* assessor training
working in pairs 182
see also self-assessment
assessor training 15, 16, 78, 136, 137, 146–7, 170, 197–206, 228
poor 13, 125, 235–6
residential 197
skills requiring 197, 200–6
timetabling of 197–9

barriers to the acceptance of centres 64–75
expense 73–4
external selection methods already adequate 65
insufficient financial benefit 64–5
internal selection methods already adequate 71–2
loss of managerial power(s) 74–5
organisation too small 74
systems for development of personnel already adequate 72–3
best-practice considerations in relation to a centre 230–2

biodata, as a means of assessment for selection 17, 19, 158, 160

breadth of awareness, as a competency/ problem-solving skill 5, 89, 118, 120, 150

briefing prior to a centre 173–4, 178
material/documentation for 162–5

budgeting for the introduction of a centre 79

business strategy
alteration of in light of assessment centre evidence 25–6
based on core competence leadership 24
based on people, their knowledge and learning 24–5
related to HR strategy (and centres) 23–6

career anchor(s), participants' insights on their own 12, 31, 154, 177

career aspirations, focusing by centre participants on their own 12, 23, 72, 209

career management, integration of centres with 28–31, 218

career (path) plans, as joint expressions by individual and organisation 14, 26, 42, 43, 206, 210
greater responsibility of the individual for 28

change, organisational 31
requiring assessment template to change too 45
requiring managers to be adaptable to 14

checks on the operation of a centre, necessary 13

classifying of behaviour, as an assessment skill 12

coaching, following centre exercises 47, 214, 216

cognitive skills 15
see also problem-solving skill(s)

cognitive tests, as opposed to assessment centre procedures 17, 18, 19, 57–8, 153
as part of pre-selection 158
greater perceived validity of 57–8
lesser perceived validity of 17, 57–8
training to apply or make use of 204
use in selection of 62, 68

see also aptitude and ability tests

collaborative model of development/ assessment centre 8, 9, 18

combining elements of assessment and development centres 31–2
inevitable antipathies involved in 32–3

commitment of an organisation to its personnel 46, 53

commitment of personnel to a centre and its objectives 20, 42, 76–8

commitment of personnel to the organisation
as a result of an assessment centre 17, 42, 43
effect of rigour in selection on 17

competence, areas of 88–90, 93, 95, 107, 108–11
current or potential 23–4
gaining information about a person's 2, 46
personal development by increasing 25, 46, 93

competency/competencies 16, 85–114
in relation to traits, motives, dispositions, etc 90, 92
organisational, as what the organisation does best 24
Russell's two classes of 5
see also competency (dimensions/ measurement)

competency (dimensions/ measurement) 2–3, 4, 5, 12, 25, 28, 30, 45–6, 47, 48, 56, 58, 67–8, 85–114, 116–17, 126, 128–9, 139, 149, 153–5, 163, 177, 182–95, 200, 202–4, 220, 222–4, 227–9, 231–49
and HR management 108–11
as incorporated into an appraisal system 16, 23
as organisational folklore 16
as statistically involved in quantitative validation of a centre 222–9
core 24, 45, 112, 214
definition(s) of 86–93
determination of 77, 79, 186–92
differentiating the successful from the average 16, 77
generic (management) 99–102
in relation to organisational change 31

in relation to psychometric/
personality tests 153–5
of similar competencies in different
organisations 66, 100–1
ownership by personnel of (the list of)
101–2
setting new standards for successful
performance 20–21, 56
training in 4
competency analysis *see* competency
(dimensions/measurement); job
analysis
competency development 45–51,
109–11, 213, 217
workshop(s) for 47, 52, 213–14
consultants in the field of development/
assessment 15, 82, 84
continuous development, by
organisations of personnel 45
by personnel of competencies 213–14
core competencies *see* competency/
competencies, core
costs of installing/operating a centre 11,
73–4
critical incidents analytical technique
96, 104, 229

debriefing session after a centre 174,
221
decision-making, the centre as a tool
for 12
de-layering, effects of 25
demotivation 8, 19, 42, 44–5, 221
designing a centre 4, 6, 31–5, 47–52, 53,
76–84
badly 13, 19
based on either selection or
development 31–5, 41, 79
consultants in 82, 84
examining the results after 78–9
flexibility in 6, 53
including a timetable/schedule for 49
matching exercises with desired job
competencies 115
need for care and rigour in 13
need to involve people in 76–8
requirement for a job analysis prior to
16, 77, 78, 80, 85–114, 115
stages and substages of 78–84
validation of the design after 78
designing a development system/
programme 78

Developmental Challenge Profile (DCP)
217
development centre(s) 44–53, 76–7, 208,
244, 250
as a collaborative process between
participant and assessors 8, 9, 14,
30, 42, 44, 49, 52–3, 191
as an extension to an assessment
centre 4, 32
as a sign of the organisation's
commitment to staff 19, 23, 46
as a strategy for choosing, developing
and retaining talent 14, 19, 23, 30,
218
as a threat to local managers 75
as opposed to a centre for assessment
or selection 44, 48, 50, 52–3
as part of an overall HR strategy
22–36, 200
costs of 73–4
debrief(ing) after 221
definition of 1–4
duration of 11
facilitators for 49
for management development 23,
27–8, 44
history (of the growth) of 8–9, 44–7
line managers' involvement in 52, 75
main features of 47–52
mislabelling an assessment centre as
19, 32
modular 196
need for complete openness during 48
purpose and objectives of 1–2, 31–2,
47
room for flexibility in 50
to help manage organisational
restructuring 20–1
'validity'/validation of 59–60, 229–32
what happens after 207
widespread use of 9–10, 14
see also assessors; development
needs; development plan
development needs, identification of 11,
23, 27, 44, 47, 51, 72, 188, 193,
210, 211
see also continuous development by
organisations of personnel
development of/by an individual *see*
personal development
development plan 8, 9, 33, 47, 51, 52,
59–60, 211–12, 221, 232

as joint expression of individual and organisation 14, 25, 27, 30, 46
design and construction of 12–13, 30, 42, 51
development actions that realise 211–18
follow-up system for 212–13, 232
line managers' involvement in 52, 194, 211–12
refinement of during development centre 51
self-perception as a first step toward 60
which the individual buys into and takes responsibility for 12, 28, 30, 47, 72, 211
development system/programme, design of *see* designing a development system
discussion groups *see* group discussion(s)
downsizing, effects of 25

economic justification for development/assessment centres 54, 61–4
utility analysis to establish 54, 61–4
emotional intelligence 58
as a description of interpersonal competencies 5, 64, 113
empathy, as an interpersonal skill 89, 118, 119, 205
equal opportunities issues
and (assessment) centres 19–20, 34, 205, 230, 244–5, 247
and briefing prior to a centre 163
and competencies 112–13, 205
statistical analysis of centre results and 224
success rates for various gender and ethnic groups 20
US law, centres and 244
executive development programme (EDP) 33
exercise design 123–33
fairness in 129–32, 176
format involved in 126
forms and documentation for 138–44
goals of 124–33
level of difficulty in 132–3, 136
revision of competency grid during 126, 139

team(s) for 123–4
to bring out the competency dimensions 127–9
see also exercises; job simulations, design of
exercise effect, the 224–7, 228, 230, 233–8, 239, 240, 244
feedback in relation to 236
exercise material, line managers as providers of 81, 123, 124
ownership by contributors of final versions of 136
exercises 115–48
customised 147–8
design and designers of *see* exercise design
forms and documentation for 138–44
grid of 115, 116–17, 118, 126
harmonising (linking and integrating) 133–5
innovations in the design of 115–16, 122–3
marking-guides for 137–8
production of 123–33
timing/scheduling of 116, 136
trying out 132–3, 136–7
types of 117–22
writing of 124–33
see also analytical exercises; assessment centre exercises; designing a centre; group exercises; in-tray exercises; job simulations/simulation exercises; off-the-shelf exercises; role-playing and role-players; written exercises
external selection centres 37–9, 148
and the necessity for feedback 37
and the undergraduate grapevine 37–8
in relation to assessment centres 38
risks of alienating participants 37–8
run by a consultancy 148

facilitators and facilitation 49, 51, 172, 177, 206
factor analysis, of assessment ratings at a centre 224–7
the statistical process of 104–5
'fast-track' development and promotion, identification for 18, 27, 33, 37, 41, 161, 171, 189, 217
feedback, as a means of personal development 8, 12–13, 19, 47, 50,

72, 150, 151, 152, 154–5, 177, 186, 197, 207–10, 216, 244
  by participants on the centre itself 53, 126, 174, 221
  combined with counselling 199, 205–6
  giving, as a skill 15, 186, 197, 198, 205–6
  in relation to the exercise effect 236
  on feedback 50
  quality of, following assessment centre 42, 184, 207–10
  rating as a summary of 184
  360-degree 19, 73, 151, 152, 177, 216, 250
  timing/scheduling of 50, 73, 165
  to the organisation 218–19
  who should give 208–9
functional analysis 95

graduate assessment centre 37, 131, 145
graphology 66
group discussion(s) 4
  as part of a centre exercise 128, 185
  unstructured/leaderless 7, 115–16
group exercises 5, 6, 7, 121–2, 126, 128, 136, 182, 185, 204, 231
  involving assigned roles 8, 121
  layout of 181
  leaderless 7, 8, 121–2
  negotiating 121, 124, 143
  observation sheets (for assessors) for 139–41, 181
  practical/physical 7
  problem-solving 121–2, 124, 126–7
  usual number of assessors/observers for 170
  usual number of people for 5
  videotaping 136, 137
  with a leader 7, 121–2, 185

human resource (HR) strategy, centres
  as integral to 22–36, 77
  choice of either assessment or development as basis for 22
  competencies as basic approach to 46
  relation to business/organisational strategy 22, 23–6
human resource (HR) system, centres as part of 26–8

in-depth psychological assessment 155–6, 189
information about people
  as an objective of development/ assessment centres 2
  collating under competency headings 4
  collating under job simulation headings 5
  collating unsystematically 13
  framework for integrating 149
  'owned' by the people themselves 44, 59
  that is non-exercise material 149–56
information decay 189
internal (assessment) centres (for existing members of staff) 4, 18–19, 27–8, 31–4, 130, 163, 189, 192–3
  reaction by participants to 33–4, 207
  what happens after 207–8
internal selection centres 39–43, 76, 192
  developmental emphasis of including feedback from 40, 42–3
  major uses of 37
  potentially threatening nature of 39, 40
  reaction by participants to 39–40, 42–3
interpersonal skills 5, 15, 66, 98
  as equated with 'emotional intelligence' 5
interview(s)
  as a classic competitor to innovation 66–8
  as a means of assessment 6–7
  as an addition or part-alternative to a centre 149–50
  as part of an assessment centre 4, 64
  as part of the prior job analysis 102–4
  pre-screening 159, 161
  pre-selection 158
  situational 17, 70–1
  structured, as sometimes superior to a centre 64, 67–8
  structured poorly 66–7
  training in giving 204
  to elicit competencies 67
  unstructured, uninformative nature of 67, 68
  utility analysis in relation to 62–3
  see also appraisal interview(s)

in-tray exercise(s) 3, 115, 117, 119, 122–3, 128, 185
  scoring of 123
  traditional instructions in 135
introducing a centre *see* project management in introducing a centre
inventory of personality see personality test(s)

job analysis 16, 69, 77, 78, 80, 85–114, 200, 238
  in terms of competencies 85–114, 116–17, 200
  interviews as part of 102–4, 171
  level of 96–7
  methods to carry out 102–8
  potential discrimination without 245
  questionnaire(s) on 104, 107
  revealing technical skills 93
job preview, involving assessment centre 18
job simulations/simulation exercises 115, 124–6, 200, 243
  as an assessment technique 2–3, 12, 46
  as an inspiration for personal development 12, 45, 51
  as essential to development/ assessment centres 1–5, 20, 46, 47–8, 68, 77, 115, 200
  design of to fit competencies of the target job 2–3, 20, 51, 115, 245

learning contract between participants/ candidates and the organisation 164–5
learning organisation
  contribution of centres to 20–1, 30
learning style, individuals' awareness of their own 12
lie scales 70
line-manager involvement in a development centre 52, 77–8, 123
  need for sense of ownership over the process 52, 75, 123, 145, 152, 170

Management Charter Initiative (MCI), the 111
management development programme/

function 23, 27–8, 41, 163, 173, 195, 206, 211–12, 218, 220
  impetus added by development centre to 12, 28, 220
management games as assessment exercise(s) 125–6, 145
managing the introduction of a centre *see* project management in introducing a centre
marking-guides for exercises *see* exercises, marking-guides for
mentor(s) and mentoring 212, 216
meta-analysis of assessment centres 56–8, 62–3
  validity coefficients in 56–7, 59, 62–3
meta-analysis of interviews 62–3
motivation, inculcation of in potential or new staff 17–19, 23
  maintenance of 14
  renewal of 19

non-exercise material nonetheless useful for centres 149–56

observation, as an assessment skill 4, 6, 12, 181–2
observation sheets *see* group exercises, observation sheets
'observers' of development centres *see* assessors
off-the-shelf exercises 74, 145–8
  and copyright issues 148
one-to-one exercise(s) *see* role-playing, for two persons (one-to-one)
organisational change see change, organisational
organisational commitment to personnel *see* commitment of an organisation to its personnel
organisational competencies *see* competency/competencies, organisational
organisational culture, centres as promoters of change in 30
  different even in apparently similar organisations 66
  impact of centre(s) upon 16, 33
organisational competencies *see* competency/competencies, organisational
organisational development

contribution of development/
assessment centres to 20–1
requiring the continuous
development of its personnel 45
organisational mission 25–6
ownership of insights by participants of
a centre 6, 52, 72
ownership of process by line managers
involved in a centre 52, 78, 136,
152, 170

peer-assessment 3, 4, 151–2
as a developmental aspect to a
centre 50
care required with feedback in/by
50, 153
centre for development 31, 162
peer nomination(s) for selection 160
personal development, as a demand of
personnel/staff themselves 46
as an increase in competence 25, 46
based on assessment centre feedback
27
responsibility of the individual for 8,
30, 52–3
through work-based learning 46, 52
personal development plan see
development plan
personality inventories see personality
test(s)
personality test(s) 66, 69–70, 72, 153–5,
189, 204, 228
and competency dimensions 153–5
as an adjunct to development centre
exercises 72, 189
feedback from 72–3, 154, 204
pre-employment training scheme 65–6
pre-screening 159, 161
pre-selection for assessment at a centre
157–162
in relation to external selection 157–8
in relation to internal selection
159–62
interview 158
probation as an assessment period 65
problem-solving skill(s) 1, 5, 68, 98
projective techniques of assessment 156
project management in introducing a
centre 76–84
personnel involved 79, 81–2
timetable for 82–3

promotion board, contrasted with an
assessment centre 34
psychological assessment in depth see
in-depth psychological assessment
psychological contract, changing as
organisation changes 46
psychological/psychometric tests 3, 5,
147, 153–5, 178, 204
psychologist as an assessor for a centre
155–6, 172
psychometric model of a centre
as favoured in the USA 9

questionnaires 5
enabling centre participants to
provide reaction/feedback 38–9

rating, as an assessment skill 4, 12,
183–6
as reliable predictor of job
performance 228–9
by line managers 152, 239
forms/documentation for 152–3
of potential 240
subject to variation according to
standards of participants 247, 249
see also assessment techniques,
rating
recruitment of staff, involving an
assessment centre 17–19, 23
remotivation see motivation, renewal
of
repertory grid analytical technique 96,
104
report at the end of a development
centre 6
written by participants 6
role-playing and role-players 3, 5, 8, 48,
78, 82, 120–1, 124, 132, 175–6, 178
for two persons (one-to-one) 8, 48–9,
82, 116, 120–1, 124, 126, 136, 182
observation sheets (for assessors) for
139, 142
supervision by a chairperson of 175
training for/of 78
running a centre, checklist for 178–9

selection centre(s) 37–43, 93
for external selection 37–9, 129, 191
for internal selection 39–43, 129,
191

in the continuum from development
to selection centres 35
selection ratio 62
self-assessment 3, 4, 150–1, 209
as a developmental aspect to a centre
12, 41, 50, 150
as a valued and useful aspect of a
centre 13, 50
centre for development 31, 162
pre-centre 166
self-confidence, as an interpersonal
skill 5
self-managed learning 215–16, 217
self-nomination for selection 159, 161
self-perception as a first step to
development planning 60
senior management development
programme 27–8
sensitivity, as an interpersonal skill 5
short-term contracts as a means of
assessing new staff 65
simulation exercises *see* job
simulations/simulation exercises
situational test(s) 70
soft skills (soft competencies) 92
solution-finding *see* problem-solving
skills
staff turnover *see* turnover of personnel
succession planning, assisted by
assessment centre feedback 26,
30–1
in relation to 'talent pools' 30
integration of centres with 28–31
in the short term 31
traditional 30
supervisor recommendation for
selection 159

talent, centres as fostering/realising 14,
19, 22, 23, 25, 30, 45, 218
talent pool(s) 30, 218
teams/team leaders, assessment as/for
selection of 19, 27, 34, 37
360-degree feedback *see* feedback, 360-
degree
training and training systems 26
using information feedback from
centres 26
turnover of personnel, impact of
organisational commitment on 17

turnover of trainees, impact of realistic
job preview on 18

UK and US approaches contrasted
7–10, 18
utility analysis to gauge the financial
benefits of centres 54, 61–4

validation of a centre 220–32
from the viewpoint of assessors 220–1
from the viewpoint of line managers
and the organisation 222
from the viewpoint of participants
221–2
from the viewpoint of potential
employees 222
qualitative 220–2
quantitative 220, 222–9
statistical analysis for quantitative
222–9
see also validity of centres
validation(s) of a(n assessment) centre
design 78
validity of centres, barriers to
acceptance of 64–75
choosing the appropriate type of
243–4
construct 238–9
content 238–9, 243
criterion 239–40, 243
in achieving purposes 54–64
'virtual' (assessment) centres 196

War Office Selection Boards (WOSBs) 6
work-based learning, leading to
personal development 46, 47, 52,
214–16
work sample tests
as opposed to cognitive tests and
assessment centres 57, 237
as opposed to job simulation
exercises 3
not unlike assessment centre
exercises 4
workshop, as opposed to a centre 5
written exercises 7, 116, 117–20, 124,
126, 137, 183, 185
indication to assessors of targeted
competencies in 138, 183
model/correct answers for 138